ELVIS

FOREVER IN THE GROOVE

Recording Career 50th Anniversary

BY SUSAN DOLL, PH.D.

PUBLICATIONS INTERNATIONAL, LTD.

Susan Doll holds a Ph.D. in radio, television, and film studies from Northwestern University and is an instructor of film studies at Oakton Community College, Des Plaines, Illinois. She also writes articles and reviews on film, pop culture, and history for various journals and magazines. In addition, Susan has appeared on TV on *The Joan Rivers Show* and has made frequent appearances on the radio, including NPR (National Public Radio), to discuss Elvis Presley as well as topics related to popular film. She is the author of the titles *Elvis: A Tribute to His Life, The Films of Elvis Presley, Elvis: Rock 'n' Roll Legend, Best of Elvis, Marilyn: Her Life and Legend,* and *Understanding Elvis.*

Publications International, Ltd., wishes to extend a special thanks to the following collectors who have so graciously shared their Elvis collections for this book: Dolores Balcom, The Steve Barile Collection, The Maria Columbus Collection, The Susan Doll Collection, Robert W. Dye, The Colin Escott Collection, The Sharon Fox Collection, Mike Freeman and Cindy Hazen, Joan and Paul Gansky, The Grand Ole Opry Archives, Bob Heis, Dwight K. Irwin, Bob Klein Photo Archives, The Ger Rijff Collection, The Robin C. Rosaaen Collection, The Dean Stephens Collection, and Opal Walker.

Acknowledgments:
Pages 54, 207: *TV Guide*® Magazine covers, September 8, 1956, and February 17, 1990. © TV Guide Magazine Group, Inc. Reprinted by permission of TV Guide Magazine Group, Inc., publisher of *TV Guide*® Magazine. *TV Guide* is a registered trademark of TV Guide Magazine Group, Inc.

Pages 77 (top), 124 (top): Photos courtesy of Mike Freeman and Cindy Hazen, authors of the book *Memphis Elvis Style.*

Page 181: *The Commercial Appeal,* August 17, 1977, "Death Captures Crown of Rock And Roll," © The Commercial Appeal, Memphis, TN. Reprinted by permission.

All BMG/RCA Victor® labels, logos, album covers, record jackets, and CD covers reprinted by permission and courtesy of BMG Strategic Marketing Group, a unit of BMG Music.

All Sun Records® labels and logos reprinted by permission and courtesy of Sun Entertainment Corporation. Sun® and the Sun Records Logo® are registered trademarks in the United States and elsewhere and are used under license from Sun Entertainment Corporation.

Louis Weber, CEO
Publications International, Ltd.
7373 North Cicero Avenue
Lincolnwood, Illinois 60712

Permission is never granted for commercial purposes.

Manufactured in China.

8 7 6 5 4 3 2 1

ISBN-13: 978-1-4127-1001-5
ISBN-10: 1-4127-1001-4

Library of Congress Control Number: 2003098107

TABLE OF CONTENTS

Hillbilly Cat....................5

Memphis Dynamite..............29

Rockin' Rebel.....................55

Pop Star............79

Million Dollar Actor..........97

Comeback Hero...................121

The King 145

Falling Star.....................165

The Legend 189

Epilogue................210

Index................214

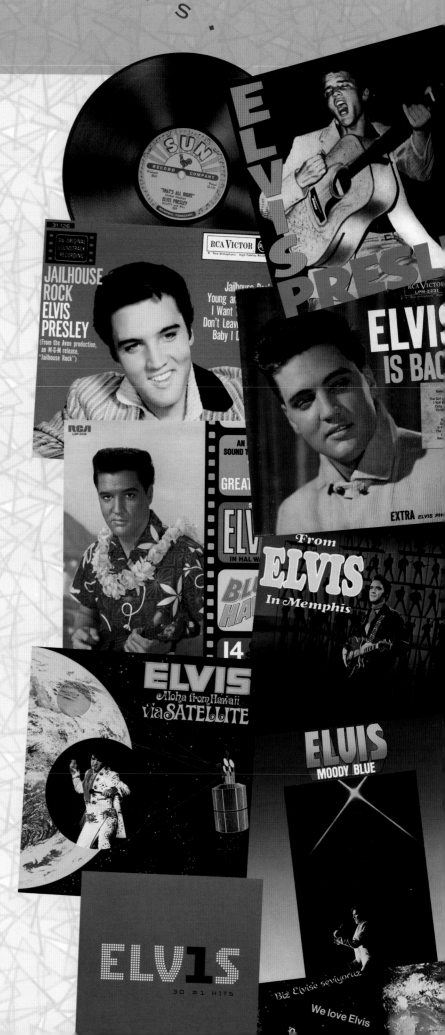

Hillbilly Cat

Chapter 1

ELVIS STARTED SINGING . . . AND MOORE AND BLACK JUMPED IN. SAM PHILLIPS'S VOICE BOOMED OUT FROM THE CONTROL BOOTH, "WHAT ARE YOU DOING?" NONE OF THEM REALLY KNEW. HOW COULD THEY KNOW THAT THEY HAD STUMBLED ONTO A NEW SOUND FOR A NEW GENERATION?

—*ELVIS: ROCK 'N' ROLL LEGEND*

The story of Elvis Presley's discovery begins with a shy, 18-year-old Elvis entering a recording studio in 1953 to cut two songs on an acetate disk at a cost of four dollars. The Memphis Recording Service was owned and operated by Sam Phillips, who had been recording rhythm-and-blues artists since 1950. By the time Elvis came to the recording studio, Sam Cornelius Phillips was known as Memphis's most important independent record producer. He had opened Sun Records in 1952 to record both rhythm-and-blues (R&B) singers and country-western artists.

Phillips enjoyed a national reputation for discovering such talented R&B artists as Rufus Thomas and Junior Parker. Phillips recorded these performers for independent record companies in other parts of the United States, including Chess Records in Chicago and the Modern label in Los Angeles. Phillips financed the recording sessions, paid the musicians, recorded the artists himself (often serving as the studio engineer), and then leased the master recordings to other record companies. His reputation was

Elvis, shown in 1955, slicked his dark blond hair into a trendy ducktail with pomade.

Sam Phillips

Born in 1923 and raised just outside Florence, Alabama, Sam Cornelius Phillips was greatly influenced by his rural Southern roots. Working in the cotton fields with African Americans, Phillips was exposed to gospel and blues music, and he experienced the poverty and hard life of many Depression-era Southern families. As a record producer, he would draw on those experiences to shape a new musical aesthetic—a purely Southern sound that combined black rhythm-and-blues and white country-western with a hardscrabble philosophy born of bad times. The new music that emerged— a Dixie-fried sound called "rockabilly"—would emanate from Phillips's Sun Records in the mid-1950s and influence all of rock 'n' roll.

Phillips's genius lay in recognizing talented singers and musicians of the region. Of his desire to record Southern-based music, Phillips mused, "I just knew this was culture, and it was so embedded in these people because of hardship.... Generation after generation, these people have been overlooked— black and white!" For his contribution in shaping modern music, Phillips was one of the first to be inducted into the Rock 'n' Roll Hall of Fame.

Sun Records

Aside from 3764 Elvis Presley Boulevard, 706 Union Avenue is probably the most famous address in Memphis. There, Sam Phillips opened the doors to Sun Records in February 1952, along with the Memphis Recording Service. Phillips had been recording such blues artists as Howlin' Wolf, B. B. King, Little Walter, Ike Turner, "Little" Junior Parker, and Bobby "Blue" Bland since 1950, but he leased those recordings to other labels, including Chess Records and RPM Records. Until Sun was established, no major studio existed in the South where artists could record. After Phillips established Sun, he could release his artists on his own label.

Many know that the legendary producer recorded blues and R&B performers, but less familiar are the country singers he began recording in 1953. He started out with the Ripley Cotton Choppers, then moved on to Doug Poindexter, Slim Rhodes, and Warren Smith.

After Elvis experienced success on the Sun label, others who would become rockabilly legends signed with Phillips, including Jerry Lee Lewis, Carl Perkins, Johnny Cash, Roy Orbison, Charlie Rich, Conway Twitty, and Charlie Feathers. Phillips sold Sun in 1969.

The original Sun building at 706 Union is now owned by the Presley estate.

Phillips's assistant, Marion Keisker, immediately recognized Elvis's talent. She called him "a hillbilly cat."

built on his recordings of blues performers, but he had just begun to work with country singers when Elvis walked into his recording studio for the first time.

Rock 'n' roll folklore relates a different version of Elvis's first trip to the Memphis Recording Service. According to older, more sentimental accounts, Elvis was a talented but inexperienced singer who simply wanted to make a record for his mother's birthday. Because Gladys's birthday was in April, the timing in this version of the story is not correct, because Elvis cut that first acetate disk in the late summer of 1953. It's more likely that Elvis knew of Sam Phillips's reputation as an independent producer and came to the Memphis Recording Service to catch his attention.

Unfortunately, on the day that Elvis decided to stop by, Phillips was not there. His tireless secretary and assistant, Marion Keisker, was running the recording studio alone. She noticed Elvis's flamboyant clothes and his long, slicked-back hair and engaged him in conversation. Marion asked Elvis what kind of music he sang and who he sang like. His prophetic answer, "I don't sound like nobody," piqued her curiosity, and while Elvis was singing "My Happiness" by the Ink Spots for his acetate record, Keisker also taped him so Phillips could hear him later.

BEFORE ELVIS, THERE WAS NOTHING.

—JOHN LENNON

As the "King of Rock 'n' Roll," Elvis personified the spirit of rebellious youth.

In the early 1950s, rhythm-and-blues had evolved from a combination of urban blues and swing. It was called "race music" because R&B musicians were predominantly African American. Phillips firmly believed that the rhythm-and-blues sound could win a mass audience. He knew that white teenagers in Memphis were listening to R&B, and he suspected this to be true in other parts of the country as well. Phillips had been known to proclaim, "If I could find a white man who had the Negro sound and the Negro feel, I could make a billion dollars." According to Marion Keisker, it was a widely known statement. Elvis's second song for the flip side of the acetate was another Ink Spots song, "That's When Your Heartaches Begin." His choice of material—two songs by the Ink Spots, an established R&B group—suggests that Elvis may have known of Phillips's statement and was hoping the producer would take notice. Phillips listened to the two songs by the unknown singer but did nothing about them, even though legend has it that Elvis's natural talent immediately blew Sam Phillips away.

Years later, after Elvis had become a major star, Phillips changed the story a little. He claimed that he was the person behind the desk at the Memphis Recording Service on that landmark day. To support his claim, Phillips pointed out that Keisker

Elvis peeked at an anxious crowd from behind the stage curtains.

Teenage girls fell hard for the good-looking young singer.

As a teenager, Elvis liked to listen to his sizeable record collection.

didn't know how to operate the recording equipment, so he was the only person who could have recorded Elvis. But Marion Keisker has told her account of the event many times in print and during television interviews, and, as far as anyone knows, Elvis never disputed her version.

Even though nothing came of his first session at the Memphis Recording Service, Elvis was determined to give it another shot. He returned to the recording service in January 1954 to record two more songs on acetate. He sang "Casual Love Affair" and a country tune called "I'll Never Stand in Your Way." This time Phillips worked the controls. Though he offered the young singer little in the way of encouragement, he did take down Elvis's phone number and address.

Sam Phillips and Elvis enjoy the good life at Taylor's Restaurant, next door to Sun Records.

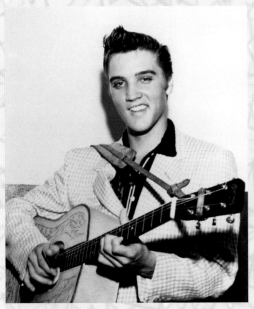

Phillips first asked Elvis to record a ballad, "Without You," which didn't suit Elvis's singing style.

Phillips didn't call Elvis until Peer Music of Nashville sent Sun Records a demo recording of a ballad called "Without You." Phillips decided to allow Elvis to record the new ballad. Unfortunately, Elvis could not seem to master the song, so Phillips asked him to sing anything else he knew. Delighted with the opportunity, Elvis eagerly ran through his extensive repertoire of country songs and R&B tunes. Phillips was impressed enough to suggest that the hopeful singer get together with Scotty Moore, a young guitarist who played with a local country-western combo, the Starlight Wranglers.

Elvis dropped by to see Moore almost immediately. Moore recalls, "He had on a pink shirt, pink pants with white stripes down the legs, and white shoes, and I thought my wife was going to go out the back door—people just weren't wearing that kind of flashy clothes at the time." (*Ed. note:* In fact, in the 1950s, pink was the hot fashion color for everything from men's clothing to cars.) Moore introduced Elvis to bass player Bill Black, and the three musicians spent the long, hot Memphis summer trying to find a sound that clicked.

Bass player Bill Black and Elvis posed in front of a train engine that was on display at a venue.

The trio worked in the recording studio at Sun Records instead of performing in front of a live audience. Recently developed magnetic recording tape made it possible for them to do one take of a song, listen to it, then make adjustments for the next take. Presley, Moore, and Black finally hit upon their sound while they were fooling around during a break one night. Elvis started singing Arthur "Big Boy" Crudup's blues song, "That's All Right," with a fast rhythm and in a more casual style than most blues songs, and Moore and Black jumped in. Phillips's voice boomed out from the control booth, "What are you doing?" None of them really knew. How could they? How could they know that they had stumbled onto a new sound for a new generation?

"That's All Right" (Sun 209) never reached the national charts, but it changed the course of popular music.

In September 1954, Scotty Moore (left), Elvis, and Bill Black played outside on a flatbed truck for the opening of Lamar-Airways Shopping Center in Memphis.

"Blue Moon of Kentucky" was the flip side of Sun's 78 rpm single, "That's All Right."

Phillips was excited about the trio's sound and recognized its potential. He asked them to refine their unique interpretation of "That's All Right," and then he recorded it. The flip side of their first record was their rendition of the bluegrass standard "Blue Moon of Kentucky," made famous by Bill Monroe and the Bluegrass Boys. Elvis's first record seemed to symbolize the roots of his musical sound; a blues song occupied one side while a country song made up the flip side.

Elvis's treatment of both songs didn't sound much like the recordings by the original artists. His approach was far more easygoing, which gave his renditions an air of spontaneity. Instead of the hard vocal delivery and tense rhythm of Crudup's version of "That's All Right," Elvis used a more-relaxed vocal style and rhythm. For "Blue Moon of Kentucky," the tempo was speeded up, and two elements were added that would make Elvis's sound famous. He syncopated certain lyrics, using a sort of hiccuping sound, while Sam Phillips added a reverberation, resulting in the famous echo effect. Elvis's style became the basis of "rockabilly," the fusion of country music (commonly called hillbilly music) with a rhythm-and-blues sound that has been relaxed and speeded up, or "rocked." The term rockabilly was not widely known until after Elvis became a household name. At the time he cut his first record for Sun, there was no word that could adequately describe his style of music. When the press attempted to explain his sound, they usually made a mess of it, often confusing their readers with inappropriate or comical comparisons

Elvis and the Blue Moon Boys played several small towns in Texas in July 1955.

Elvis sang "That's All Right" in a relaxed style compared to Arthur "Big Boy" Crudup's rendition.

to other types of music. Elvis was referred to at various times as a "hillbilly singer," "a young rural rhythm talent," a "white man…singing Negro rhythms with a rural flavor," and "a young man [with a] boppish approach to hillbilly music."

Not long after Elvis's success, other rockabilly and country-western singers showed up on the doorstep of Sun Studio, hoping that Phillips could work the same magic with them as he had with Elvis. Phillips eventually recorded Johnny Cash, Jerry Lee Lewis, Carl Perkins, Roy Orbison, Charlie Feathers, Billy Lee Riley, Dickie Lee, and other artists. With their flashy clothes, raw sound, and fervent delivery, these singers forged a new sound and style that was intensely Southern, or "Dixie-fried." As Bill Williams, Sun Records publicist, recalled, "I think every one of them must have come in on the midnight train from nowhere. I mean, they came from outer space." Yet, the influence of Sam Phillips and Sun's recording artists on the development of rock 'n' roll can never be overestimated.

Sam Phillips took a copy of "That's All Right" to popular disc jockey Dewey Phillips (no relation) for the latter's *Red Hot and Blue* radio program. At first Memphis's hottest deejay hesitated to play the Sun recording because his show was usually reserved for the music of black artists, but on July 7, 1954, he played the record on the air. The station received dozens of requests for both sides of the disk, and Phillips played the two songs over and over. After receiving 14 telegrams and almost 50 phone calls in a matter of hours, he decided to interview the unknown singer on his program that very night. Elvis was supposedly too nervous to stay at home and listen to himself on the radio, so he had gone to the movies. His parents, Vernon and Gladys, dashed to the theater to pick him up and then rushed him to station WHBQ. Dewey Phillips asked Elvis a variety of questions about his life and

Country star Johnny Cash and Elvis visited backstage at the Grand Ole Opry, Nashville, in 1956.

"I lose myself in my singing."

Memphis disc jockey Dewey Phillips, of WHBQ, was the first to play "That's All Right" on the radio.

his interests, including what high school he had attended. This was a careful tactic on Phillips's part, for as soon as Elvis said "Humes" the audience knew he was a white man because the school was all white. At that time in 1954, Memphis schools were not yet integrated.

"That's All Right" became a fast-selling record in the Memphis area. Elvis's first single steadily climbed up the country-western charts by the end of July 1954.

Elvis's second record was released on September 25, 1954. It included the R&B tune "Good Rockin' Tonight," first made popular in 1948 by Wynonie Harris, and a country pop song called "I Don't Care If the Sun Don't Shine." This record moved up the charts even more quickly than his first single. It sold 4,000 copies in the Memphis area in two and a half weeks. By this time, Elvis was singing with Scotty and Bill at such Memphis night spots as the Eagle's Nest. At first, the talented newcomer made guest-star appearances with the Starlight Wranglers, but soon Elvis, Scotty, and Bill were performing on their own. They were called Elvis Presley and the Blue Moon Boys but often billed as the Hillbilly Cat and the Blue Moon Boys.

In September 1954, Elvis's second Sun single, "Good Rockin' Tonight," was released.

By this time, the three men had decided they needed to hire a professional manager. Bob Neal, a disc jockey at country station WMPS in Memphis, accepted the job and began pushing their Sun recordings, booking tours in the country-western clubs across the South and the Southwest, and handling all their business arrangements.

Bob Neal encountered a double problem in getting radio stations to play Elvis's records. The country-western stations thought Elvis sounded too much like a rhythm-and-blues singer, and blues stations found him too country. Also, audiences on the smaller country circuits considered the trio's

IN PERSON
★ *Elvis* ★
PRESLEY
SCOTTY and BILL
The "Blue Moon" Boys

For Dates—Write—Wire—Call
BOB NEAL
Exclusive Personal Management
160 Union Ave.   Memphis, Tenn.

Radio stations were reluctant to play Elvis's music as he didn't totally fit either the country or the R&B markets.

Overton Park Shell

On July 30, 1954, a hot summer night, Elvis made his first billed appearance at the Overton Park Shell in Memphis. The headliner was Slim Whitman, a country singer who incorporated yodeling into his style. Also on the bill were Billy Walker, Curly Harris, Sugarfoot Collins, Tinker Fry, and Sonny Harville. The newspaper ads promoting the event misspelled Elvis's name as "Ellis Presley." Elvis's first single, "That's All Right," backed by "Blue Moon of Kentucky," had been released just 11 days earlier, and most have speculated that he sang both sides of his new single that night. Elvis was clearly nervous for the first show, and he moved constantly while he was singing. The girls in the audience began to scream and make noise. After it was over, Elvis asked band member Scotty Moore what they were "hollering" at, and Moore replied, "It was your leg, man. It was the way you were shakin' your left leg."

In August 1955, Elvis appeared with Bill Strength at Overton Park Shell in Memphis.

By 1955, D. J. Fontana, a staff drummer on Louisiana Hayride, *had joined the Blue Moon Boys.*

frenzied performances to be too wild. Aside from Elvis's personal performing style, bass player Bill Black liked to clown around by dancing with his huge bass fiddle or rolling across the floor with it. By 1955, these problems began to take care of themselves as Elvis's sound became more widely known, thanks to his weekly performances on the *Louisiana Hayride* radio show. Also, his newfound fame brought the band better bookings in larger towns where their act was more acceptable. They added a drummer, D. J. Fontana, and began to appear with well-established country acts, such as the Wilburn Brothers, Faron Young, Ferlin Huskey, Roy Acuff, Kitty Wells, and the Carter Family.

Elvis signed a management contract with Bob Neal (right) as Sam Phillips looked on.

Louisiana Hayride *manager Horace Logan and Elvis stage a showdown with deejay Ed Franklin caught in the middle.*

During 1955, Sun released three more Elvis singles: "Milkcow Blues Boogie"/ "You're a Heartbreaker" in January; "I'm Left, You're Right, She's Gone"/ "Baby Let's Play House" in April; and "Mystery Train"/ "I Forgot to Remember to Forget" in August. Like his early records, these singles featured a rhythm-and-blues song on one side and a country-western tune on the other. Elvis was still considered to be a regionally based country-western performer, but his popularity was beginning to soar.

Elvis's fourth single for Sun Records, "Baby Let's Play House," became the first Elvis Presley effort to chart nationally. Backed by "I'm Left, You're Right, She's Gone" on the flip side, it stayed on *Billboard*'s country chart for ten weeks, reaching No. 10.

"Baby Let's Play House" (Sun 217) charted nationally on Billboard's country list, peaking at No. 10.

The 1950s: The Hillbilly Cat and the Blue Moon Boys

Essential to Elvis's sound in the 1950s were the musicians who backed him up. Elvis, guitarist Scotty Moore (near right), and bassist Bill Black (far right) were dubbed the Hillbilly Cat and the Blue Moon Boys. Moore and Black had previously played with the country-western band the Starlight Wranglers, but they hitched their wagons to Elvis's star after recording "That's All Right" with the inexperienced young singer. Moore's driving guitar sound helped create Elvis's style, while Black's antics on his stand-up bass added humor and excitement to their live act. After appearing with the group on *Louisiana Hayride*, drummer D. J. Fontana joined them on the road, although he never played on any of Elvis's Sun recordings. After Elvis became a household name, Moore, Black, and Fontana were not given the respect and salary they were due. Moore and Black split with Elvis in September 1957 over this issue. Both were wooed back, but things were never quite the same after that. Moore and Fontana recorded with Elvis after he returned from the army in 1960, but Black had already struck out on his own in 1958, enjoying moderate success with his own combo.

The Opry and Louisiana Hayride

Fall of 1954 was eventful for Elvis. He was invited to perform on the oldest and most successful country music radio program in America, the *Grand Ole Opry*. On October 2, the Hillbilly Cat and the Blue Moon Boys, as Elvis, Scotty, and Bill called themselves, drove from Memphis to Nashville to appear on the show. The audience was not enthusiastic. However, because the *Opry* had always been reluctant to accept changes in country music, including the use of electric guitars and drums, it's not surprising that Elvis's highly charged performance of blues-inspired music was not appreciated. The *Opry*'s talent coordinator Jim Denny went so far as to suggest that Elvis should go back to driving a truck.

In mid-October, Elvis performed for the first time on *Louisiana Hayride*, a radio program broadcast from the Municipal Auditorium in Shreveport, Louisiana. *Hayride*, unlike the *Opry*, had always encouraged new country talent, including Hank Williams, Slim Whitman, Jim Reeves, and Webb Pierce. The Hillbilly Cat and the Blue Moon Boys sang "That's All Right" and "Blue Moon of Kentucky" during the "Lucky Strike Guest Time" segment, which was devoted to new artists. The trio was so well received that they were asked to return the next week. On November 6, *Louisiana Hayride* offered them a one-year contract to perform every weekend. The show paid scale wages, but it gave the trio valuable exposure to country fans outside the Deep South.

Elvis and his band cut loose on Louisiana Hayride.

Elvis put on an energetic show.

Rhythm-and-blues singer Arthur Gunter had written and recorded "Baby Let's Play House" in 1954, basing it on country singer Eddy Arnold's 1951 hit "I Wanna Play House with You." As an R&B reworking of a country-western song, "Baby Let's Play House" was perfect for Elvis's rockabilly repertoire. Gunter himself had been influenced by rockabilly artists, and he made a good model for Elvis, who had purchased a copy of Gunter's version the previous December at the House of Records in Memphis. Elvis made the song his own with the inclusion of the syncopated phrasing "babe-babe-baby" in the verse. He also tinkered with the lyrics, changing "You may have religion" to "You may drive a pink Cadillac," a humorous foretelling of the car with which he would come to be identified. Sam Phillips added drums to the recording session for the song, marking the first time drums were used on a Presley single. As "Baby Let's Play House" received national exposure, trade publications called it a country song, so few people connected it with the relatively unknown rhythm-and-blues artist who had inspired Elvis.

By mid-1955, Elvis had developed a large following made up mostly of teenagers.

Elvis added "Baby Let's Play House" and "I'm Left, You're Right, She's Gone" to his act in the spring of 1955. Less than a year later, he sang "Baby Let's Play House" on television for his second appearance on The Dorsey Brothers *Stage Show* (February 4, 1956), just as his sensual performing style was beginning to create a national controversy. If his hip-swinging performance on *Stage Show* raised eyebrows, then the lyrics to "Baby Let's Play House" added to the provocative connotation. Basically a proposition, the song is a plea from the singer to his girlfriend to return to him because he wants to "play house"

Early on, Elvis was billed as the "freshest, newest voice in country music," although he did not sound country.

THE FRESHEST, NEWEST VOICE
IN COUNTRY MUSIC

ELVIS PRESLEY

"Howdy to all my friends at the Jimmie Rodgers Memorial!"

Featuring His
Latest Hit

"YOU'RE RIGHT, I'M
LEFT, SHE'S GONE"
b/w
"BABY, LET'S
PLAY HOUSE"

SUN-217

For available dates

WRITE
WIRE
PHONE

BOB NEAL Exclusive Personal Management
160 Union Ave. Memphis, Tennessee
Phone: Office 8-3667 ■ Home 4-4029

Featured Star,
KWKH Louisiana Hayride

with her, a slang term for an unmarried couple living or sleeping together. Despite the singer's plea, he takes a confrontational stance, telling his girl, "I'd rather see you dead than with another man."

In the spring of 1955, Bob Neal booked the Hillbilly Cat and the Blue Moon Boys on a tour with country singer Hank Snow. The tour was organized by Hank Snow Jamboree Attractions, which was owned by Snow but operated by a former carnival barker named Colonel Tom Parker. Many colorful stories exist about Parker; some are no doubt true, while others have been

Manager Bob Neal and his young client enjoyed an issue of The Cash Box.

Elvis used the guitar as a prop, saying, "Can't play it. Use it as a brace."

exaggerated through the years. It's been said that he once covered a hot plate with straw and set baby chickens on top of it to make them "dance" to the tune "Turkey in the Straw." Another carny story tells of Parker painting sparrows yellow and selling them as parakeets. Parker's country-western experiences included guiding country singer Eddy Arnold's career from relative unknown to star. Parker's title of "Colonel" does not refer to military rank but is an honorary title, which was bestowed upon him by the state of Louisiana in 1953. Later he was made an honorary Colonel of Tennessee as well. Much has been written about Colonel Tom Parker, not the least of which is that he was a very shrewd man.

Elvis toured with country star Hank Snow in Snow's All-Star Jamboree.

Throughout 1955, Elvis continued to tour with established country acts, including Faron Young (far right). About this time, Colonel Tom Parker (second from right) became Elvis's manager.

A large portion of Elvis's audience by mid-1955 was made up of teenage girls. They were extremely enthusiastic during his stage performances, and Elvis learned to play to the girls, teasing them with his body movements and making them scream each time he swiveled his hips. During a summer performance in Jacksonville, Florida, Elvis jokingly invited all the girls in the audience to meet him backstage. But the joke was on Elvis: A swarm of screaming girls chased him all the way to his car and literally ripped most of his clothes off his body. The incident terrified his mother, surprised the press, and delighted the Colonel, who had begun to monitor Elvis's career quite closely. Parker's position at Jamboree Attractions allowed him to quietly observe the young singer's steady rise in popularity.

As with other important events in Elvis's career, there are many versions of the story about how Colonel Tom Parker became Elvis's sole manager. Parker was supposed to have had a close working relationship with Hank Snow, but when he finally signed Elvis to a contract, Parker did not include Snow in the deal. Parker and Snow broke up their partnership over this matter, but Snow did not sue.

> I'D RATHER TRY AND CLOSE A
> DEAL WITH THE DEVIL.
> —HAL WALLIS, COMMENTING ON THE COLONEL

"My fans want my shirt, they can have my shirt. They put it on my back."
Illustrated, *September 7, 1957*

When the Colonel and Elvis signed their first contract in August 1955, Bob Neal still had a contract as Elvis's manager. Parker initially signed on as "special adviser," and his duties were to "assist in any way possible the buildup of Elvis Presley as an artist." Parker was also given the right to negotiate renewals on all existing contracts. At this point, Neal was kept on merely as a courtesy. When Neal's contract expired on March 15, 1956, he was completely out of the picture, and Parker became Elvis's full-time manager for a 25 percent cut.

Colonel Tom Parker

The Tupelo birthplace of Elvis Presley.

Opposite page: *Movie publicity portrait of Elvis Presley.*

One of the two rooms in the Tupelo house served as a bedroom and sitting area. The furnishings are not the original pieces.

When Parker began to take part officially in Elvis's career, Elvis was just a country-western singer. Though his style wasn't traditional and many of his most loyal fans were teenagers, Elvis still toured the country-western circuits and performed with other country stars. His records were played almost exclusively on country stations. If Elvis was going to live up to the potential the Colonel saw in him, he was going to have to be exposed to audiences outside the South on a wide scale.

As logical as this seems, the Colonel's plan was actually a bold move. After all, Elvis had never stepped foot outside the South, and northern audiences were unaccustomed to Southern musical traditions and sounds.

Elvis had been absorbing those traditions since his birth in Tupelo, Mississippi, on January 8, 1935. From gospel hymns in church to country-western tunes on local radio station WELO, Elvis and his parents, Vernon and Gladys, loved to sing and listen to music. Years later Gladys recalled that when Elvis was only a toddler he would run up to the front of the First Assembly of God church and try to sing along with the choir.

Elvis learned about traditional country music from Mississippi Slim, whose real name was Carvel Lee Ausborn. Slim was a native of Tupelo and a fixture on WELO for more than 20 years. Elvis, who was friends with Slim's younger brother James, may have learned several guitar chords from Slim. Elvis's uncle Vester Presley also taught the young boy how to handle and play a guitar. It's possible that Elvis sang on WELO's amateur radio show called *Black and White Jamboree* (also known as *Saturday Jamboree*). Named for the Black and White hardware store, the Saturday afternoon program featured a live studio audience. Locals were allowed to perform on the program on a first-come, first-served basis. Elvis attended the show regularly, and he may have sung the traditional ballad "Old Shep" on the air when he was eight or nine.

Mississippi Slim was a country music mainstay of Tupelo radio station WELO.

23

In September 1948, the Presleys moved to Memphis, probably because the employment opportunities for Vernon were much better there than in tiny Tupelo. A few weeks after the move, Vernon's mother, Minnie Mae Presley, journeyed north to join the little family. For the next four years, the Presleys lived in the poor districts of Memphis.

Elvis attended L. C. Humes High School, where he majored in industrial arts/wood-shop. While he was in school, Elvis held a variety of part-time jobs to help the family make ends meet. He ushered at Loew's State Theater, worked in the table department at Upholsteries Specialities, and worked for MARL Metal Products. One summer, he labored for a short time in the hot, cramped facilities of the Precision Tool factory, along with cousins Travis, Gene, and John Smith. He was eventually fired for being underage.

While in school, Elvis became a target of ridicule from some of his fellow students because of his unusual appearance. When he was 16, Elvis grew his hair longer than the other boys and greased it down with pomade. He started dressing in flashy clothes, including brightly colored shirts turned up at the collar and gabardine slacks pegged at the bottoms and ballooned at

Elvis in his senior class photo from the Herald, *the Humes High yearbook.*

The Presleys lived at a two-story brick apartment building on Alabama Street when Elvis recorded "My Happiness" at the Memphis Recording Service in 1953. Ruth Black, mother of bassist Bill Black, lived in an apartment nearby.

Elvis attended L. C. Humes High School, which is now a junior high.

While in high school, the teenager worked as an usher at Loew's State Theater, among other part-time jobs.

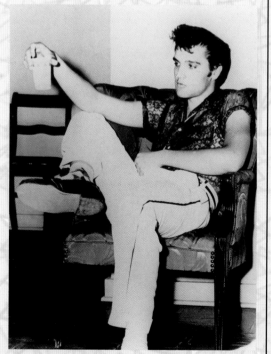

Elvis's taste in clothing was a constant source of amusement and criticism in the popular press.

the knees. This style, which was popular in the big cities of the North, was prevalent among Memphis's black rhythm-and-blues musicians. Never a particularly popular student, Elvis did enter a talent contest during his high school years, and he felt honored when he was allowed the show's only encore. Elvis graduated from Humes in 1953 and went to work at Crown Electric as a truck driver. It is said he brought home about $41 per week.

Elvis's personal taste in clothes seemed an outward manifestation of his interest in music—particularly gospel and rhythm-and-blues. Elvis's musical interests and influences during this period of his life have been widely debated and disputed, but he is known to have attended all-night gospel sings in the Memphis area and to have collected recordings by rhythm-and-blues artists. In addition, the diversity of music on Memphis's radio stations had a great deal of impact on the development of his musical style, especially stations WDIA and WHBQ. Station WDIA broadcasted music aimed at black audiences. Although owned by two white men (Bert Ferguson and John R. Pepper), WDIA was staffed with black disc jockeys who played the blues, with special emphasis on local blues performers. WHBQ was a white station that played a variety of music, but it's best remembered for disc jockey Dewey Phillips's *Red Hot and Blue* radio program that featured the rhythm-and-blues recordings of black artists.

Memphis was the headquarters for white gospel music in the 1950s. During 1951 and 1952, Elvis frequently attended all-night gospel sings at Ellis Auditorium. Male quartets most often headlined at these sings, and Elvis's

Elvis shared top billing with Hank Snow on May 15, 1956, for the Memphis Cotton Festival at Ellis Auditorium. Elvis drew such a crowd that both sides of the auditorium were opened, forcing him to turn constantly to face each audience.

favorite groups included the Blackwood Brothers and Hovie Lister and the Statesmen. The lead singer of the Statesmen was the colorful Jake Hess. Many people remember this quartet for their emotional, highly stylized manner of singing and their flamboyant wardrobes, which undoubtedly made an impression on the young Elvis.

The Blackwood Brothers attended the same Assembly of God church as the Presleys, and along with a junior quartet called the Songfellows, they had a significant influence on Elvis. Cecil Blackwood, the youngest Blackwood brother and a member of the Songfellows, was in Elvis's Sunday school class. After he left the junior quartet to join his brothers as part of the Blackwoods, Cecil suggested that Elvis join the Songfellows. For reasons not entirely known, nothing ever came of this opportunity.

Personal accounts of Elvis's life from family members and close friends, including Priscilla Presley and Red and Sonny West, confirm that his love of gospel music was a major influence on his musical style. But other versions of Elvis's career, particularly rock 'n' roll histories, emphasize the effect that the notorious Beale Street area had on his music and performing style. The

The Tupelo Hardware Company, where Elvis bought his first guitar, maintains the atmosphere of an old-fashioned hardware store from an era gone by.

Elvis entered a teen auto rodeo with a 1953 Plymouth Cranbrook. A friend measured how close he came to the line.

Poplar Tunes

Founded by hardworking Joe Cuoghi, Poplar Tunes epitomizes the 1950s record shop. Located near Lauderdale Courts, where Elvis once lived, the one-story brick building was a hangout for Elvis and his friends during their high school years. Elvis purchased singles at Poplar Tunes to add to his ever-growing record collection. When he became a recording artist, the music shop began selling his Sun singles. Most claim it was the first store to sell an Elvis Presley record. Because Elvis was from the neighborhood, his singles sold like wildfire, and he enjoyed signing autographs at the store.

Poplar Tunes still sells Elvis's records, and it looks much the same as it did in 1954. The walls of the store are lined with dozens of rare and interesting photos, including a telling shot of Elvis, Dewey Phillips, and Cuoghi (see page 33) that captures the fleeting moment when Elvis—standing between obscurity and legend—was just a boy from the neighborhood who made good.

As a teen, Elvis was close to his parents, Vernon and Gladys.

seedy joints and small clubs of this famous stretch of Memphis were home to many well-known rhythm-and-blues musicians. According to some accounts of Elvis's life, he frequented Beale Street regularly, eventually incorporating the sound he heard there into his own. However, despite his visits to the clubs on Beale Street, it is likely that Elvis's knowledge of blues and rhythm-and-blues also came from listening to the radio.

Elvis was familiar with the music of some well-known R&B artists in Memphis, including the sounds of B. B. King, Rufus Thomas, and Big Memphis Ma Rainey. King, a disc jockey at that time, recalls meeting Elvis on Beale Street after seeing the teenager hanging around the clubs and pawn shops. Elvis bought most of his flamboyant wardrobe at Lansky Brothers Clothing Store, located at the end of Beale Street.

The country influence on Elvis's music often takes a back seat to the more colorful Beale Street stories. Aside from Elvis's personal acquaintance with country singer Mississippi Slim in Tupelo, Elvis and his family often listened to Memphis's many country-western radio stations. Gladys Presley loved to listen to the radio and was a big fan of country artist Hank Snow. Elvis had grown up with country music, listening to the radio with his mother.

The style and sound of country-western music had changed by 1950. Singer Ernest Tubb, known as the "Texas Troubadour," introduced the electric guitar to the *Grand Ole Opry* during the 1940s. Also in that decade, boogie-woogie fused with country to form a more raucous country sound called "western swing." The enormous popularity of Hank Williams, whose honky-tonk style had been influenced by the

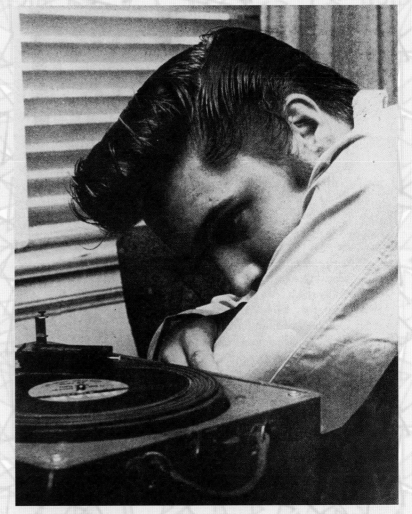

In a rare quiet moment, a youthful Elvis relaxes at home by listening to a record on his portable record player.

Ernest Tubbs and the Texas Troubadors were among the first to use amplification at the *Grand Ole Opry*.

blues, also affected the sound of country music. By the early 1950s, some of the fans and many members of the country-music establishment had not yet embraced these innovations, but they did provide a precedent for Elvis's music.

Elvis also admired the singing styles of such mainstream pop singers as Dean Martin and Eddie Fisher. Although the pop music establishment and the traditions of Tin Pan Alley seem diametrically opposed to Elvis's early music, he felt a kinship with pop singers and would later profess a desire to sing in their style.

A crowd waited to be let in to a show at the Ryman Auditorium in downtown Nashville in the 1950s.

The Ryman Auditorium was home to the Grand Ole Opry.

"Mystery Train" proved to be Elvis's last single for Sun.

Elvis Presley's early singing and performing style was marked by a true fusion of sounds. This fusion of gospel, country-western, and rhythm-and-blues, with a little pop thrown in here and there, makes him unique and important in the annals of popular music—a full integration of contemporary musical styles into a totally new sound. Of course, no one knew this when Elvis walked into Sam Phillips's Memphis Recording Service in 1953.

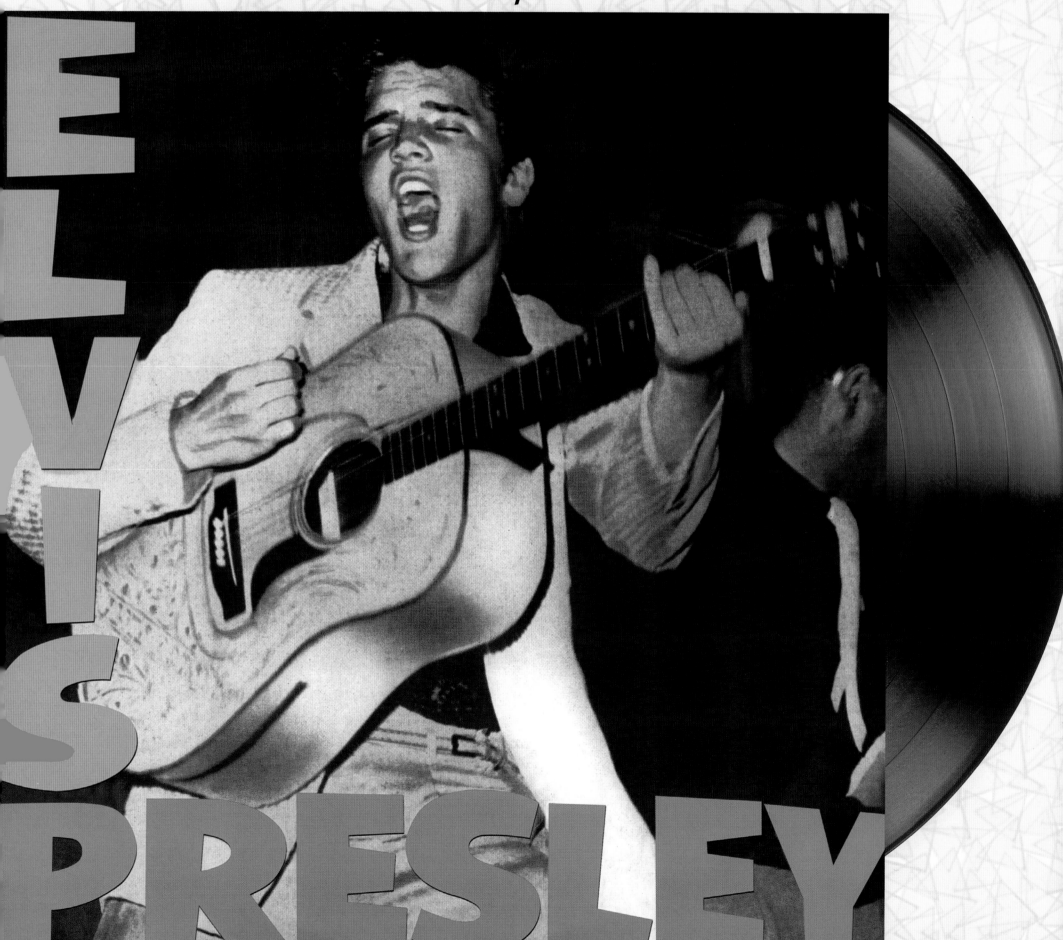

07863 67735 1 LC 00316

ELVIS PRESLEY

Side One
Heartbreak Hotel
I Was The One
Blue Suede Shoes
I'm Counting On You
I Got A Woman
One-Sided Love Affair
I Love You Because
Just Because
Tutti Frutti

Side Two
Trying To Get To You
I'm Gonna Sit Right Down And Cry (Over You)
I'll Never Let You Go (Little Darlin')
Blue Moon
Money Honey
Shake, Rattle And Roll
My Baby Left Me
Lawdy, Miss Clawdy
I Want You, I Need You, I Love You

Compilation Produced by
Ernst Mikael Jorgensen and **Roger Semon**
Original Engineer: **Sam Phillips**,
Bob Ferris and **Ernie Oehlrich**
Executive Directors: **Mike Omansky**
and **Klaus Schmalenbach**
Project Director: **Dalita Keumurian**

Elvis Presley zoomed into big-time entertainment practically overnight. Born in Tupelo, Mississippi, Elvis began singing for friends and folk gatherings when he was barely five years old. All his training has been self-instruction and hard work. At an early age, with not enough money to buy a guitar, he practiced for his future stardom by strumming on a broomstick. He soon graduated to a $2.98 instrument and began picking out tunes and singing on street corners.

After earning some money by working at part-time jobs, Elvis walked into a small recording company studio and asked to make a record, at his own expense. In a few months his first record was released and became an overnight sensation. Following his graduation from high school, Elvis began an extended round of personal appearances and then signed his contract with RCA Victor. The rest is history.

Elvis is the most original protagonist of popular songs on the scene today. His style stands out vividly on records and in personal appearances and accounts for the universal popularity he has gained.

DESPITE REPEATED EFFORTS BY CRITICS TO COOL HIS SEX-HOT FLAME, ELVIS PRESLEY HAS REMAINED THE MOST INCENDIARY FIGURE IN THE WORLD OF ROCK 'N' ROLL.

— "INEXTINGUISHABLE," *NEWSWEEK,* AUGUST 27, 1956

The Colonel's pursuit of the big time for Elvis—his sole client—began with a search for a recording contract with a nationally based company. Columbia and Atlantic expressed interest in the unusual new singer, but the Colonel had several contacts at RCA Victor, making a deal with this company preferable.

In November 1955, Sam Phillips sold Elvis's contract to RCA Victor for $35,000, plus $5,000 in back royalties he owed Elvis. It was the largest amount paid for a single performer up to that time. Steve Sholes, RCA's premier A&R (artist and repertoire) man, had helped sign Elvis to the label. Sholes oversaw the company's specialty singles, which included country-western, gospel, and R&B, so he served as the producer of Elvis's first recordings for RCA. Moving to RCA was a major step in Elvis's career and a major investment for the company; at the very least, it meant going national and international in promotion and distribution. Sholes was aware that the executives at RCA were closely watching their unusual new artist, who didn't fit into any of the company's existing categories of music.

Legendary guitarist Chet Atkins played rhythm guitar on Elvis's first RCA recordings in Nashville.

Elvis's deal with RCA made everyone smile. From left: Elvis's former manager Bob Neal, Sun's Sam Phillips, RCA attorney Coleman Tilly, Elvis, and the Colonel.

ELVIS PRESLEY

HEARTBREAK HOTEL

and

I WAS THE ONE

Elvis's voice, combined with an exaggerated echo effect, perfectly conveyed the despair in the lyrics of "Heartbreak Hotel" (RCA 47-6420).

RCA re-released Elvis's Sun singles in December 1955; the reissue of "Mystery Train" did not sell well. Then the company arranged for Elvis to begin recording new material in Nashville the next month. Chet Atkins, RCA's head man in Nashville, organized the sessions, which started on January 10, 1956. Scotty Moore and Bill Black, who had worked with Elvis on the road and at Sun from the beginning, accompanied Elvis as usual. D. J. Fontana, who played with Elvis on tour, checked in as Elvis's drummer, although he had never recorded with the trio before. Atkins played rhythm guitar, Floyd Cramer was added at the piano, and gospel singers Ben and Brock Speer of the Speer Family and Gordon Stoker of the Jordanaires provided backing vocals.

Moore and Black, who were used to the down-home atmosphere of Sun, found the detached, professional air at the RCA sessions intimidating, while Sholes was unsure of how to duplicate Elvis's Sun sound. Stoker was unhappy because the rest of the Jordanaires had not been asked to join the session. In fact, everyone was nervous or unsettled except Elvis, who attacked his first number, Ray Charles's "I Got a Woman," with everything he had. In effect, Elvis performed the song while he recorded it, which so impressed the typically cool Atkins that he called his wife to come down to the studio because "it was just so damn exciting."

"Heartbreak Hotel" was the second song Elvis recorded that day in January, and it became the first record he released on his new label, RCA.

*Elvis and deejay Dewey Phillips (center) visited Joe Cuoghi, owner of Poplar Tunes in Memphis. **Upper right:** The biggest show the singer gave in Memphis in the 1950s occurred on the Fourth of July, 1956, at Russwood Park, a baseball stadium.*

HEARTBREAK HOTEL

Words and Music by MAE BOREN AXTON, TOMMY DURDEN and ELVIS PRESLEY

AS RECORDED BY ELVIS PRESLEY FOR RCA VICTOR

ELVIS PRESLEY

TREE PUBLISHING CO., INC.

Elvis first heard "Heartbreak Hotel" when songwriter Mae Boren Axton pitched it to him in November 1955. The song became Elvis's first million-seller.

Elvis had come across the song—written by Gainesville songwriters Mae Boren Axton and Tommy Durden—at a Nashville disc jockey convention the previous November. Durden had gotten the impetus for "Heartbreak Hotel" after reading a newspaper article about the suicide of a young man who had left behind a bitter note that read simply: "I walk a lonely street."

Axton had asked Gainesville singer Glen Reeves to record the demo and emulate Elvis's style, and Elvis copied the vocal intonations of Reeves for his recording. This story shows that Elvis's style was familiar enough to be recognized as his at the time. It also illustrates Elvis's pattern when recording a demo. He copied the interpretation of the demo singer whenever he recorded his version of a song.

At the New York RCA session, Elvis covered Carl Perkins's 1956 hit, "Blue Suede Shoes." It was the first single, recorded by different artists, to top the pop, R&B, and country charts.

"Heartbreak Hotel" borrowed the echo sound that was associated with Elvis's Sun releases, perhaps even exaggerating it. The effect is eerie, downright ghostly, especially during the opening lines to each verse when Elvis sings without accompaniment. His voice is penetrating, and the sound is despondent, perfectly capturing the alienation of disaffected youth.

Steve Sholes was disconcerted by Elvis's off-handed, instinctual approach to recording, in which he sang a take, played it back, discarded it, and then sang another, repeating the process until he felt he had captured the tune. Elvis did not read music, nor did he have any professional experience at arranging it. He just instinctively knew what to do and when to do it. RCA executives in New York were also troubled with the Nashville session. The recordings did not sound as much like Elvis's Sun records as they had wanted, and the two ballads were nothing like his previous releases.

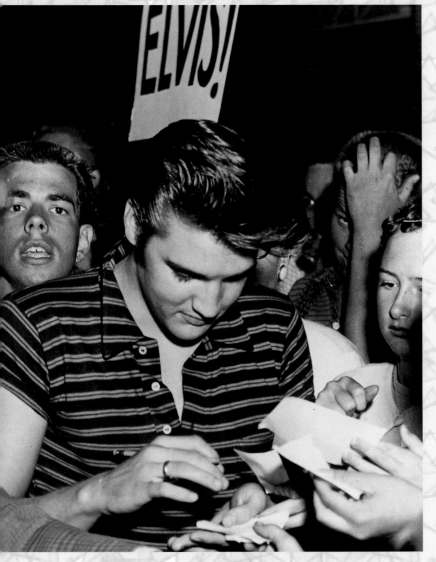

Elvis showed consideration to his fans, and they repaid him with intense loyalty.

Elvis visited Sam Phillips at Sun Records and got an impromptu guitar lesson from his original mentor.

Elvis's informal approach to recording sessions flustered RCA executive Steve Sholes.

A second recording session was arranged in New York, in which Elvis covered Carl Perkins's "Blue Suede Shoes" and Little Richard's "Tutti Frutti." This time only piano player Shorty Long was used in addition to Scotty, Bill, and D. J., and the focus was on explosive rock 'n' roll numbers. Seven tracks from the Nashville and New York sessions were chosen for Elvis's first long-playing album, *Elvis Presley*. These were combined with five songs previously recorded at Sun but never released. Interestingly, "Heartbreak Hotel" was not included on the first album.

Released on March 13, 1956, *Elvis Presley* sold over 360,000 copies by the end of April. At $3.98 per album, this made it RCA's first million-dollar album by a single artist. *Elvis Presley* also became the first album in music history to sell over a million copies. It reached No. 1 on *Billboard*'s Top LPs chart.

THE COLORED FOLKS BEEN SINGING IT AND PLAYING IT JUST LIKE I'M DOIN' NOW, MAN, FOR MORE YEARS THAN I KNOW. THEY PLAYED IT LIKE THAT IN THE SHANTIES AND JUKE JOINTS AND NOBODY PAID IT NO MIND 'TIL I GOOSE IT UP. I GOT IT FROM THEM. DOWN IN TUPELO, MISSISSIPPI, I USED TO HEAR OLD ARTHUR CRUDUP BANG HIS BOX THE WAY I DO NOW, AND I SAID IF I EVER GOT TO THE PLACE I COULD FEEL ALL OLD ARTHUR FELT, I'D BE A MUSIC MAN LIKE NOBODY EVER SAW.
—ELVIS PRESLEY, *CHARLOTTE OBSERVER*, JUNE 26, 1956

Country Song Roundup was the first national magazine to include a feature on Elvis.

Elvis fielded questions at a press conference at the Sports Arena, Philadelphia, where he played April 5–6, 1957. At the concerts, 100 police were on hand for crowd control.

Some critics have claimed that the quality of Elvis's music began to deteriorate at RCA. They blame the decline on commercial calculation, the tightly structured schedule for recording at RCA (compared to the makeshift, down-home atmosphere at Sun), or Elvis's own desire to follow in the footsteps of Dean Martin. Elvis's music did undergo some changes once he moved to RCA, but the word "decline" is too harsh to use to describe the modification of his sound. Elvis's music did not decline at RCA, but it did move away from rockabilly to more mainstream rock 'n' roll. By the 1960s, it would mellow into a bona fide pop sound.

Part of the modification of his music was the result of deals Elvis and the Colonel made with music publisher Hill and Range, which was affiliated with RCA. After the deal was finalized, Hill and Range set up two new music publishing companies: Elvis Presley Music and Gladys Music. These companies were responsible for obtaining the rights to all the songs Elvis recorded. This setup was financially advantageous for Elvis because he received not only his performer's royalty every time he recorded a song but also a publishing royalty. Hill and Range received half the income generated by Elvis Presley Music and Gladys Music. The songwriters who published their songs through the two smaller companies gave up a large percentage

Elvis named one of his publishing companies Gladys Music after his mother.

Elvis's first RCA recording session took place in January 1956 in Nashville.

Vernon, Elvis, and Gladys relax at the first home Elvis bought, a $40,000 house on Audubon Drive.

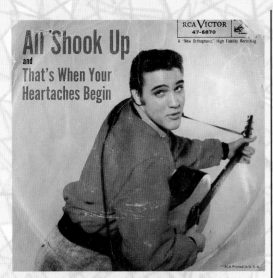

The flip side to "All Shook Up" (RCA 47-6870) was "That's When Your Heartaches Begin," one of the songs Elvis recorded when he first walked into Sam Phillips's Memphis Recording Service in 1953.

of their royalties to music publishers for the opportunity to write songs for Elvis. They were also required to give Elvis a cowriting credit, even though he never wrote a song or any part of a song in his entire career. But the songwriters didn't complain because even with reduced royalties they made a lot of money. It soon became apparent that every song Elvis recorded sold millions of copies.

On the patio of Elvis's Audubon Drive house, Vernon and Gladys Presley hosted fans who stopped by. This hospitable gesture was one they could not continue as their son became more and more famous.

Thanks to his success, Elvis began car collecting in earnest. A 1955 pink Cadillac was among his first purchases.

Obviously, it was best for all parties financially if Elvis recorded only those songs published by his own companies, although contractually he was not prevented from recording other songs. Ultimately, the Hill and Range deal limited Elvis because the material it obtained for Elvis Presley Music and Gladys Music sometimes came from songwriting hacks who had been employed by Hill and Range for years. Any writer with an exclusive agreement for another publisher was restricted from having his work recorded by Elvis. Consequently, Elvis was sometimes saddled with lackluster material from mediocre writers.

Throughout the rest of 1956, as Elvis recorded more material at RCA, he moved further away from the pure rockabilly of Sun Records and closer to a fully integrated rock 'n' roll style. By July 1956, when he stepped back into the RCA studios, Elvis seemed to be seeking a bigger, more explosive sound. It was in this session that he recorded two of his signature singles—"Hound Dog" and "Don't Be Cruel."

Jerry Leiber and Mike Stoller wrote "Hound Dog" in 1952 for blues singer Willie Mae "Big Mama" Thornton at the request of Johnny Otis, a hustling bandleader, producer, composer, and R&B deejay. Otis invited the team to watch Thornton rehearse in his garage-turned-studio. After watching the mighty singer belt out a few numbers, Leiber and Stoller composed "Hound Dog"—a song about a gigolo—in about ten minutes. Thornton growled the saucy lyrics to a hard-driving blues beat, and "Hound Dog" sold over a half million copies, climbed to No. 1 on the R&B charts, and became a top-selling record in the R&B market during 1953.

HOUND DOG

WORDS AND MUSIC BY JERRY LEIBER AND MIKE STOLLER

The sheet music for "Hound Dog" featured a photo of Elvis in rehearsal for The Steve Allen Show. *"Hound Dog" was the first record on which Elvis used the background vocals of the Jordanaires.*

Famed rock 'n' roll songwriters Leiber and Stoller were barely in their 20s when they wrote "Hound Dog" in 1952 for blues singer Willie Mae "Big Mama" Thornton.

Million Dollar Quartet

On December 4, 1956, Carl Perkins was recording at Sun Studios with Jerry Lee Lewis on piano. Some time in the afternoon, Elvis walked in with Las Vegas dancer Marilyn Evans on his arm. According to the album notes, Johnny Cash's contribution that day was mainly visual. Sam Phillips had put a bug in Johnny Cash's ear about the rare photo opportunity taking place, and Cash came in for the newspaper snapshot but did not stay for the extended jam session. A bootleg version of 17 of the 37 songs on the famous tape was released in 1980; in 1990, RCA released a legitimate version under the title *The Million Dollar Quartet.*

The famed Million Dollar Quartet (left to right): Jerry Lee Lewis, Carl Perkins, Elvis, and Johnny Cash.

Vegas Flop

Elvis and his band enjoyed some sun before a show.

In April 1956, the Colonel booked Elvis into a two-week engagement at the New Frontier Hotel in Las Vegas, a venture that turned out to be a disaster. Perhaps Parker should have known better than to book Elvis into a major engagement outside the South with an audience made up mostly of adults. After a few performances, Elvis was bumped to second billing in favor of a more typical Vegas entertainer, comedian Shecky Green. Stung by the rejection, Elvis would remember his failure in Las Vegas for many years. However, he did have a stroke of luck during the Vegas trip: Elvis was introduced to "Hound Dog" when he saw Freddie Bell and the Bellboys perform the song in the hotel lounge. A few months later, "Hound Dog" became Elvis's signature song, ultimately bringing him as much controversy as fame.

Las Vegas audiences gave Elvis the cold shoulder.

Elvis kidded around with manager Tom Parker for a publicity shot for Elvis's first Las Vegas appearance.

Several performers covered "Hound Dog," including country artists Tommy Duncan, Betsy Gay, Jack Turner, and Billy Starr, and lounge act Freddie Bell and the Bellboys. Bell enlivened the tempo and tampered with the lyrics in a humorous way, adding the line, "You ain't never caught a rabbit, and you ain't no friend of mine." Elvis caught the Bellboys' act in April 1956 when he was booked into the New Frontier Hotel in Las Vegas. Although Elvis flopped in Vegas, he brought back a little souvenir—Bell's comedic version of "Hound Dog."

A male singer belting out the opening line to "Hound Dog" seems odd because the song was clearly written for a female voice, and Elvis's decision to add "Hound Dog" to his repertoire has been interpreted variously by rock music historians. Some insist that Elvis must have been familiar with the Thornton version because he was an R&B enthusiast, and they speculate that he recorded Bell's version because he recognized its humor. Detractors suggest that he appropriated the blues tune without realizing its roots. It seems likely, however, that Elvis did know of Thornton's record. Although Elvis's recorded version was a rock 'n' roll interpretation patterned after Bell's, his rendition on the Berle show owes something to the growling, bump-and-grind vernacular of Thornton's bluesy "Hound Dog."

Pressured by producer Steve Sholes to record the tune, Elvis finally captured "Hound Dog" after about 30 takes in RCA's New York studios. Backed by "Don't Be Cruel," the record became the biggest two-sided hit in history. It climbed to No. 1 and held that position for 11 weeks, longer than any other single release of the rock 'n' roll era. It also reached No. 1 on the country-western and rhythm-and-blues charts.

> WHEN I FIRST KNEW
> ELVIS, HE HAD A MILLION
> DOLLARS' WORTH OF
> TALENT. NOW HE HAS A
> MILLION DOLLARS.
> —COLONEL TOM PARKER, 1956

Elvis liked to tickle the ivories to warm up before a session, but he seldom played the piano on any of his recordings. Shorty Long played piano on "Don't Be Cruel."

"Don't Be Cruel" was the flip side of "Hound Dog." A relatively new tune, "Don't Be Cruel" had not been recorded by any singer prior to Elvis. As the song was not associated with any singer's specific style, Elvis could make it entirely his own. The recording's easygoing but fast-paced rhythm, light tone, and harmonious backup vocals by the Jordanaires indicate how far Elvis had drifted from the sounds of pure R&B and country music.

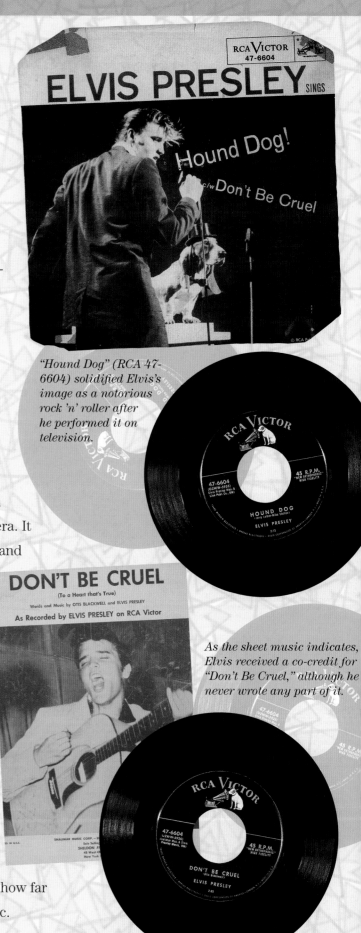

"Hound Dog" (RCA 47-6604) solidified Elvis's image as a notorious rock 'n' roller after he performed it on television.

As the sheet music indicates, Elvis received a co-credit for "Don't Be Cruel," although he never wrote any part of it.

Despite his controversial image, on September 26, 1956, Elvis returned as a hometown hero to Tupelo, Mississippi. Mayor James Ballard proclaimed it Elvis Presley Day, and Mississippi Governor J. P. Calamine awarded a scroll to Elvis. The singer performed at the Mississippi-Alabama Fair and Dairy Show.

"Don't Be Cruel" was written by rhythm-and-blues singer-songwriter Otis Blackwell. He had sold the song to a music publisher, Shalimar Music, for $25 on Christmas Eve 1955. Elvis's parent publisher, Hill and Range, had acquired the song, and the demo was one from a stack the hot new singer listened to during an RCA recording session in July 1956. When Elvis wanted to record the song, Blackwell was told that he would have to cut a deal and share the writer's credit with him, though Elvis did not contribute anything to writing the song. Blackwell was uneasy about the deal, but he realized he stood to make a great deal of money from royalties—even at half-interest—if Elvis recorded the song. This would not be the last time Elvis received a writing credit on a song he did not originally compose.

Elvis's concert was a huge change from the time when, at age 10, he had crooned "Old Shep" in the same fair's talent show and won second prize.

Otis Blackwell

Respected singer-songwriter Otis Blackwell composed many rock 'n' roll standards in the 1950s and 1960s. Born in Brooklyn in 1932, Blackwell grew up admiring country-western singer and actor Tex Ritter. Otis became a staff writer for Shalimar Music in early 1956 after he sold six songs, including "Don't Be Cruel," for $25 each to that company. Blackwell had been standing in front of the Brill Building (home to rock 'n' roll music publishing) in New York City on Christmas Eve when an arranger asked him if he had any songs to sell. The man then took Blackwell to meet Shalimar's owners, who purchased the songs and hired him after the holidays. Elvis recorded ten Blackwell compositions, including "Fever" (written with Eddie Cooley), "All Shook Up," "Paralyzed," and "Return to Sender" (cowritten with Winfield Scott). Among Blackwell's other rock 'n' roll classics are Jerry Lee Lewis's "Great Balls of Fire" and "Breathless." Blackwell sang on the demos of his songs for Elvis and Jerry Lee and imitated their styles, but he and Elvis never met.

During the recording session, Elvis rehearsed "Don't Be Cruel" a couple of times with his regular backup musicians, a piano player hired by RCA, and the Jordanaires. Then the group worked on the song, finessing it as they went through almost 30 takes. All the musicians contributed something in their own way. D. J. Fontana used Elvis's leather-covered guitar as a makeshift drum to capture a snare effect by laying it across his lap and hitting the back with a mallet. Their efforts resulted in one of Elvis's most beloved songs and one of his personal favorites. Total sales for any Presley single are often difficult to calculate, but by March 1992, the "Hound Dog"/"Don't Be Cruel" single had been awarded triple platinum status by the Recording Industry Association of America (RIAA).

But it was more than just a new promotional strategy and some minor developments in his music that transformed Elvis Presley

In 1956, Elvis burst onto the national scene amidst controversy and fanfare, making it a pivotal year in the life of the young Southern boy.

Elvis's gold lamé suit was made by Nudie Cohen, who designed flamboyant clothing and automobiles for celebrities.

The Jordanaires

Formed in 1948, gospel quartet the Jordanaires have backed many diverse performers, including Kitty Wells, Hank Snow, and Ricky Nelson. The members have changed several times over the years. The four men who backed Elvis Presley were (clockwise from top left) Hoyt Hawkins (baritone), Gordon Stoker (first tenor), Hugh Jarrett (bass), and Neal Matthews (second tenor). In January 1956, Stoker was included as a backup singer on Elvis's first RCA recording session in a makeshift group with Ben and Brock Speer of the gospel-singing Speer Family. On another session later that year, Stoker was again hired to back Elvis without the rest of the quartet. When Elvis asked the tenor where the rest of the Jordanaires were, Stoker replied that he had been the only one asked. Elvis told him, "If anything comes of this, I want the Jordanaires to work all my sessions from now on, and my personal appearances, too." With that verbal agreement, the Jordanaires became the "Sound Behind the King" for more than a decade.

into a rock 'n' roll singer. A vital part of this change occurred because of the image of Elvis the media constructed at that time, particularly after his controversial appearances on television.

Two weeks after Elvis's first RCA recording session, he made his first television appearance on Tommy and Jimmy Dorsey's weekly *Stage Show*. During the next eight weeks, he appeared on this variety series five more

Fame launched Elvis into a whirlwind schedule of concert bookings in 1956.

Elvis introduced his provocative performing style to a national audience on TV's Stage Show. *With each successive appearance on* Stage Show, *Elvis grew more confident and his performing style became more explosive.*

times, and each time the show received better ratings. The first show, however, was only moderately successful and was beaten in the ratings by *The Perry Como Show*.

Stage Show was typical of television variety programs in the mid-1950s. Understanding the nature of these variety shows helps us to understand why Elvis created such a stir. With an hour-long format, *Stage Show* featured performances by a diverse group of entertainers, ranging from popular singers to animal acts to ballet dancers. Each week a guest host introduced some of the acts for that particular program. On Elvis's first appearance, he was introduced by Cleveland disc jockey Bill Randle,

Acclaimed swing musicians Tommy and Jimmy Dorsey starred in the movie The Fabulous Dorseys, *released in 1947.*

who was supposedly the first radio personality to play an Elvis record outside the South. Randle, however, would be the only person featured on any of Elvis's *Stage Show* appearances who had any connection with the young singer. The other hosts and guest stars who appeared with Elvis included jazz singers Sarah Vaughan and Ella Fitzgerald, stand-up comedians Joe E. Lewis and Henny Youngman, a chimpanzee act, an acrobatic team, and an 11-year-old organist. Compared to these types of entertainers—who were considered suitable for family audiences—Elvis's new, high-powered music and dynamic

Elvis's first performance on The Milton Berle Show *was aboard aircraft carrier USS Hancock at the San Diego Naval Station.*

In June 1956, the singer's second appearance on Milton Berle's program created a show business scandal when he performed his provocative rendition of "Hound Dog."

performing style seemed alien. The young singer's Beale Street clothing and ducktail haircut made him stand out even more.

On his first appearance, Elvis was visibly nervous. He sang "Shake, Rattle, and Roll" and "Heartbreak Hotel," doing a little shaking and shimmying, and then quickly moved offstage. By his final appearance, more of an interaction between Elvis and his audience took place as the young man worked hard to drive the girls in the crowd into a screaming frenzy. When he strummed the

Elvis's ducktail haircut was emulated by teenagers but criticized by adults.

Scotty Moore, D. J. Fontana, and Bill Black backed Elvis for the popular Berle TV shows.

opening chord of "Heartbreak Hotel" on his guitar, a burst of screams and applause broke out. Elvis hesitated for a moment, tantalizing the audience with anticipation. As he broke into song, he moved across the stage, shaking his shoulders and swinging his legs. Certain moves were obviously designed to elicit emotional responses from the girls, and Elvis's smiles proved he was delighted at this explosive effect on his female fans. The interaction between Elvis and his fans was much like a game: He teased the women with his provocative moves; they screamed for more; he promised to go further; sometimes he did.

> IN A PIVOTING STANCE, HIS HIPS SWING SENSUOUSLY FROM SIDE TO SIDE AND HIS ENTIRE BODY TAKES ON A FRANTIC QUIVER, AS IF HE HAD SWALLOWED A JACKHAMMER.
> —*TIME* MAGAZINE, MAY 15, 1956

In late spring of 1956, Elvis appeared on *The Milton Berle Show* for the first time. The show was broadcast from the USS *Hancock*, which was docked at the San Diego Naval Station. Despite the novel location, this television appearance is barely mentioned in biographies or other accounts of Elvis's career because his second appearance on the Berle program has completely overshadowed it. This appearance on June 5 fanned the flames

Unlike some other personalities, Milton Berle always had kind words to say about Elvis.

Elvis's sex appeal came across loud and clear during the bluesy final chorus of "Hound Dog"; it stirred the studio audience into a frenzy.

of the nationwide controversy over his hip-swiveling performing style. Elvis sang "Hound Dog" for the first time on television that spring night. When he began the song, no one knew what to expect because the tune was new. But the audience responded immediately with enthusiasm. Elvis then went a bit further in his performance: He slowed down the final chorus of the song to a blues tempo, and he thrust his pelvis to the beat of the music in a particularly suggestive manner. The studio audience went wild with excitement.

HE'S JUST ONE BIG HUNK OF FORBIDDEN FRUIT.

—ANONYMOUS

The Florida tour included an engagement at the Olympic Theater in Miami.

The reaction of teenage girls to Elvis's sensual performing style roused the anger of the PTA, civic groups, church leaders, and the mainstream press.

The next day, the press nicknamed him "Elvis the Pelvis." Many described his act by comparing it to a striptease. Jack Gould of *The New York Times* declared, "Mr. Presley has no discernible singing ability," while John Crosby of the *New York Herald Tribune* called Elvis "unspeakably untalented and vulgar." The criticism prompted parents, religious groups from the North and South, and the Parent-Teacher Association to condemn Elvis and rock 'n' roll music by associating both with juvenile delinquency. Elvis could not

Elvis didn't understand the furor in the press over his performances.

Steve Allen, who disliked rock 'n' roll, booked Elvis on his show solely for the high TV ratings.

understand what all the fuss was about: "It's only music. In a lot of papers, they say that rock 'n' roll is a big influence on juvenile delinquency. I don't think that it is. I don't see how music has anything to do with it at all.... I've been blamed for just about everything wrong in this country."

After *The Milton Berle Show*, Colonel Parker booked Elvis on *The Steve Allen Show*, a new variety program that aired at the same time as Ed Sullivan's immensely popular show. Allen hated rock 'n' roll, but he was aware of the high ratings Berle's show received when Elvis appeared. He was also aware of the controversy. To tone down Elvis's sexy performance, Allen insisted that he wear a tuxedo during his segment, and he introduced him as "the new Elvis Presley." Elvis sang one of his latest singles, a slow but hard-driving ballad called "I Want You, I Need You, I Love You." Immediately after that number, the curtain opened to reveal a cuddly basset hound sitting on top of a tall wooden stool. Elvis sang "Hound Dog" to the docile creature, which upstaged the singer with his sad-eyed expressions. Allen used humor to cool down Elvis's sensual performing style, prohibiting him from moving around much on stage and even preventing him from wearing his trademark Beale Street clothes. The fans were furious, and they picketed NBC-TV studios the next morning with placards that read, "We want the gyratin' Elvis."

Later in the program, Elvis joined Allen, Imogene Coca, and fellow Southerner Andy Griffith in a comedy sketch that satirized country-western programs, not unlike *Louisiana Hayride*. Many of the jokes were condescending toward Southern culture. Allen's presentation of Elvis singing to a dog plus the appearance of the "hayseed" sketch actually ridiculed Elvis. Steve Allen was the real winner that night because his show beat Sullivan in the ratings.

In rehearsal for his appearance on The Steve Allen Show, *Elvis sang "Hound Dog" to Sherlock, a basset hound.*

In December 1956, the end of his first year as a national sensation, Elvis performed for the last time on Louisiana Hayride. *The show had helped make him a big draw in the South.*

Elvis cuts loose during the show that made TV history when Ed Sullivan and the CBS censors ordered that the cameras shoot him only from the waist up.

Ed Eats His Words

"I'll not have him at any price—he's not my cup of tea."

—*Ed Sullivan, before Elvis's ratings-busting appearance on* The Steve Allen Show, TIME, *July 23, 1956*

"I want to say to Elvis Presley and the country that this is a real decent, fine boy, and we've never had a pleasanter experience on our show with a big name than we've had with you."

—*Ed Sullivan, to Elvis in front of the studio audience after Elvis's third appearance on* The Ed Sullivan Show, *January 6, 1957*

Elvis had established himself as an entertainer who could attract a large television audience and boost ratings, so it's not surprising that after many rejections, the Colonel finally arranged for Elvis to appear on *The Ed Sullivan Show,* a highly rated, prime-time variety program. Sullivan, who was a powerful figure in the industry, had stated publicly that he would not allow Elvis to appear on his show because it was a family program. But ratings speak louder than scruples, and Sullivan backed down from this stance after *The Steve Allen Show* was so successful. Elvis was paid an unprecedented fee of $50,000 for three appearances on *The Ed Sullivan Show*. This was a lot more than the $5,000 per show Colonel Parker had asked for only a few weeks earlier when Sullivan turned him down.

Elvis's performance on *The Ed Sullivan Show* is cemented in the annals of rock music history because of the censors' decision to shoot the volatile young singer only from the waist up. However, contrary to popular belief, this decision was not made until his third appearance. Actor Charles Laughton served as

After declaring that Elvis Presley would never appear on his program, Ed Sullivan backed down and signed Elvis for three shows.

Above and far right: On Elvis's first two appearances on The Ed Sullivan Show, *CBS did not censor his act.*

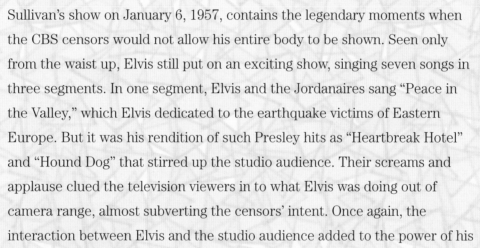

substitute host the night of Elvis's first appearance because Sullivan was recuperating from an auto accident. In kinescopes and video footage of that performance, Elvis can be seen in full figure, crooning "Love Me Tender" and "Don't Be Cruel," then later belting out "Hound Dog" and "Ready Teddy."

Elvis's third and final appearance on Sullivan's show on January 6, 1957, contains the legendary moments when the CBS censors would not allow his entire body to be shown. Seen only from the waist up, Elvis still put on an exciting show, singing seven songs in three segments. In one segment, Elvis and the Jordanaires sang "Peace in the Valley," which Elvis dedicated to the earthquake victims of Eastern Europe. But it was his rendition of such Presley hits as "Heartbreak Hotel" and "Hound Dog" that stirred up the studio audience. Their screams and applause clued the television viewers in to what Elvis was doing out of camera range, almost subverting the censors' intent. Once again, the interaction between Elvis and the studio audience added to the power of his performance. After Elvis's final number, Sullivan declared him to be "a real decent, fine boy"—a rather hypocritical statement considering what he and the censors had just done to Elvis's act.

For years people have wondered why Elvis was censored during his third appearance on Sullivan's show. The simplest and most probable explanation is that Sullivan received negative criticism about Elvis's earlier appearances. Other, more outrageous explanations include the theory that the Colonel forced Sullivan to apologize publicly for remarks he'd made about Elvis to the press the previous summer, and the waist-up-only order was Sullivan's way of getting back at Parker. The wildest explanation was offered by a former director of *The Ed Sullivan*

Before the show, Ed Sullivan spoke with his guests, Elvis Presley and Brazilian singer Leny Eversong.

Show, who said that during his second appearance, Elvis put a cardboard tube down the front of his trousers and manipulated it to make the studio audience scream. To avoid a repeated occurrence of that behavior, Sullivan supposedly insisted on the above-the-waist coverage for Elvis's final appearance. None of these explanations offers any real insight into Sullivan's motivations but all add to the folklore surrounding this event, thereby enhancing Elvis's image as a notorious rock 'n' roller.

After rehearsal for his third appearance on The Ed Sullivan Show, *Elvis chatted with members of the audience.*

Fans greet their idol's train upon his arrival in Miami in August 1956.

Looking back, it all seems so harmless, but Elvis appeared on the scene at a time when rock 'n' roll was coming under fire in the popular press. The controversy centered on whether this new style of music associated with teenagers led to teenage sex and crime. During the spring and summer of 1956, many national magazines published articles that claimed there was a link between rock 'n' roll and juvenile delinquency. At the same time, Elvis was often featured in these same magazines in articles that sensationalized the effect of his sensual performing style on teenage girls. Headlines blared

The attire of R&B Memphis musicians inspired Elvis to dress in the "cool cat" fashions of the day.

"Presley's Impact Piles Up Fans, Fads—and Fear," while trumped-up stories declared his "sex-hot flame" to be inextinguishable. It did not take a great leap of imagination for journalists, reviewers, and critics to relate Elvis's personal appearance and sensual performing style to the decadence of rock 'n' roll and the horrors of juvenile delinquency.

When the popular press was not openly criticizing Elvis, they were ridiculing him. Despite the fact that his music was identified as rock 'n' roll, journalists and reporters often referred to him disparagingly as a "hillbilly singer." He

Frequently photographed, Elvis puckered up for the camera.

Elvis was on his toes, his famous move, at Miami's Olympic Theater.

Florida Theater

The controversy over Elvis's sensual performing style reached a fever pitch during his 1956 summer tour. When Elvis played Jacksonville, Florida, in mid-August, he sold out all three shows for both nights at the Florida Theater. Reacting to the publicity surrounding "Elvis the Pelvis," Juvenile Court Judge Marion W. Gooding attended the first show, in which Elvis moved to his music as usual. Gooding met with Elvis and Colonel Tom Parker afterward and warned the young singer to "quieten" his act. The police attended to film the show to ensure that Elvis obeyed the judge's directive. In an atypical public display of sarcasm, Elvis reacted to the directive by wiggling only his little finger during the performance. *LIFE* magazine centered its August 27 article on Elvis around the Jacksonville incident, sensationalizing the stories about the judge's threats and the tales about the crazed fans who tore off Elvis's clothes after one of his shows.

was maligned for his Southern accent, his flashy clothes, his long sideburns, and his ducktail haircut so heavily laden with pomade that his blond hair looked black. The latter in particular seemed to raise the ire of the press and public alike. Never before had an entertainer's hair been the subject of so much attention; Elvis's hairstyle was criticized because of its length, its use of pomade, and the fact that so many teenagers emulated it.

Despite the predominance of negative stories about Elvis in the press, another type of publicity began to emerge slowly but surely. This new pattern of publicity presented a different Elvis Presley, a persona that was contradictory to the high-profile figure who had caused so much controversy. This gentler side of the singer's image has come to be known in Elvis lore and literature as the "other Elvis" or "good Elvis."

The "other Elvis" surfaced on July 1, 1956, on the television interview program *Hy Gardner Calling.* The program consisted of syndicated columnist Gardner calling one or two celebrities on the telephone each week. A split-screen technique allowed viewers to watch both Gardner and the celebrity as they talked on the phone. The episode featuring Elvis gave the young singer an opportunity to dispel some of

From the time he cut his first record, in the summer of 1954, until the day he died, Elvis rarely refused an autograph, and fans were always eager to take advantage of the opportunity to get one.
Far left: *Movie publicity portrait of Elvis Presley.*

Hy Gardner hosted the TV interview show Hy Gardner Calling. Via split-screen broadcast, he interviewed Elvis to give the young man a chance to respond to the negative publicity being thrown at him.

Elvis and merchandiser Hank Saperstein showed off a new Elvis canvas sneaker for girls.
Below: *In August 1956, after a visit to his barber, Elvis clowned with one of Memphis's finest. In the '60s and '70s, Elvis rented the Malco Theater, seen behind him, after-hours so he could watch movies in peace with his friends.*

the vicious rumors that were circulating about him, including one that purported he often smoked marijuana to reach the frenetic state necessary for his performing style and another that stated he had once shot his mother. Viewers saw a down-to-earth Elvis, who expressed that he was experiencing confusion over the enormity of his success. He also professed disbelief that critics could find his music to be a negative influence on anyone.

Stories about Elvis's close relationship with his parents began to appear in print. The fact that he didn't smoke or drink was brought out in some articles. Elvis was known to be polite during interviews, referring to his elders as "sir" or "ma'am." Parker publicized Elvis's strong feelings about helping less-fortunate people and booked him for many charity benefits, including those for the American Cancer Society and the March of Dimes.

IN THE '50S ELVIS CAME TO ONE OF MY SHOWS IN MEMPHIS, AT THE CITY AUDITORIUM. YOU COULD HAVE LIT A CIGARETTE FROM HIM—THAT'S HOW HOT HE WAS. THE MONEY FROM THE SHOW WENT FOR LITTLE LEAGUE BASEBALL UNIFORMS AND STUFF FOR THE CHILDREN OF MEMPHIS, BLACK, WHITE AND OTHERWISE. [ELVIS] WAS INTO THAT. THEY CALL HIM THE KING, AND I AGREE.
—B. B. KING, "THIS IS ELVIS," *TV GUIDE* SPECIAL COLLECTORS ISSUE

Still, publications touted singer Pat Boone as a more clean-cut—therefore a more appropriate—teenage idol than

The rock and blues royalty of Memphis—Elvis and B. B. King.

Elvis Presley. Parker then tried to make Elvis seem more wholesome by getting his name and picture on a line of children's products. The Colonel sealed a deal with promoter extraordinaire Hank Saperstein to merchandise Elvis along the same lines as his other famous clients, who included Wyatt Earp, the Lone Ranger, and Lassie. Every child in the country could find these all-American heroes on everything from lunch boxes to T-shirts. The Colonel wanted them to find Elvis's image on such products as well. In addition to the usual line of children's items, girls were able to buy Elvis Presley lipstick in colors of Hound Dog Orange, Tutti Frutti Red, and Heartbreak Pink. They could also get Elvis Presley charm bracelets to wear. Parker exploited this "other Elvis" image to counter the portrayal of Elvis as a hedonistic rock 'n' roller and to push the singing idol closer toward respectability.

Colonel Tom Parker established Elvis Presley Enterprises in the summer of 1956. As a result, 18 licensees produced about 30 Elvis products, including shoes, jewelry, and cosmetics.

Reporters of the mainstream press had saddled Elvis with what they thought was a clever nickname, "Elvis the Pelvis"—a name the serious young singer despised. On Hy Gardner's television interview program, Elvis complained, "I don't like being called Elvis the Pelvis—I mean it's one of the most childish expressions I have ever heard coming from an adult." By referring to his gyrating hips, the moniker became shorthand for the accusations of tastelessness that dogged Elvis during this time. The Colonel hoped to erase "Elvis the Pelvis" from the public consciousness by showcasing the "other Elvis" at every turn.

Sincerely touched by the devotion of his fans, Elvis interacted with them in an intimate, physical way that few stars ever dared.
Inset (top): *Elvis made the cover of* TV Guide *for his first appearance on* The Ed Sullivan Show.

Another step in Elvis's transformation occurred with his career move into Hollywood movies. During the years 1956 to 1958, four films featuring Elvis Presley were released to enthusiastic audiences. The films recast Elvis the Pelvis into Elvis the Rebel, a subtle but significant change. As Hollywood's newest rebel, Elvis eased into a more recognizable persona, already made acceptable by Marlon Brando and James Dean.

Elvis's controversial image triggered damaging coverage from the mainstream press.

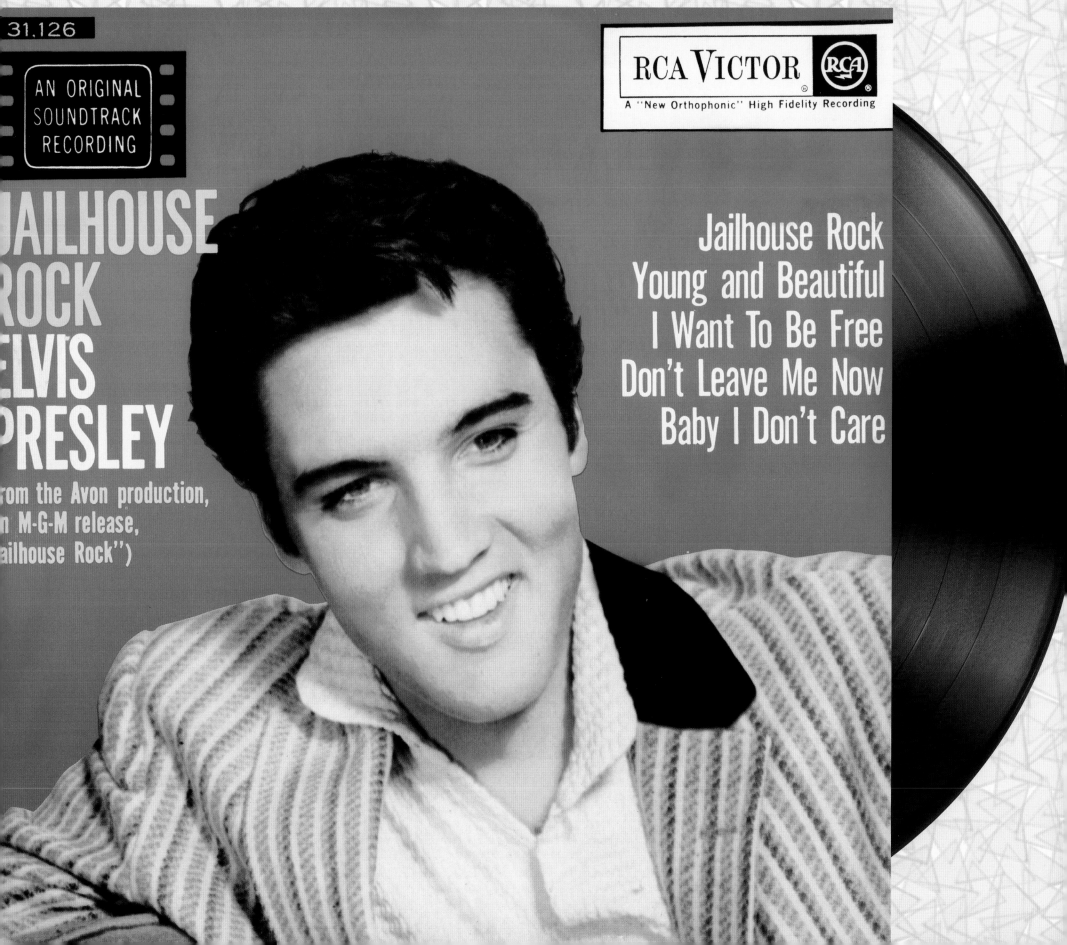

ELVIS PRESLEY

SINGS THE SONGS FROM
THE AVON PRODUCTION, AN M.G.M. RELEASE,

"JAILHOUSE ROCK"

SIDE 1. JAILHOUSE ROCK :: YOUNG AND BEAUTIFUL :: I WANT TO BE FREE :: DON'T LEAVE ME NOW
:: BABY I DON'T CARE :: TREAT ME NICE

SIDE 2. I BEG OF YOU :: DON'T :: PLAYING FOR KEEPS :: SHAKE RATTLE AND ROLL
:: GOOD ROCKIN' TONIGHT :: I DON'T CARE IF THE SUN DON'T SHINE

THE FABULOUS MR. PRESLEY DOES IT AGAIN! FOLLOWING THE FANTASTIC SUCCESS OF *LOVING YOU* (31,097), MOST OF THOSE IN THE KNOW THOUGHT THAT THE PEAK HAD BEEN REACHED IN THE ALREADY UNBELIEVABLY SUCCESSFUL CAREER OF THIS YOUNG MAN. BUT BROTHER, WERE THEY WRONG! THIS FILM, RELEASED BY M.G.M. LOOKS LIKE BREAKING ALL PREVIOUS RECORDS.

JAILHOUSE ROCK is Elvis Presley's third appearance before the movie cameras. An Avon Production released through M-G-M, this film goes far beyond anything Elvis has done to date. Cast in the role of a well-meaning but fiery-tempered young Southerner, Elvis — Vince Everett in the film—finds himself sent to prison after he accidentally kills a man. The changes wrought by his prison life and his relentless ambition to gain wealth and fame after his release are other aspects of this emotionally charged film.

Needless to say, when Vince Everett looks for a means to gain wealth he naturally turns to singing, which gives Mr. Presley an excellent chance to utilize his voice while staying in character.

In this album, on side one, Elvis sings all the songs which were written especially for the film. There is the throbbing title song, *Jailhouse Rock*, which opens the album, followed by *Young and Beautiful, I Want to be Free, Don't Leave Me Now*, and *Baby I Don't Care* . . . all in the inimitable style of this exceptional young singer and actor, Elvis Presley.

Side two features old Presley favourites (how old can they be?) plus numbers not previously released in Southern Africa.

THEM AIN'T TACTICS, HONEY; IT'S JUST THE BEAST IN ME.

—VINCE (ELVIS), IN *JAILHOUSE ROCK*

The extended-play (EP) album released as the soundtrack for *Jailhouse Rock* serves as a snapshot of the times. EP albums were a fixture in the recording industry during the 1950s, tapering off in popularity during the 1960s. Generally containing four to five songs, an EP offered the listener something more than a single, but it cost less than a long-playing album, which averaged ten to twelve songs. Elvis's last commercially released EP was the soundtrack for *Easy Come, Easy Go* in 1967. The *Jailhouse Rock* EP also indicated the enormity of Elvis's popularity in the winter of 1957–1958, charting for an astounding 49 weeks and remaining at No. 1 for 28 weeks. *Billboard* named it EP of the Year for 1958. The highlight of the EP was the famous title song—the embodiment of the Presley persona during that era.

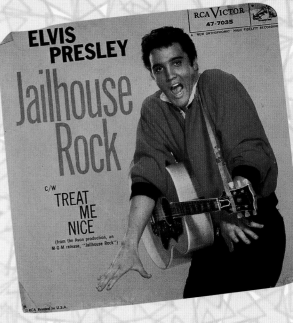

Leiber and Stoller, who wrote "Jailhouse Rock" and "Treat Me Nice" (RCA 47-7035), served as unofficial producers on the two songs.

Penned by the legendary Jerry Leiber and Mike Stoller, "Jailhouse Rock" became another No. 1 record for Elvis. It entered the British charts at No. 1, making it the first single ever to do so. The rock 'n' roll songwriting duo was commissioned to write most of the songs for the movie *Jailhouse Rock,* though they were less than enthusiastic about the assignment.

Elvis's controversial performing style formed the basis of the choreography in the "Jailhouse Rock" production number.

Prior to "Jailhouse Rock," Elvis had recorded a handful of songs from Leiber and Stoller, including "Hound Dog," "Love Me," and a couple of tunes from *Loving You.* The two songwriters were not impressed with Elvis's interpretation of their material. Leiber and Stoller had a tendency to write hard-driving, R&B-flavored tunes with satiric or tongue-in-cheek lyrics that could be understood at more than one level. Elvis, on the other hand, performed most of his material straight, as when he recorded the duo's "Love Me,"

In Jailhouse Rock, *Mickey Shaughnessy costarred as the convi[ct] who teaches Elvis's character to play the guitar.*

which they had originally intended as a lampoon of country-western music. Leiber and Stoller also felt that Elvis's foray into R&B territory was a fluke, and they were suspicious of his interest in blues and rhythm-and-blues.

When the three met during the April 1957 recording session for "Jailhouse Rock," Leiber and Stoller quickly changed their minds about Elvis. They realized he knew his music and he was a workhorse in the studio. The pair took over the recording sessions, serving as unofficial producers of "Jailhouse Rock," "Treat Me Nice," "(You're So Square) Baby, I Don't Care," and other tunes. Their collaboration with Elvis and his musicians on "Jailhouse Rock" resulted in the singer's hardest-rocking movie song. D. J. Fontana said of his drum playing, "I tried to think of someone on a chain gang smashing rocks."

Elvis clowns around during a recording session for the Jailhouse Rock *soundtrack.*

The "Jailhouse Rock" single.

Leiber and Stoller

Jerry Leiber (right) and Mike Stoller (far right) adapted aspects of blues and rhythm-and-blues when writing for rock 'n' roll performers. Their integration of these musical genres in the 1950s expanded the commercial possibilities of rock 'n' roll. The pair met in Los Angeles in 1950 when they were just 17 years old. Stoller the musician and Leiber the songwriter found they shared an interest in blues and R&B, so they spent the summer writing songs in these styles. Lester Sill, sales manager for Modern Records, took them under his wing and introduced them to performers and industry reps. Despite their youth, the pair fared well because the prominent Tin Pan Alley songwriters of the day thought rock 'n' roll was beneath them. Leiber and Stoller are noted for structuring their songs like playlets. That is, they tell a story—usually with wit or satire—within the three-minute length of a popular song. Elvis recorded about two dozen Leiber and Stoller tunes, including "Hound Dog" and "Jailhouse Rock."

The short period of time that Leiber and Stoller worked with Elvis proved beneficial to both sides. The irony and ambiguity in the lyrics of "Jailhouse Rock" gave Elvis one of his most clever rockers, while the singer's sincere and energetic delivery prevented the song from becoming too much of a burlesque—a tendency with some of the Leiber and Stoller songs written for the Coasters. These songwriters hung with Elvis long enough to contribute to the *King Creole* soundtrack, among other projects, but eventually they ran afoul of Elvis's management for trying to introduce him to new challenges.

With its combination of hard-rocking tunes and romantic ballads, the *Jailhouse Rock* EP ably supported the film of the same title. *King Creole* boasts a powerful cast and a skilled director, and *Blue Hawaii* features slick production values, but the gritty, low-budget *Jailhouse Rock* remains Elvis Presley's best film. If Elvis the rock 'n' roll rebel liberated a generation from the values, tastes, and ideals of their parents, then *Jailhouse Rock* is the only Presley film that speaks directly to the feral, sensual, and unruly nature of rock 'n' roll music.

Elvis's musicals belong to that genre known as the "teenpic" or the teen musical, in which rock 'n' roll performers were showcased in musical vehicles designed to cash in on the immense popularity of youth-oriented music. From *Rock Around the Clock*, featuring real-life rocker Bill Haley, to *Rock, Pretty Baby*, starring actors pantomiming to ersatz rock tunes, producers and studios pandered to the teenage audience by combining teen fashion, teen jargon, and teen idols with a healthy dose of generational conflict.

Could the hound dogs that appeared in this scene with Elvis and Mickey Shaughnessy be visual reference to Elvis's most famous song? **Left:** *Movie publicity photo of Elvis Presley.*

Costar Judy Tyler was killed in a car crash just after production wrapped on Jailhouse Rock. *Because of this tragedy, Elvis could never bring himself to watch the film.*

Above and right: Stills from Jailhouse Rock tried to capture Elvis's rebel image.

Released in 1957, *Jailhouse Rock* offers more than a superficial rundown of the latest fads and fashions, however, and it excludes the standard clash between generations. The plot features an insider's look at the rock 'n' roll record business (as interpreted by Hollywood) through the character of Peggy Van Alden, a record exploitation "man" (1950s title for a record promoter) who helps ex-con Vince Everett (Elvis's character) launch a singing career. Because the audience sees the business through Peggy's point of view, the film's treatment of rock music differs from other teenpics. For example, rock 'n' roll is an established, accepted style of music when the story begins, and there is no organized resistance to it by authority figures. In general, the attitude toward the music in the script is both knowing and respectful, serving to validate rock 'n' roll as a popular art form— an important consideration to teenagers of the era.

One scene does acknowledge the conflict in musical tastes between the generations. Vince and Peggy drop in on a cocktail party hosted by Peggy's parents. Mr. Van Alden is a college professor, so his friends and associates are depicted as upper-middle–class professionals. Bored and out of place, Vince is standing beside a group talking about music. A woman exclaims, "Some day they'll make the cycle back to pure old Dixieland. I say atonality is just a passing phase in jazz music. What do you think, Mr. Everett?" Vince snarls, "Lady, I don't know what the hell you're talking about!" The scene curtly draws a line between the two types of music by generation and by class, and it concludes

Tough-minded businesswoman Peggy Van Alden and streetwise Vince make a formidable pair when they negotiate with a slick lawyer to manage Vince's financial affairs.

without the two sides attempting to reconcile, which was unusual for teenpics of this era. Instead, the jazz fans come off as snobbish and dull, while Vince's ultimate success with records, television, and movies validates his style of music. For once, rock 'n' roll bests another type of music and its proponents without a character having to explain or defend rock 'n' roll's existence.

The heart of *Jailhouse Rock* is the character of Vince Everett, who swaggers and prowls through the film with attitude and magnetism. Despite his Hollywood-style conversion in the final moments, it is Vince's impudence and haughty defiance that stay with the viewer long after the final fadeout. The character embodies the rebellious spirit and sexuality of rock 'n' roll, in much the same way that Elvis did in his career. This close identification between real-life performer and fictional character is the film's strength.

Several scenes and shots illustrate the similarities between the performing styles of Elvis and Vince and help audiences make the connection. Of particular interest is a scene in which Vince spends time in a recording studio searching for a singing style. Listening to himself croon "Don't Leave Me Now," he realizes that he lacks a personal style. After rocking the tune just a bit, Vince discovers how "to make the song fit him." The scene echoes Elvis's efforts to work through a personal style at Sun Records back in the summer of 1954, an often repeated tale in Elvis's publicity. To make the connection between Vince and Elvis even stronger, the musicians used in the scene were Elvis's own backup band.

A theater lobby card from the movie.

Sherry (after kissing Vince/Elvis):
I'm coming all unglued. —Jailhouse Rock

One of the singer's sensational dance moves was a tiptoe squat.

A recording scene from Jailhouse Rock.

Also, Vince's costume in this scene duplicates Elvis's unique style of clothing. With his baggy black pants held in place by a thin belt and his tight-fitting shirt with turned-up collar and rolled-up sleeves, Vince sports the type of ultrahip attire Elvis purchased at Lansky's clothing store on Beale Street in Memphis. Similarly, Vince's hairstyle is a slightly cleaned-up version of Elvis's notorious ducktail and sideburns. Costuming and hairstyle might seem like minor details now, but to fans and audiences of the era, the similarities would have been obvious and meaningful. Most of the songs were written especially for the film by Jerry Leiber and Mike Stoller, with Stoller making a brief appearance as a studio pianist during the scene in which Vince records "Don't Leave Me Now." The participation of these famous rock 'n' roll scribes in the making of the film adds an authenticity to it, as does the elaborate choreography for the title tune. Elvis participated in choreographing "Jailhouse Rock," with the steps based on his controversial performing style.

Behind the scenes on the set of Jailhouse Rock, *lifelong movie fan Elvis Presley snaps some candids of his costars in action.*

The Haircut

The scene in which the prison barber shaves off Elvis's infamous ducktail made fans weep and parents cheer. Over the years, much speculation existed as to whether it was his real hair or a wig that was cut. A glance at the production schedule, as reprinted in Jim Hannaford's *Inside Jailhouse Rock*, reveals the truth: Two wigs were used to represent Elvis's atrocious prison do. The schedule indicates that Elvis had to film three scenes in one week—one with the butch haircut, one with the hair partially grown back, and one with his regular style. Obviously, his real hair could not have grown back in that short span of time. In later years, makeup artist William Tuttle revealed that a series of plaster casts of Elvis's head allowed them to make wigs that fit so well they were nearly impossible to detect.

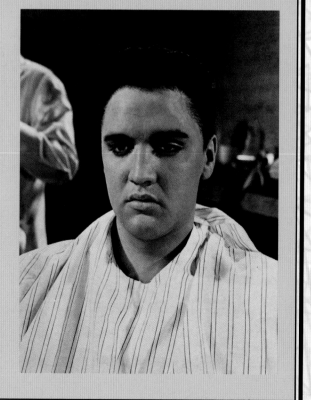

Thus, Elvis's image defined the role of Vince Everett as much as Vince perpetuated Elvis's image as a rebellious rock 'n' roller. For MGM and the producers, this guaranteed a sizable audience of Elvis fans. For audiences of the era, it added credibility and authenticity to the film. For contemporary audiences, it captured Elvis in his most popular incarnation—the young rebel who not only changed the course of popular music but also gave a generation an identity and an attitude.

A brooding, overdressed Vince (Elvis) rocks a poolside party with his rendition of "(You're So Square) Baby, I Don't Care."

In retrospect, *Jailhouse Rock* may be Elvis's best film because of the way it captures the rebellious rock 'n' roll attitude of the 1950s. Yet, Elvis appeared in three other films between 1956 and 1958, and each of them spawned hit singles and chart-topping albums.

Despite the obvious attempt to cash in on Elvis's popularity as a recording phenomenon, these four films are decidedly different from those associated with Elvis during the 1960s. Musical dramas with solid supporting casts, the 1950s films benefited from the contributions of veteran Hollywood producers and directors. Chief among them was Hal Wallis.

The first time that independent movie producer Hal Wallis saw Elvis perform, he was convinced Elvis was going to become a major star. A veteran of the movie business for 25 years, Wallis had a stellar reputation. He had worked as an executive producer at Warner Bros. for several years before forming Hal Wallis Productions in 1944. In early 1956, Wallis happened to catch Elvis's act on one of the *Stage Show* episodes. The electrifying effect Elvis had on the women in the studio audience spelled movie magic to the keen-eyed producer. Wasting no time, he called Colonel Parker the next morning to set up a screen test for the controversial young singer. Parker was cool, playing Wallis like the experienced

Elvis behind the scenes of a movie set.

Elvis helped choreograph the famous cell block production number.

dealmaker he was, before casually replying that Elvis was planning to be on the coast soon and perhaps a meeting could be arranged.

On April 1, 1956, Elvis took a screen test with respected character actor Frank Faylen. They performed a scene from N. Richard Nash's play *The Rainmaker,* which was later made into a major movie. Although it happened on April Fools' Day, Elvis's screen test was taken quite seriously. His screen presence was powerful enough for Wallis to arrange a three-picture deal. If starmaker Hal Wallis had confidence in Elvis as an actor, then Hollywood was willing to accept that the young singer was well on his way to motion picture stardom.

Vince realizes the heated effect he has on women when he reads his fan mail.

WHEN I RAN THE TEST, I FELT THE SAME THRILL I EXPERIENCED WHEN I FIRST SAW ERROL FLYNN ON THE SCREEN. ELVIS, IN A VERY DIFFERENT, MODERN WAY, HAD EXACTLY THE SAME POWER, VIRILITY, AND SEXUAL DRIVE. THE CAMERA CARESSED HIM.

—HAL WALLIS, *STARMAKER*

After seeing Elvis perform on Stage Show, *producer Hal Wallis knew he could turn the young singer into a movie star.*

Elvis had always loved the movies. When he was in high school, he had worked as an usher at Loew's State Theater in Memphis. Later in his life, when his superstar status prevented him from going out in public, Elvis often rented an entire theater just to watch a movie in peace. From the beginning of his career, Elvis had aspired to be a movie actor. When his sudden notoriety opened the door for this to happen, he was eager to do whatever it took to make a career in the movies. "Singers come and go," Elvis said, "but if you're a good actor, you can last a long time."

Love Me Tender was Elvis's first movie.

Hal Wallis was working exclusively for Paramount Pictures at the time, but the studio had no suitable script for Elvis when he signed with Wallis. So Elvis was loaned to Twentieth Century-Fox for a Civil War drama called *The Reno Brothers*. His part in the movie was a secondary role, and both Robert Wagner and Jeffrey Hunter had originally been considered for the part. It was the first and last film in which Elvis appeared that was not specifically designed as a vehicle for him.

The Discoverer

Hal Wallis, a respected veteran of the film industry, worked in Hollywood from the silent era through the 1970s. He began as a publicity man for Warner Bros., working his way up to executive producer in charge of production by 1933. There he produced several classics, including *Little Caesar*, *Sergeant York*, and *The Maltese Falcon*. In 1944, he became an independent producer, releasing his films through Paramount and later Universal. As an independent, Wallis had a reputation for fostering new talent and was dubbed "the Discoverer." Among those whose screen careers he helped were Kirk Douglas, the team of Dean Martin and Jerry Lewis, Shirley MacLaine, and Elvis Presley.

Wallis produced nine films starring Elvis, and his personal favorite was *King Creole*. He once said that one of the biggest regrets in his career was not being able to follow through on his idea for a western starring John Wayne as an old gunfighter and Elvis as his protégé. Wallis died in 1986.

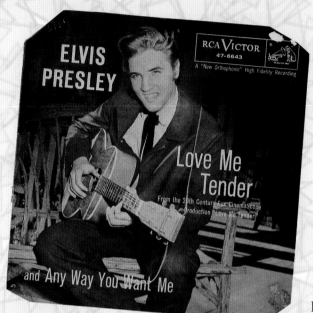

The "Love Me Tender" single.

The movie's theme song was taken from a Civil War ballad called "Aura Lee" and reworked as "Love Me Tender." Elvis released the song as a single, which became immensely popular and gained wide exposure after he sang it on *The Ed Sullivan Show*. Because the tune was such a hit, the name of the movie was changed to *Love Me Tender* before it opened in New York on November 16, 1956. The storyline follows the fortunes of a farm family after the Civil War. Elvis plays the youngest son, Clint Reno, who marries his eldest brother's girl. Everyone presumes that the brother has been killed in the war, but he returns unexpectedly. The family is torn apart by the consequences of the marriage, and in the end, Clint is shot and killed.

The producers of *Love Me Tender* worried that Elvis's fans would have a negative reaction to the movie's ending. Elvis's real-life mother, Gladys, was said to be shocked by his on-screen death. No one knew if people would stay away from theaters once word got out that Elvis's character was going to die in the last few frames. In the movie's original ending, Mother Reno, played by Mildred Dunnock, rings the bell for dinner as the remaining Reno brothers come to supper. The pain and sadness on their faces indicate that Clint has gone to the Great Beyond. The end credits immediately follow this poignant but downbeat scene. After the shooting of *Love Me Tender* was completed, Elvis was called back to make another ending for the movie. In this version, his character survives. However, the ending that was actually used in the final version of

Elvis and costar Richard Egan take direction from Robert Webb on the set of Love Me Tender.

Elvis's death scene in Love Me Tender *upset not only his mother but also his fans.*

the film represents a compromise between the two. Clint Reno is killed, but Elvis's face is superimposed over the final scene as he sings "Love Me Tender." This version rings true to the original script, but fans are left with a more positive image of their idol.

Love Me Tender has only four musical numbers, but the song "Love Me Tender" was such a big hit for Elvis that no one seemed to notice how few songs were in the movie. Some people have claimed that Hal Wallis hinted that Elvis's faithful backup musicians, Scotty Moore, Bill Black, and D. J. Fontana, were not welcome in Hollywood. Supposedly, he thought the trio was too unsophisticated to participate in a Hollywood recording session. A group called the Ken Darby Trio backed up Elvis in the soundtrack recording sessions, but this was not Wallis's decision. He had nothing to do with the production of *Love Me Tender* because it was released by Twentieth Century-Fox. The story about the musicians is either untrue or it is about another Hollywood producer. In fact, Moore, Black, and Fontana appear in later movies that Elvis made for Wallis.

A Love Me Tender costar adjusts the brim of Elvis's hat between takes.
Opposite page: *A movie publicity photo of Elvis Presley.*

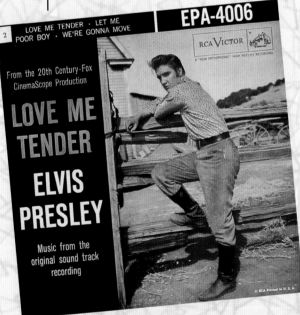

Elvis got along well with his costars, and he often deferred to their greater experience in making movies. Richard Egan, who played elder brother Vance Reno, said about Elvis: "That boy could charm the birds from the trees. He was so eager and humble, we went out of our way to help him." Years later, during Elvis's 1972 engagement in Las Vegas, Egan stood up after the final number and began

"Love Me Tender" was based on a Civil War–era ballad called "Aura Lee," written by W. W. Fosdick and George R. Poulton. Elvis's single achieved a first in music history with advance sales of over 1 million copies. The movie version of the song had slightly different lyrics and an additional verse.

Elvis and costar Debra Paget posed for a publicity photo.

an ovation for his former costar. Throughout the production of *Love Me Tender*, Elvis nursed a crush on costar Debra Paget, beginning a career-long habit of falling for his female costars. In this case, however, his attentions went unnoticed because Paget was not interested. A couple of years older than Elvis, Paget was dedicated to her career at this point. Her mother, who was often on the set, had big plans for Debra, none of which involved Elvis.

Elvis's first screen performance got brutal reviews, which was no surprise considering the criticism by the popular press before he turned to acting. A reviewer for *TIME* magazine compared Elvis's performance at various times in the movie to a sausage, a Disney cartoon figure, and a corpse. A review in *Variety* was more to the point: "Appraising Presley as an actor, he ain't. Not that it makes any difference." But the critics' sarcasm fell on deaf ears. When a huge promotional cutout of Elvis as Clint Reno was unveiled atop a New York City theater, thousands of fans showed up to see Elvis's image larger than life.

The first movie Elvis made for Hal Wallis was *Loving You*. It was developed by Wallis and writer/director Hal Kanter specifically for the young star. Not only was this musical drama designed to showcase Elvis's best talents, but the storyline was rather

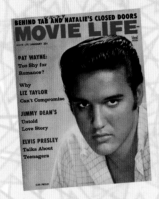

Thousands of fans swarmed New York's Paramount Theater to see the three-story cutout of Elvis promoting the debut of Love Me Tender.

ingeniously based on his own life. *Loving You*, released by Paramount in July 1957, stars Elvis as an unknown but talented singer who has a totally new sound. His character, Deke Rivers, hails from the South, but he doesn't fit in with the country-music crowd. A ruthless music promoter, played by Lizabeth Scott, recognizes Deke's unique talent and exploits him as a fresh face who appeals to teenage audiences. The media misrepresents his appeal and brands him a dangerous hothead until Deke proves he has simply been

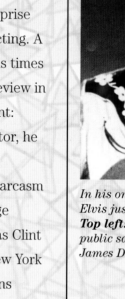

In his onscreen performance in Loving You, *Elvis just wants to be your "Teddy Bear."*
Top left: *When Elvis became a star, the public saw him as a rebel in the mold of James Dean and Marlon Brando.*

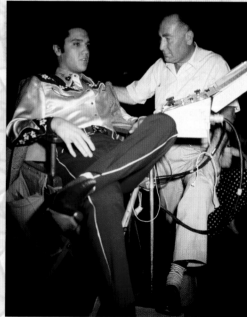

Elvis and Hal Wallis relax on the set of Loving You.

First Kiss

Elvis received his first screen kiss in his second feature film, *Loving You*. Actress Jana Lund bestowed the legendary kiss, which was the one act that made her minor screen career memorable. Other films she appeared in included the teen flicks *Don't Knock the Rock*, *High School Hellcats*, and *Hot Rod Girl*. Her last screen appearance was in *Married Too Young* in 1962.

The movie Loving You *was released in July 1957.*

misunderstood. The storyline and the well-written tunes tailored to Elvis's musical style were guaranteed to attract his fans. Contrary to popular belief, Elvis received his first on-screen kiss in *Loving You,* not in *Love Me Tender*. The honor went to a young actress named Jana Lund. She had a small role in the movie as a sexy Deke Rivers fan who, unfortunately for Deke, has a jealous boyfriend.

To get the script as close as possible to real-life events, Wallis sent director Hal Kanter to Memphis to observe Elvis's act and lifestyle while he was on the road. Kanter was in Shreveport when Elvis gave one of his last performances on *Louisiana Hayride*. Kanter's movie attempts to capture the excitement Elvis generated in his audience during a concert. The performance scenes in *Loving You* were accurate down to the constant popping of flashbulbs, the hysterical screaming of the audience, and the almost unbearable tension that built up before Elvis appeared on stage. In an article Kanter later wrote for

Director Hal Kanter cuts up with Elvis between takes of Loving You.

Variety, he referred to Elvis's position in this mass hysteria as "the eye of the hurricane." It was a position Elvis would hold for the rest of his life.

Kanter also managed to depict the unpleasant side of Elvis's fame in *Loving You.* Fans are shown swarming around Deke Rivers in the film, just as Elvis was often followed and mobbed after he became famous. Fans infringe on Deke's personal life, making demands on his time and badgering him with selfish requests. Deke's fancy new automobile is covered with lipstick messages and phone numbers in the same way that Elvis's cars were sometimes defaced by female fans desperate to get his attention.

Elvis's cars were often ruined by messages from fans, a fact incorporated into Loving You.

Other titles considered for Loving You *included* Lonesome Cowboy, Something for the Girls, *and* Running Wild.

While making *Loving You,* Elvis went out with Yvonne Lime, an actress in the movie. Yvonne revealed what it was "really" like to date Elvis in the movie magazine *Modern Screen.* The article was just a publicity piece that presented Elvis as a shining example of wholesome living: He was the perfect gentleman, devoted to his mother, and liked to sing religious songs at parties. His rock 'n' roll image, long hair, and sideburns were explained away as a case of nonconformity.

Elvis asked his parents, Vernon and Gladys, to join him in Hollywood for the filming of *Loving You* because he had missed their company so much while making *Love Me Tender.* Hal Kanter arranged for them and some family friends to make a cameo appearance near the end of the movie as members of a concert audience. After Gladys's death, Elvis refused to watch *Loving You* because it was such a painful reminder

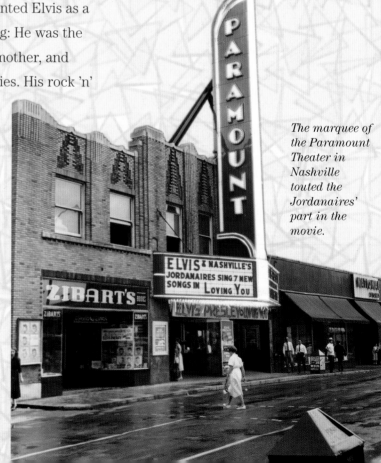

The marquee of the Paramount Theater in Nashville touted the Jordanaires' part in the movie.

The King Creole *45 EP (extra play) offered four songs.*

of his mother. In addition to his parents, Elvis's longtime backup musicians, Scotty Moore, Bill Black, and drummer D. J. Fontana, appeared in the movie as members of a country-western band. Even the Jordanaires popped up in the movie for a brief appearance.

The soundtrack for *Loving You,* which was Elvis's third long-playing album for RCA, reached No. 1 on some pop charts. This particular record also established a pattern in which songs from Elvis's latest film would be combined with tracks from recording sessions to make up an album. Elvis's films then served as elaborate promotions for his albums and vice versa. This was part of the Colonel's plan to get as much mileage from Elvis's movies as possible. One vehicle promoted the other for the maximum exposure of both.

Elvis's next movie, *King Creole,* was produced by Hal Wallis for Paramount. Based on Harold Robbins's novel *A Stone for Danny Fisher,* this musical drama stars Elvis as troubled teenager Danny Fisher. Dean Jagger costars as Danny's father, a man who has fallen apart emotionally since the death of his wife, letting his family slip into dire poverty. Determined to help his family regain the security and status it once had, Danny quits school to earn money by sweeping floors in a nightclub. A local mobster, played by Walter Matthau, takes an interest in Danny after he hears the talented young man sing. Danny becomes a regular performer in the mobster's club, packing in the crowds with his explosive performing style. But Danny seals his tragic fate when he becomes romantically involved with the mobster's girl.

King Creole *was considered a major Hollywood production. Director Michael Curtiz (far left) and producer Hal Wallis confer with Elvis behind the scenes.*

A movie poster (left) and a publicity photo of Elvis for the movie King Creole.

Graceland

Elvis Presley was proud of his home, Graceland, but not because of its grandeur or value. When Elvis first experienced success as a singer, he used his newfound fortune to improve the quality of life for his parents. Always struggling in poverty, the Presleys had never owned a permanent home and always scrambled for menial jobs to survive. As soon as Elvis realized that his singing career was solid, he told his father, Vernon, to quit his job as a laborer. In May 1956, Elvis paid $40,000 for the first real home his family ever knew—a ranch-style house on Audubon Drive in the suburbs of Memphis. He bought two Mixmaster mixers for Gladys so she would not have to do as much walking in the kitchen. In March 1957, Elvis purchased Graceland on the outskirts of Memphis to protect his family's privacy and to give his mother her dream home. Elvis was gratified he could share the fruits of his success with his parents, because he could return to them the sense of security they had always given him throughout his youth.

Graceland was Elvis's home for 20 years. It served as his retreat from the personal and professional pressures of an increasingly demanding career. The small Southern-style mansion with a white-columned portico was built in 1939 by Dr. Thomas Moore and named after his wife Ruth's aunt, Grace Toof. Elvis bought the 13.8 acres of land with its house, barn, smokehouse, and wellhouse in 1957 for slightly over $100,000. He renovated the house and gradually made additions to the property until Graceland consisted of 23 rooms and the grounds included the Trophy Room and Meditation Garden, as well as a carport, bath house, and racquetball court. Opened to the public in 1982 and placed on the National Register of Historic Places in 1991, Graceland draws approximately 700,000 visitors per year. On almost any given day, flowers and mementos from fans are left on Elvis's grave in the Meditation Garden—a testimonial to the passion and loyalty of his fans. A visit to Graceland offers a glimpse of both Elvis the man and Elvis the phenomenon.

Gladys and Vernon Presley board the train in Memphis to visit their son in Hollywood.

Wallis had other intentions for this property when he first purchased it in 1955. At that time, a play version of *A Stone for Danny Fisher* was running off-Broadway, and Wallis may have originally intended the title role to go to Ben Gazzara, with more of the novel left intact. Rumor has it that James Dean was also considered a possibility for the role. When Wallis decided to use Elvis for the part of Danny Fisher, the original storyline had to be changed to accommodate Elvis's rock 'n' roll image. The setting was changed from New York City to New Orleans, although few characters other than Elvis speak with Southern accents. In the novel, Danny is an aspiring boxer; in the movie, he's an exciting young singer with a new sound.

She was the most wonderful mother anyone could ever have. She was always so kind and good. –Elvis Presley, Memphis Press-Scimitar, *August 15, 1958*

Gladys Presley

Elvis suffered the tragedy of his mother's death on August 14, 1958, possibly caused by a heart attack related to the acute hepatitis that had hospitalized her. Gladys was 46 when she died, although many accounts list her age at death as 42. (She was embarrassed to be older than Vernon and often said that she was four years younger than she actually was.) Devastated by her passing, Elvis broke down in front of reporters many times during the days before her funeral. The Blackwood Brothers gospel group sang Gladys's favorite hymns at the funeral, and many celebrities sent condolences, including Marlon Brando, Dean Martin, Ricky Nelson, Tennessee Ernie Ford, and Sammy Davis, Jr. Gladys was originally buried at Forest Hill Cemetery in Memphis, but after Elvis died her remains were moved next to his at Graceland.

HE WAS AN INSTINCTIVE ACTOR...
HE WAS QUITE BRIGHT... VERY
INTELLIGENT.... HE WAS NOT A PUNK.
HE WAS VERY ELEGANT, SEDATE, AND
REFINED, AND SOPHISTICATED.
—WALTER MATTHAU, ON COSTARRING WITH ELVIS
IN *KING CREOLE*, 1987 INTERVIEW

Elvis worked with a cast of top Hollywood talent in King
Creole. *Walter Matthau had begun his film career playing
villains such as Maxie Fields.*

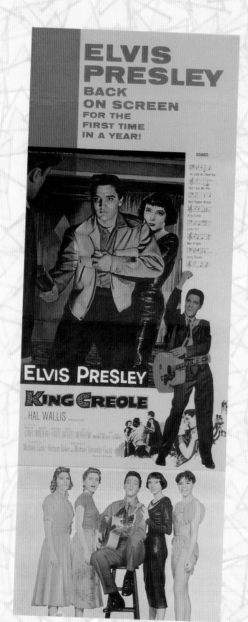

Both Wallis and Paramount considered this movie to be an
important project. The supporting cast features many notable
actors, including Carolyn Jones, Dean Jagger, and Walter
Matthau, and the director was respected veteran Michael
Curtiz, who made *Casablanca, Yankee Doodle Dandy, Angels
with Dirty Faces,* and many other Hollywood classics. The
high-quality production values plus the care taken in selecting
the cast and crew paid off; *King Creole* earned Elvis his best
movie reviews. Many critics agreed that Elvis had improved

Dolores Hart

If Ann-Margret and Tuesday Weld represented the sensual or
provocative contemporary woman, then Dolores Hart was the
girl next door. According to Elvis, Hart "was the nicest girl I've
ever met." Born Dolores Hicks, Hart was seen by producer Hal
Wallis in a school production of *Joan of Lorraine* just weeks
before *Loving You* went into production. She was only 18 years
old, and Wallis was charmed by her youthful innocence. She
made her screen debut in *Loving You* and also played the good
girl in *King Creole,* where her wholesome, blond looks were
contrasted with Carolyn Jones's sultry, dark-haired beauty.

After ten films, including the memorable teen flick *Where the
Boys Are* (1961), Hart retired from screen acting to become a
nun in 1963. Years later, mean-spirited rumors claimed that she
joined a convent after being spurned by Elvis, but these tales are
wholly unfounded. Now known as Mother Dolores, she is a
member of the Benedictine Order.

Elvis greeted fans in front of his Audubon Drive house in Memphis. His guest, Nick Adams, star of the TV series The Rebel (*in the background wearing a white shirt*)*, also spoke to the crowd. Actress Natalie Wood was visiting Elvis as well, but she chose to stay hidden in the house.*

The career of well-respected character actor Dean Jagger (far right) spanned 50 years.

tremendously as an actor, while others noted that he was "no longer depicted as the churlish, egotistical singing idol."

King Creole was shot in part on location in New Orleans. The film made effective use of such local sites as the French Quarter, Lake Pontchartrain, and a local high school. During location shooting, Elvis had a major problem with fans mobbing him at the Roosevelt Hotel, where he was staying. Hal Wallis arranged for heavy-duty security so Elvis could get enough rest to look fresh on camera. Pinkerton guards patrolled the hallways, the elevators, and even the fire escapes of the hotel to keep well-intentioned but troublesome fans away. When he returned to his hotel in the evening, Elvis had to go to the top of an adjacent building, cross over the roof, and enter the Roosevelt by way of a fire escape. He was unable to enjoy New Orleans' celebrated nightclubs or famous restaurants because of the persistence of his fans. Shooting in the city's streets was even worse; city policemen had to be used for crowd control. By this time, Elvis Presley had entered a new phase of his career that would keep him in seclusion, away from the fans who not only made him a star but also made him a recluse.

Elvis, as Danny Fisher, scuffles with Vic Morrow's character, Shark.

Elvis's first four movies are nothing like his later musical comedies. Aside from *Love Me Tender,* the plots of his early movies echo aspects of Elvis's image or actual events in his life. *Loving You* was a conventional Hollywood treatment of Elvis's rise to fame. *Jailhouse Rock* capitalized on Elvis's sensual, bad-boy image, and *King Creole* made use of certain details that paralleled Elvis's own life. In these movies, Elvis was clearly being groomed to take over for actor James Dean, who died in September 1955. Elvis appealed to teenage audiences in much the same way as Dean and the young Marlon Brando. An article in *Photoplay* magazine, published during the shooting of *Love Me Tender,* indicated that David Weisbart, the producer of Dean's best-known movie, *Rebel Without a Cause,* was talking to Elvis about portraying Dean in a movie biography. Elvis's role in *King Creole* had supposedly been offered to Dean. In 1956, a special single-issue magazine called *Elvis and Jimmy* showed how closely the two young men were linked in the popular imagination. The magazine designated Elvis to take up the fallen hero's leather jacket and become the premier teen rebel.

The photogenic Elvis was snapped for a publicity photo for Jailhouse Rock.

The first motorcycle Elvis bought for himself was a 1956 Harley KH. It is currently on display at the Harley-Davidson Motor Company Museum and Archives in Milwaukee, Wisconsin. Four more of his Harleys can be seen at the Graceland Museum in Memphis.

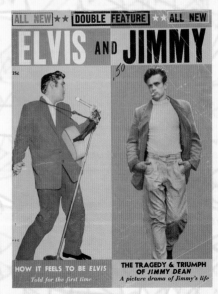

Elvis was groomed to replace the late James Dean.

RCA
LSP-2231 STEREO

ELVIS!
IS BACK!

FEVER • GIRL NEXT DOOR WENT A'WALKING • SOLDIER BOY
MAKE ME KNOW IT • I WILL BE HOME AGAIN • RECONSIDER BABY
IT FEELS SO RIGHT • LIKE A BABY • THE GIRL OF MY BEST FRIEND
THRILL OF YOUR LOVE • SUCH A NIGHT • DIRTY, DIRTY FEELING

UNFAIRLY CRITICIZED BY MANY BEFORE HE ENTERED THE ARMY, ELVIS RESURFACED AFTER HIS TOUR OF DUTY AS A SHINING EXAMPLE OF YOUNG ADULTHOOD. EVEN CONGRESS NOTICED THE CHANGE. IN MARCH 1960, SENATOR ESTES KEFAUVER READ A TRIBUTE TO ELVIS INTO THE CONGRESSIONAL RECORD.

—*ELVIS: A TRIBUTE TO HIS LIFE*

As soon as Elvis set foot on American soil after his discharge from the army, reporters descended on him with questions about his career. Newspaper interviews revealed that he did not intend to abandon rock 'n' roll "as long as people wanted it." Yet, almost immediately, Elvis and Colonel Parker embarked on a course designed to do just that; they altered Elvis's image by using the same entertainment arenas that had constructed his image in the first place—recordings, television, and the movies.

Elvis and Colonel Parker were no longer interested in rock 'n' roll, which had changed between 1958 and 1960. If anything, rock musicians were more controversial than ever: Little Richard was in trouble with the IRS; Chuck Berry had been arrested for violating the Mann Act; and Jerry Lee Lewis was ostracized for running away with and marrying a 13-year-old girl. To make matters worse, at least in the eyes of the press, the girl was Lewis's cousin and he was already married at the time. All these scandals served to temporarily put those rockers' careers on hold and damage rock 'n' roll's already tarnished reputation.

Little Richard gave energetic performances on the piano.

While scandal claimed some rockers, death claimed others, including Buddy Holly, Ritchie Valens, the Big Bopper (J. P. Richardson), and Eddie Cochran. The loss of these rock pioneers from the music scene contributed to the rise in popularity

When in Germany during a European tour, Bill Haley received a backstage visit from Elvis.

Chuck Berry wowed the crowds with his guitar playing.

Elvis smiled at his screaming fans as he stepped off the plane that brought him home from the army.

of ballad singers. As early as 1958, articles in music magazines began to note with pleasure that ballad singers were replacing the more frenzied performers who had been on the charts.

When Elvis returned home in 1960—amid headlines blaring "Chorus of Teenage Squeals Rocks Elvis Out of the Army" and "The Army's Made a New Man Out of Elvis"—the stage was set for him to take up a more mellow style. The Colonel took advantage of the good publicity over Elvis's tour of duty to promote a more mature Elvis who he hoped would attract a larger audience. Rock 'n' roll critics and fans view this change as a decline, but in reality it was a deliberate change in Elvis's image. Elvis and his manager abandoned the notoriety of rock 'n' roll for the wider appeal of movies and pop music. In terms of financial success and overall popularity, they made the right decision.

His scandalous marriage caused Jerry Lee Lewis's popularity to plummet.

Colonel Tom Parker

In the Elvis legend, the Colonel is often portrayed as the villain—a sinister, underhanded force who controlled the singer's every move and influenced his every decision. Those who see him in this light point to his background as a carnival hustler, his unsophisticated approach to promotion, and the questionable movie deals Elvis became locked into during the 1960s as proof of Parker's notorious character. In the early 1980s, information came to light that bolstered this negative depiction of the Colonel. During the course of a lawsuit filed against Parker by Elvis's estate, which stemmed from a court-ordered investigation of Parker's management of Elvis, the Colonel admitted that he was not Thomas Parker from Huntington, West Virginia, but Andreas van Kuijk from Breda, Holland. This information had surfaced earlier, but Parker did not admit his true identity until it was to his advantage to do so. He used the information to declare he was not an American citizen but "a man without a country," and therefore he could not be sued under federal laws. The case was later settled out of court. Parker died in 1997 after suffering a stroke.

A single image sums up the ramifications of this important switch in the young singer's career: Elvis's long ducktail haircut, which had been so ceremoniously shorn for his army induction, was never grown back.

ELVIS DIED WHEN HE WENT INTO THE ARMY.
—JOHN LENNON

Two weeks after his discharge, Elvis journeyed to Nashville for his first recording session in almost two years. Elvis was joined in the studio by two of his oldest friends, guitarist Scotty Moore and drummer D. J. Fontana. Bill Black, who had played doghouse bass for Elvis, was no longer part of his band. Moore, Black, and Fontana had been Elvis's backup musicians during most of his early career, but in the fall of 1957, Moore and Black resigned as regular members of Elvis's band. Money probably had a lot to do with their decision as Scotty and Bill were paid only $100 a week while they were in Memphis and $200 a week while they were on the road. It is assumed that the Colonel was responsible for the

Elvis waits to board the bus he rented for the trip to Nashville to record Elvis Is Back! *It was the first album he released after his tour of duty in the army.*

Elvis danced in his socks while recording for King Creole. *The King of Rock's moves have been copied by the King of Pop Michael Jackson.*

Scotty Moore on Guitar

Born Winfield Scott Moore in tiny Gadsden, Tennessee, Scotty moved to Memphis to learn more about music. Asked by Sam Phillips in 1955 to season young Elvis Presley, Moore used a driving guitar sound to help create Elvis's rockabilly style. However, Scotty's insistence that a musician's job is to help the singer get the song across relegated his accomplishments to the background for many years.

During the 1960s, Scotty founded his own label, Fernwood Records, which produced Thomas Wayne's modest hit "Tragedy." Moore's 1964 album for Epic, *The Guitar That Changed the World*, hinted at his significance to rock 'n' roll, but it wasn't until after Elvis's death that his accomplishments were appreciated. Younger generations of rockers began to openly acknowledge him, including Keith Richards who dubbed him "the midwife of rock 'n' roll" for giving birth to Elvis's sound. In 2000, Scotty Moore was inducted into the Rock 'n' Roll Hall of Fame.

Bill Black on Bass

A member of the country band Starlite Wranglers, bass player Bill Black found Elvis's fast-paced rockabilly sound better suited to his ebullient performing style. The Memphis native, who slapped his doghouse bass hard and fast, was also known to get on top of the instrument and ride it around the stage while still playing. After Elvis became a national sensation, Black was unhappy with the low wages paid by the Colonel, and he and Scotty Moore quit in 1957. Although lured back into the fold, Black was more than glad to strike out on his own after Elvis was drafted.

The Bill Black Combo specialized in R&B instrumentals and quickly scored a Top-Ten hit with "Smokie." Between 1959 and 1962, the combo produced eight Top-Ten singles, and in 1964, they opened for The Beatles. Sadly, Black died of a brain tumor the following year at the age of 39.

Scotty Moore, Elvis, D. J. Fontana, and Bob Moore (on bass) gave a show for charity at Ellis Auditorium, Memphis, on February 25, 1961.

Renowned piano man Floyd Cramer played for the Nashville sessions.

skimpy wages, but throughout his career Elvis was never known to pay very high wages to any of the people who worked for him. Black eventually formed his own group, the Bill Black Combo, and in 1959 they recorded an instrumental tune called "Smokie." Moore continued to record with Elvis in the studio on a freelance basis until 1969. D. J. Fontana, who had been recruited from *Louisiana Hayride,* had a separate arrangement with Elvis, which allowed him more leeway in his career.

Moore and Fontana were not the only musicians hired for the Nashville recording sessions. The famed country pianist Floyd Cramer signed on, and once again the Jordanaires sang backup vocals. During the first session, Elvis cut a single featuring "Stuck on You," with "Fame and Fortune" on the flip side. In early April,

D. J. Fontana on Drums

Born Dominic Joseph Fontana in Louisiana in 1934, D. J. was a teenager when he signed on as a staff drummer for *Louisiana Hayride* in 1953. He hooked up with Elvis and the Blue Moon Boys after they played *Hayride* in 1955. While he did not play on the Sun recordings, he backed Elvis at RCA throughout the 1950s and part of the 1960s. Fontana later played with such diverse performers as Carl Perkins, Waylon Jennings, and Charlie Pride. In 1997, Fontana and Scotty Moore recorded *All the King's Men*, an award-winning CD featuring guest appearances by several rock 'n' roll giants, among them Jeff Beck, Keith Richards, and Ron Wood.

In an interview, Fontana claimed that before *Louisiana Hayride* he had worked at several seedy nightclubs where scantily clad dancers required a drumbeat every time they moved provocatively. Apparently this experience made it easy for him to accompany Elvis's notorious onstage gyrations.

Chubby Checker (far left) did the Twist with singer Paul Anka and actress Sandy Dennis. After three weeks of dancing to his song "The Twist," Checker had lost almost 30 pounds.

Elvis returned to the RCA studio in Nashville to record the additional tracks that were needed to make an album. By the end of April, *Elvis Is Back!* had been released. In less than two months, RCA had cut and pressed this brand-new Elvis Presley album and it was playing on the radio.

Elvis returned to a music scene very different than the one he had left. Smooth-sounding teen angels, such as Bobby Vee, Bobby Rydell, Frankie Avalon, and Connie Francis, caught the ears of young listeners, while the dance craze the Twist propelled them across the dance floor. Elvis and his manager, Colonel Tom Parker, embarked on a campaign to mold his image around current trends and away from the controversy that had followed him before the army. The rebellious persona was cast aside for a mature public image; in his music, the innovation of his Sun Studio roots was replaced by the calculation of mainstream ambitions.

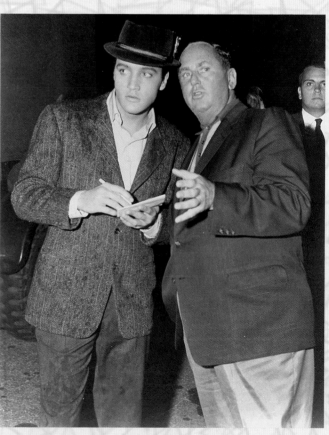

Colonel Parker decided to broaden Elvis's audience by turning him into a pop singer and movie star.

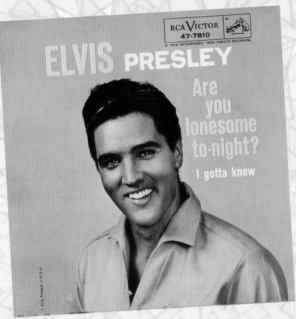

Tin Pan Alley songwriters Lou Handman and Roy Turk composed "Are You Lonesome Tonight?" in 1926, and Al Jolson recorded it the next year. Elvis's rendition of the song was released in 1960 and became nominated for three Grammy Awards.

Singer Jaye P. Morgan recorded "Are You Lonesome Tonight?" in 1959.

While many have criticized this change, it did not represent a decline in the quality of Elvis's music. On the contrary, *Elvis Is Back!* represents a peak in the singer's career, when his maturity and confidence led to a control and focus in his music. Like the pre-army Elvis recordings, this album offered an eclectic collection of musical genres, from a sentimental duet with Charlie Hodge called "I Will Be Home Again" to the gritty "Reconsider Baby" with a bluesy sax solo by Boots Randolph. Once again, Elvis's talent for unifying disparate styles of music resulted in an innovative and successful album, and it reached No. 2 on the charts.

HE IS NO LONGER THE SNEERING, HIP-TWITCHING SYMBOL OF THE UNTAMED BEAST THAT RESIDES IN 17-YEAR-OLD BREASTS. HE HAS COME BACK FROM THE ARMY EASYGOING, UNASSUMING . . .
—*LIFE,* OCTOBER 10, 1960

Not all the songs that Elvis recorded in Nashville were included on the *Elvis Is Back!* album. RCA held back for later release two of his highly acclaimed ballads: "It's Now or Never" and "Are You Lonesome Tonight?" The melancholy tune "Are You Lonesome Tonight?" was a clear departure from the kind of music that Elvis sang before he went into the army. In the 1920s, Al Jolson had made the song popular, but Elvis was probably more familiar with a 1959 version of the song that was recorded by pop singer Jaye P. Morgan. She had borrowed her arrangement from a 1950 rendition by the Blue Baron Orchestra. It is believed that Colonel Parker urged Elvis to record "Are You Lonesome Tonight?" even though it was unusual for him to interfere with Elvis's choice of music. The song perfectly suited Elvis's new image as a mainstream pop singer.

Elvis returned from the army without sideburns, a look he kept in order to soften his image as a notorious rock 'n' roller.

Who could have guessed that "It's Now or Never," a reworked version of the 1901 Italian opera-style classic "O Sole Mio," would become the King of Rock 'n' Roll's biggest-selling single? But then, in 1956, when Elvis was skewered by most newspapers in the country for thrusting his hips to the bluesy beat of "Hound Dog," no one would have known that he would become a press favorite in just four years. By quietly serving his country in the army from 1958 to 1960, Elvis had won the hearts and minds of the mainstream press and general public. "It's Now or Never" received airplay on conservative radio stations that previously wouldn't have touched a Presley record, thus exposing Elvis to a wider, more adult audience.

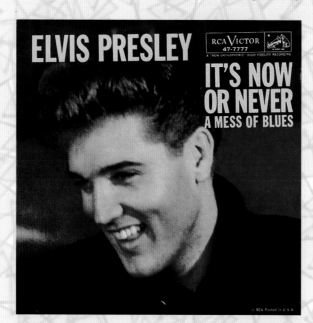

Above and below: "It's Now or Never" (RCA 47-7777) was an international success, with global sales exceeding 20 million copies. It entered the British charts at No. 1 and remained there for eight weeks.

Yet Elvis did not record the song just to gain a broader audience. "O Sole Mio" was written by G. Capurro and Eduardo di Capua at the turn of the twentieth century, but it had been made popular much later by Mario Lanza. Elvis was a fan of Lanza and undoubtedly heard the opera singer's recording, but he had also heard the English version "There's No Tomorrow" by Tony Martin. While still in the army, Elvis asked his music publisher, Freddie Bienstock of Hill and Range (part of RCA), to find someone to write new lyrics for the song. The only songwriters available at Hill and Range to do it were Aaron Schroeder and Wally Gold, who jumped at the chance because they knew the royalties on an Elvis Presley song would be enormous. They composed the lyrics in less than 30 minutes. A singer named David Hill (aka David Hess) recorded the demo with a cha-cha arrangement, and Elvis loved it. He was challenged by its operatic style and attracted to its drama.

"It's Now or Never" charted for 20 weeks, holding the No. 1 spot in the U.S.A. for five weeks. Worldwide sales of the tune, according to *The Guinness Book of Recorded Sound,* eventually exceeded 20 million copies.

A Feud with Pat Boone

The entertainment press in the 1950s frequently contrasted the notorious, hip-swiveling Elvis Presley with the clean-cut Pat Boone, but in fact the two singers maintained a friendly acquaintance. In 1963, with a wink toward the media-made rivalry, Boone released an album of Elvis songs done in a soft pop style, including "It's Now or Never" and "Hound Dog." Cleverly titled *Pat Boone Sings . . . Guess Who?,* the 1964 album featured Pat Boone on the cover in a replica of Elvis's famous gold lamé suit.

In 1960, Elvis's appearance on Frank Sinatra's TV variety special helped to sell him to a mainstream audience.

On May 8, 1960, Elvis appeared on TV for the first time since his discharge from the army. He was a guest on *The Frank Sinatra-Timex Special,* also known as *Welcome Home Elvis.* Colonel Parker had made the deal with the show's producers months before Elvis was released from active duty. He had hoped that appearing with Frank Sinatra would introduce Elvis as a pop singer to a wide audience made up of adults and pop enthusiasts as well as teenagers and country-western fans. Never one to take chances, the Colonel made sure Elvis would make a big splash by packing the studio audience with 400 members from one of Elvis's biggest fan clubs. The program received phenomenal ratings, giving ABC-TV a 41.5 share for that evening. Elvis was paid a staggering $125,000 for a total of six minutes on the air.

Sammy Davis, Jr., Peter Lawford, and Joey Bishop, members of Sinatra's famed "Rat Pack," also appeared on the television special. In addition, the cast included Sinatra's daughter Nancy, whom the gossip columns had recently linked with Elvis. Elvis sang his two latest hits, then later in the show he joined Sinatra for a short duet. Dressed in a conservative but stylish tuxedo, the former teen idol sang Sinatra's "Witchcraft," while Sinatra crooned Elvis's "Love Me Tender." His choice of clothes, shorter hairstyle, and connections with the Rat Pack indicated that Elvis's career was taking a new direction. When Elvis and Sinatra sang each other's songs, it seemed Sinatra was passing on his position as pop idol to the next generation: The Voice, as Sinatra was known in the 1940s, was making way for the King.

Joey Bishop (far left), Frank Sinatra, and Nancy Sinatra applauded Elvis on The Frank Sinatra-Timex Special, *aka* Welcome Home Elvis.

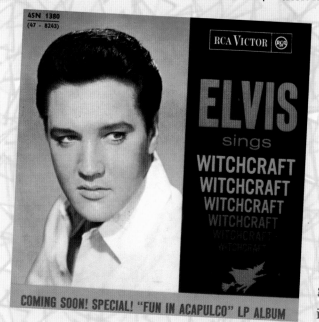

45N 1380
(47 - 8243)

RCA VICTOR

ELVIS
sings

WITCHCRAFT
WITCHCRAFT
WITCHCRAFT
WITCHCRAFT

COMING SOON! SPECIAL! "FUN IN ACAPULCO" LP ALBUM

"Witchcraft" had been one of Sinatra's hit songs.

Memphis Mafia

(Left to right) Jerry Schilling, Red West, Elvis, Sonny West, Lamar Fike, and Joe Esposito

After Elvis's discharge from the army, the entertainment press discovered that he was accompanied by an entourage of about 20 friends and associates wherever he traveled. The press dubbed them the "Memphis Mafia" or the "Tennessee Mafia," just as they had called Humphrey Bogart's group of buddies and cohorts the "Holmby Hills Rat Pack" and Frank Sinatra's gang of celebrity friends the "Rat Pack." However, the differences between the Rat Pack and the Memphis Mafia became apparent as Elvis's career in Hollywood continued, and the press never quite grasped the gang's relationship to Elvis.

Most of the members of the Memphis Mafia were hometown boys from Memphis, family members, or friends Elvis had met in the army. Many of them actually lived with Elvis, whether he was in Memphis or Hollywood. They accompanied Elvis to the set, drove him to and from the studio, and worked as bodyguards to keep fans and press away from him. The closeness of this group of friends and employees made Elvis feel at home in Hollywood or on the road, but it also isolated him from industry insiders and fellow entertainers who could have been a positive influence on him.

ASK ANYONE. IF IT HADN'T
BEEN FOR ELVIS, I DON'T
KNOW WHERE POPULAR MUSIC
WOULD BE. HE WAS THE ONE
THAT STARTED IT ALL OFF,
AND HE WAS DEFINITELY THE
START OF IT FOR ME.

—ELTON JOHN

In Ed Sullivan's syndicated newspaper column in the *New York Daily News*, May 1960, the crusty show business luminary spoke harshly of Elvis's appearance on the *The Frank Sinatra-Timex*

On October 17, 1960, Elvis Presley fractured a finger playing touch football at Graceland. After being treated, he relaxed in a hospital room with Anita Wood (left) and a few of his Memphis friends.

On March 8, 1961, Elvis drove with Red West and Lamar Fike to Nashville where a joint session of the Tennessee State Legislature made him an honorary colonel in the Tennessee Volunteers.

Special. Lingering bitterness over his dealings with Colonel Parker crept into his account. Sullivan blasted Parker for allowing Elvis to sing only two songs in the special, stating, "Col. Tom, using the logic of a farmer, is a firm believer in not giving a hungry horse a bale of hay." Sullivan seemed to forget that it was Sinatra's special, not Elvis's, and there were four other guests to showcase as well. Some jabs at how Elvis looked rounded out the column as Sullivan noted that the young singer, "minus his sideburns, has substituted what the ladies probably would call a 'high hair-do.' His hair is so high in front that it looks like a ski jump."

Less than a year later, on March 25, 1961, Elvis performed live at the Bloch Arena at Pearl Harbor, Hawaii. The show was a fundraiser to build a memorial for the USS *Arizona,* the largest of the eight battleships that had been sunk on December 7, 1941, during the surprise Japanese air attack on Pearl Harbor. Ticket prices for Elvis's performance ranged from $3 to $10 a seat, with 100 ringside seats reserved for people who donated $100. Elvis and Colonel Parker bought 50 of these special seats and donated them to patients from Tripler Hospital in Hawaii. Elvis's benefit raised more than $52,000 for the memorial fund. On March 30, the Hawaii House of Representatives passed Special Resolution 105 thanking Elvis and the Colonel.

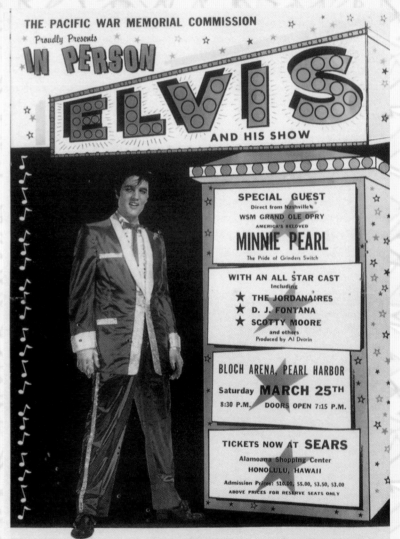

In 1961, Elvis performed at a benefit at Pearl Harbor to raise money for a memorial for the USS Arizona. *It was to be his last live concert until 1969.*

Memphis Mayor Henry Loeb declared February 25, 1961, "Elvis Presley Day" and hosted a luncheon tribute to Elvis at the Claridge Hotel.

The benefit for the *Arizona* memorial could be considered a good career move in that it helped Elvis become more acceptable to an adult audience, but his career was not the only reason Elvis agreed to do the concert. He had a sensitive, generous nature, and throughout his entire life, Elvis gave freely to charities and other worthy causes, whether he received publicity for it or not. Five years after this benefit, while in Hawaii filming *Paradise, Hawaiian Style*, Elvis visited the completed memorial and placed a wreath there. Photographers and reporters rushed in to record the event, but Elvis sent them away. He did not want his visit to the memorial to become a publicity stunt.

This 1961 concert in Hawaii marked Elvis's last live performance until 1969, and he made no television appearances after the Sinatra special until December 1968. Throughout most of the 1960s, if Elvis's fans wanted to see him, they had to see him on the silver screen.

Wherever he went in public, Elvis's fans sought to get close to their idol.

During the 1960s, the Jordanaires provided background vocals on most of Elvis's recordings.

The 1960s: Stalwarts in the Studio

For most of the 1960s, Elvis did not perform live. The musicians who backed him did so in the studio, not on the stage. Despite a falling out with Elvis in 1957, guitarist Scotty Moore played with Elvis until 1968. Drummer D. J. Fontana stayed with Elvis until 1969. During the two years Elvis served in the army, Moore produced and played on some of Jerry Lee Lewis's records. Bassist Bill Black left Elvis's employ in February 1958 and formed the Bill Black Combo. Black's successful records included the instrumental "Smokie—Part 2" and "White Silver Sands." In addition to Moore and Fontana, several Nashville session musicians contributed a consistent sound to Elvis's smooth, pop-styled music and soundtrack recordings. Nashville pianist Floyd Cramer, known for his slip-note style of playing, worked with Elvis from 1956 through 1968; Boots Randolph played saxophone and vibes on 21 recordings from 1960 through 1968; and Charlie McCoy, a member of the *Grand Ole Opry* house band, played harmonica from 1965 to 1971.

French release of the soundtrack album

Song List

WHAT'S SHE REALLY LIKE
G.I. BLUES
DOIN' THE BEST I CAN
FRANKFORT SPECIAL
SHOPPIN' AROUND
TONIGHT IS SO RIGHT FOR LOVE
WOODEN HEART
POCKETFUL OF RAINBOWS
BIG BOOTS
DIDJA EVER

In May 1960, Elvis had returned to Hollywood to begin shooting *G.I. Blues*. The movie's storyline is about a singer serving in the army in Germany. Producer Hal Wallis borrowed details from Elvis's own life to flesh out the script just as he had done in the two previous films he made with Elvis. In *G.I. Blues*, Elvis's character is not only stationed in Germany, he's also a member of a tank division just as Elvis had been.

Like the movies Elvis made before going into the army, *G.I. Blues* is based on the events of his own life, but it is a musical comedy instead of a musical drama. *G.I. Blues* was aimed at a family audience, and Elvis's controversial performing style had been toned down. Even though most of the songs are fast-paced, they don't have the same hard-driving sound, sexual connotation, or emotional delivery of Elvis's prior soundtrack recordings. Elvis's screen image was deliberately softened for *G.I. Blues*. In one scene, he sings a Bavarian-sounding folk tune during a children's puppet show, while in another he baby-sits an adorable infant. The movie's ads perfectly sum up these changes: "See and Hear the New Elvis: The Idol of the Teenagers Is the Idol of the Family."

G.I. Blues was enormously successful, ranking fourteenth in box-office receipts for 1960. The soundtrack album reached No. 1 quickly, remaining on the charts longer than any other Elvis Presley album. Movie critics applauded the new Elvis. They approved of his new image and predicted he

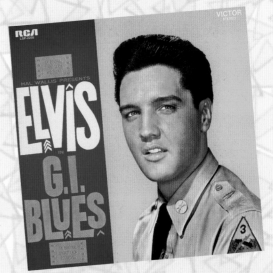

The single of "G.I. Blues" was taken from the film's soundtrack and released in Europe.

Theater lobby card

In G.I. Blues, Elvis's character served in the army in Germany in the tank division, mirroring what Elvis had done in real life.

would find plenty of new fans among older women. Elvis didn't share the critics' enthusiasm for *G.I. Blues.* He felt that there were too many musical numbers and believed some of them made no sense within the context of the plot. He was concerned that the quality of many of these songs was not as good as the music for his earlier movies.

Elvis was eager to move on to more demanding and serious roles. The western *Flaming Star* gave him the chance to prove himself as an actor. The movie brought together some of Hollywood's most notable actors and creative personnel. In this tense drama, Elvis was able to hold his own with veteran performers John McIntire and Dolores Del Rio. Newcomer Barbara Eden, who later starred in the TV series *I Dream of Jeannie,* was also featured in the film. Director Don Siegel, who later won critical acclaim for his work on the original *Dirty Harry,* fashioned a strong statement on racial prejudice out of the script, which had been based on a popular novel by Clair Huffaker. Nunnally Johnson, a longtime Hollywood producer and screenwriter, cowrote the script with Huffaker. Established composer Cyril Mockridge produced the background music.

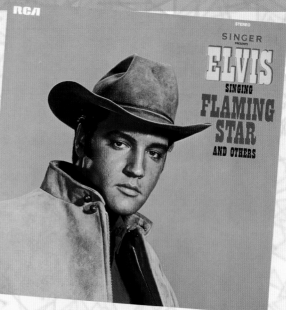

The film's title song peaked at No. 14 on Billboard's Hot 100 *chart.*

Barbara Eden, with costars Steve Forrest and Elvis, played the only ingenue role in Flaming Star *but did not end up with Elvis's character.*

HE'S THE BEST-MANNERED STAR IN HOLLYWOOD, AND HE'S IMPROVED AS A PERFORMER AND HAS DETERMINATION TO BE A FINE ACTOR. [ELVIS] WAS SMART ENOUGH TO SIMMER DOWN THAT TORRID ACT OF HIS.
—HEDDA HOPPER, EARLY 1960S

Above and opposite: *Elvis, dressed to kill in Western garb in 1948 at age 13 and in 1960 for* Flaming Star.

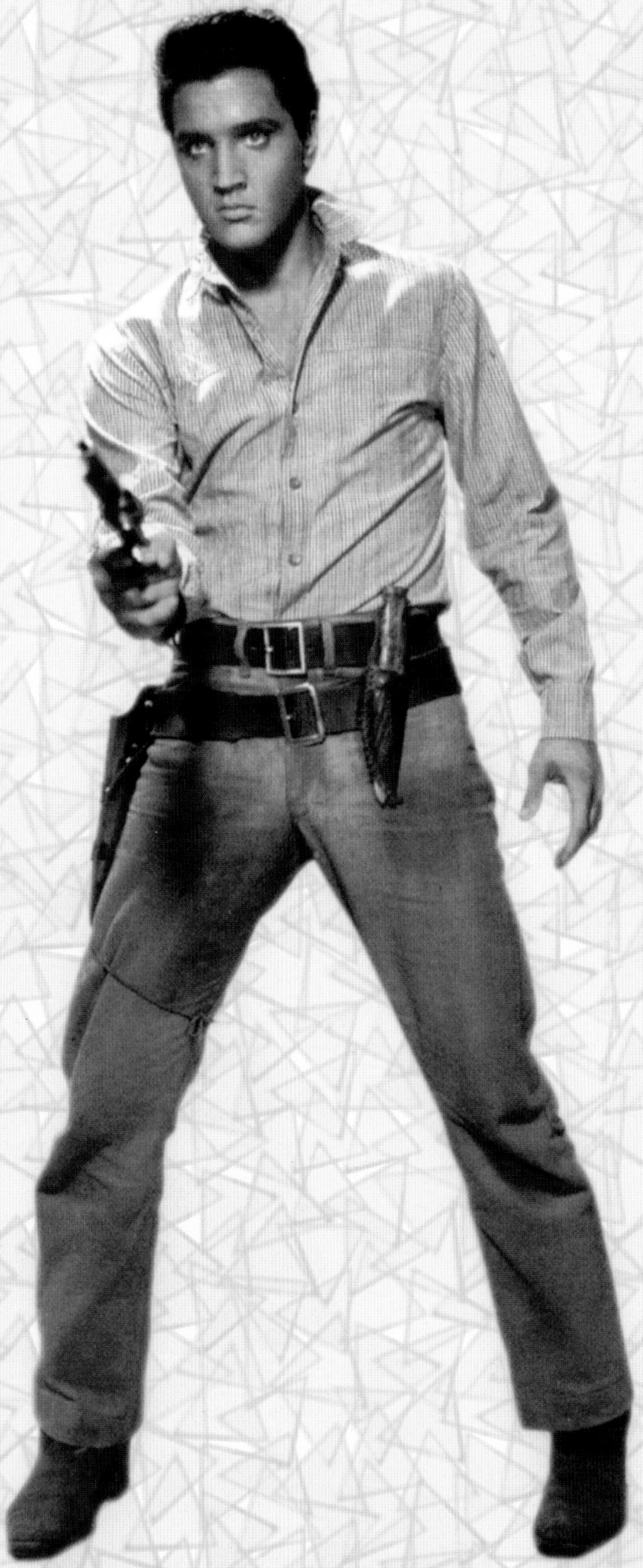

Elvis got one more shot at serious acting when he was signed to star in the drama *Wild in the Country*. The film, directed by Philip Dunne, was from a script by playwright Clifford Odets. It features Elvis as Glenn Tyler, a young hothead from the rural South who tries to straighten out his life after serving time in a juvenile hall. The original script for this movie had no original songs, but after *Flaming Star*'s poor showing at the box office, they added six musical numbers to *Wild in the Country*. Only four of them made the final cut. In addition to the title tune that is sung over the opening credits, Elvis sings a song to each of the three women in the movie. Even with the musical numbers, the film was deemed a disappointment by Elvis's fans. Like *Flaming Star*, the movie didn't lose money at the box office, but it wasn't a smash success either. Both Elvis and costar Tuesday Weld were voted the Damp Raincoat Award as the most disappointing performers of 1961 by *Teen* magazine. While awards such as this can hardly ruin anyone's career, they indicated to Elvis and the Colonel that this type of film was not what Elvis's most devoted fans wanted to see. Elvis did not accept another serious role until the end of his film career.

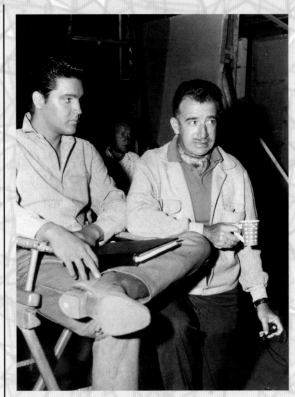

Director Don Siegel fought to keep musical numbers out of his serious western Flaming Star, *but it ended up with two.*

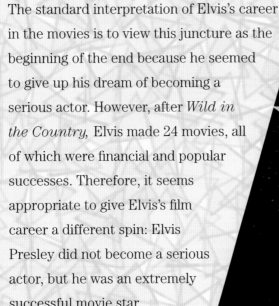

Elvis danced with costar Tuesday Weld in this scene from Wild in the Country.

The standard interpretation of Elvis's career in the movies is to view this juncture as the beginning of the end because he seemed to give up his dream of becoming a serious actor. However, after *Wild in the Country*, Elvis made 24 movies, all of which were financial and popular successes. Therefore, it seems appropriate to give Elvis's film career a different spin: Elvis Presley did not become a serious actor, but he was an extremely successful movie star.

The Walk of Fame on Hollywood Boulevard was dedicated on February 9, 1960. More than 1,500 performers received stars, including Elvis Presley. Each star is identified by one of five icons: a movie camera, theatrical masks, a radio microphone, a TV, or a record on a record player. Elvis earned his star on the Walk of Fame for his contributions to the recording industry.

Million Dollar Actor

Chapter 5

RCA

LSP-2426

VICTOR
STEREO

AN ORIGINAL
SOUND TRACK ALBUM

14 GREAT SONGS

SEE

ELVIS

IN HAL WALLIS'

BLUE HAWAII

14 GREAT SONGS

Stereo LSP-242●

PARAMOUNT PRESENTS

ELVIS PRESLEY

IN

BLUE HAWAII

A Hal Wallis Production

Co-starring

JOAN BLACKMAN • ANGELA LANSBURY

Nancy Walters

TECHNICOLOR® and PANAVISION®

Directed by NORMAN TAUROG

Screenplay by HAL KANTER

SIDE 1

1. BLUE HAWAII   (ASCAP   2:35)
2. Almost Always True   (ASCAP   2:24)
3. Aloha Oe   (BMI   1:54)
4. No More   (ASCAP   2:22)
5. Can't Help Falling in Love   (ASCAP   2:59)
6. Rock-A-Hula Baby   (ASCAP   1:58)
7. Moonlight Swim   (ASCAP   2:18)

SIDE 2

8. Ku-u-i-po   (ASCAP   2:20)
9. Ito Eats   (ASCAP   1:25)
10. Slicin' Sand   (ASCAP   1:34)
11. Hawaiian Sunset   (ASCAP   2:30)
12. Beach Boy Blues   (ASCAP   2:00)
13. Island of Love (Kauai)   (ASCAP   2:40)
14. HAWAIIAN WEDDING SONG   (ASCAP   2

A Presley picture is the only sure thing in Hollywood.

—Hal Wallis, producer of nine Elvis films

On March 14, 1961, Elvis and assorted friends, assistants, and bodyguards flew to Los Angeles so he could begin production on his next film, *Blue Hawaii.* Upon his arrival, he spent a few fun-filled days with friends Juliet Prowse, Joan Blackman, and Pat Fackethal, a real-life stewardess selected to play a bit part as a stewardess in the film. Afterward, he buckled down to record the songs that would comprise the soundtrack. Elvis recorded the tunes for the modestly budgeted musical comedy in Hollywood as opposed to Nashville, where much of his nonsoundtrack music was produced.

Theater lobby card

Norman Taurog (left) directed nine of Elvis's movies. Elvis liked working with the Hollywood veteran and once gave him a new Cadillac.

While this was business as usual for Presley that year, in retrospect it marks a juncture in his career. His management team, made up of Colonel Parker, Elvis, Hal Wallis, and Abe Lastfogel, Elvis's William Morris agent, had already determined that movies should be the focus of his career, but *Blue Hawaii* would narrow that focus further. Because it was Elvis's highest-grossing film at the box office, it became the model for the type of musical comedy associated with him during the 1960s. As the decade progressed, all other Elvis recordings took a backseat to the music for the movies.

The beautiful blue waters of Hawaii gave the film its name.

The soundtrack to *Blue Hawaii* may have been miles away from rock 'n' roll or rhythm-and-blues, but it gave Elvis the song with which he would close most of his 1970s concerts: "Can't Help Falling in Love." Recorded at Radio Recorders in Hollywood in 1961, *Blue*

Hawaii featured 14 songs, more than any other Elvis soundtrack. The material was not particularly creative, nor did it have the mix of sounds found on *Elvis Is Back!,* but it is a solid example of that blend of pop and rock that defined Elvis's movie music. *Blue Hawaii*—the album and the movie—was aimed at a far wider audience than his studio recordings. Elvis's management was interested in appealing to the mainstream audience and generating spectacular sales. They were less concerned with the impact of his music or his role as a musical innovator. This and other soundtrack albums were meant to serve a different purpose and to appeal to different audiences. Unfortunately, as the 1960s wore on, the movie material declined in quality, reflecting poorly on all the soundtracks.

Above and below: Whether crooning on the beach or dancing at a club, Elvis's character usually impressed the ladies.

Most of the 14 songs on the album are pop-style tunes. Some of these were not written for the film but had been recorded and released previously, including "Moonlight Swim," "Blue Hawaii," and "Hawaiian Wedding Song." "Aloha Oe" was composed by Queen Liliuokalani of Hawaii in 1878. The title tune and the song "Aloha Oe" had been recorded in the 1930s by Bing Crosby during a craze for the allure of the tropical isles. The songs composed for the film were not rock 'n' roll either, although "Rock-a-Hula Baby" is a playful pastiche of rock 'n' roll dance crazes. To capture a Hawaiian-style sound, special musicians were employed for the recording sessions. Percussionist Hal Blaine, whose expertise involved

The inviting locales were so heavily featured in the film that the state of Hawaii practically became a character.

Hawaiian instruments, joined drummers D. J. Fontana and Bernie Mattinson. Steel guitar and ukelele players were also added.

Blue Hawaii became Elvis's biggest-selling movie soundtrack. It topped the *Billboard* albums chart two months after its October 1961 release. It was the No. 1 album in the country for 20 weeks, which set a record for a rock performer or group that lasted until 1977 when Fleetwood Mac's *Rumors* broke it. *Blue Hawaii* remained on the albums chart for 79 weeks and was awarded double platinum status by the RIAA in March 1992.

A backstage practice session included the Jordanaires, Bill Black, and D. J. Fontana, with Scotty Moore (in background) and singer Patti Page (third from right) looking on.

"Can't Help Falling in Love"

Written especially for *Blue Hawaii* by George Weiss, Hugo Peretti, and Luigi Creatore, "Can't Help Falling in Love" is remembered as the ballad with which Elvis closed his concerts during the 1970s. In the film, Elvis's character sings it to the grandmother of his girlfriend for her birthday, but that context has long since been forgotten. Because Elvis sang it so many times in concert, it is more fitting to suggest that the song belongs to the fans. It speaks to the way the fans felt about Elvis, and it was his love song to them.

Just as "It's Now or Never" was based on "O Sole Mio," "Can't Help Falling in Love" was adapted from an 18th-century melody called "Plaisir d'Amour" by Italian composer Giovanni Martini. A handful of songs from Elvis's career were based on classic compositions or melodies, and he rose to the occasion by offering earnest, tender, or passionate interpretations of them. The single hit the charts in December 1961. It peaked at No. 2 on *Billboard*'s Hot 100 listing and remained on the charts for 14 weeks. The RIAA certified a gold record for "Can't Help Falling in Love" in March 1962 and a platinum record exactly 30 years later.

Record collectors should note that the movie version of "Can't Help Falling in Love" was not the one released as a single or on the album. Two takes of the movie version were recorded along with one take of the single release. The movie version of "Can't Help Falling in Love" was not released until after Elvis's death.

After the soundtrack was recorded, Elvis and his entourage flew to Honolulu for a month's worth of location shooting. Hawaiian fans were as enthusiastic as those on the mainland, persistently trying to get into Elvis's hotel to see their idol. A few pretended to be mail messengers with special delivery packages that only Elvis could sign for; others managed to climb the fire escape. Fans gathered on the beach by his hotel and scratched messages in the sand that Elvis could see from his window. Finally, a 24-hour guard was posted outside Elvis's room, and Elvis curtailed his off-set activities. Elvis's personal time in Hawaii was anything but the fun-filled, action-packed adventure portrayed in the film.

Elvis reprises a dramatic version of "Drums of the Islands" during the colorful finale of Paradise, Hawaiian Style.

The exotic locale was a key element in the promotion of *Blue Hawaii* and in its success. The scenery provided more than just beautiful cinematography. As a tropical paradise, Hawaii was the perfect setting for romance, and it represented an escape from the mundane everyday world of most viewers. Even the title reinforced the locale, reminding audiences of the beautiful paradise that had become America's 50th state amid much fanfare in 1960. The entertainment industry had taken advantage of the public interest in Hawaii's admittance to the union with the release of *Blue Hawaii* and *Gidget Goes Hawaiian* on the big screen in 1961 and the TV series *Hawaiian Eye* on the small screen in 1959.

Elvis returned to Hawaii for Paradise, Hawaiian Style. *His character risks losing his pilot's license to rescue young costar Donna Butterworth from a deserted island.*

The romance and escape that went with these settings became an essential ingredient in the formula for Elvis's later movies. He returned to Hawaii to make *Girls! Girls! Girls!* and *Paradise, Hawaiian Style* and went to Florida to make *Follow That Dream; Girl Happy; Easy Come, Easy Go;*

French movie poster

and *Clambake.* The movies *Fun in Acapulco, It Happened at the World's Fair,* and *Viva Las Vegas* provide action in obvious places. The films *Harum Scarum* and *Double Trouble* offer fabulous adventures in distant countries.

Any viewer familiar with Elvis's movies recognizes the prevalence of unique and exotic locations, but not all realize the extent to which these settings affect the whole film. For example, Elvis's characters were independent spirits who worked as race-car drivers, pilots, tour guides, entertainers, or boat captains—unusual occupations, to say the least. Yet they seem almost appropriate given the exotic settings. In a way, the settings determined the occupations of Elvis's characters, which indirectly helped define them as free souls who reject the conventional, nine-to-five lifestyle. In addition, exotic and vacation settings convey the idea of slipping off to paradise for romantic escapades. For decades, travel brochures have used this very notion to entice tourists to distant lands. As soon as viewers recognized the setting of an Elvis film as exotic, unique, or a haven for fun-seeking vacationers, the stage was set for romance. And romance was the main attraction in an Elvis Presley movie. The plot may center around a quest or an adventure, but it parallels the pursuit of a beautiful woman by Elvis's carefree hero. The story concludes when the goal is completed or the quest fulfilled, which is represented by the union of Elvis's character with his leading

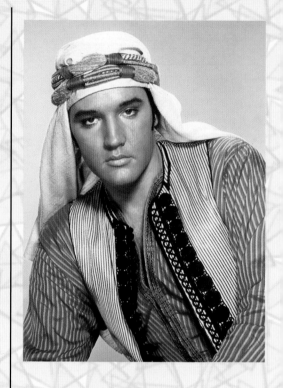

Elvis's character in Blue Hawaii *was a free spirit. This photo reveals how movie magic turned Elvis into a hang-ten surfer.*

Above and below: *Little time or money was spent on props, costumes, or set design for* Harum Scarum. *Many of the costumes that had been used in the 1944 version of* Kismet *were retailored for this 1965 remake.*

lady. The complete closure of the film in terms of fulfilling the goal and winning the girl is generally indicated by the final musical number in which the couple are united via song and/or dance.

Blue Hawaii firmly established this pattern. Here, Elvis played Chad Gates, an ambitious young man just out of the army who refuses to go into the family business. By the end of the film, after several misadventures, he has formed his own tour-guide service. The fact that he is a success is indicated by his marriage to his girlfriend, Maile, because he refused to marry her until he had proven himself. "Hawaiian Wedding Song," which concludes *Blue Hawaii,* is part of their wedding ceremony and serves to announce their union. The fulfillment of Chad's dream and the winning of Maile are neatly tied together in this final number.

"Hawaiian Wedding Song" provides an excellent example of how Elvis's music changed from his pre-army movies to the Presley travelogues. Elvis does not sing this song in a stage setting; he sings to someone who shares the spotlight with him, and the song advances the story. Most of the production numbers in the film are presented in a similar fashion, which was the exact opposite of the musical numbers in his pre-army films. *Blue Hawaii* established the formula for the presentation of the songs in Elvis's movies thereafter. In Elvis's post-army vehicles, the songs are integrated into the storyline, helping to advance the story or

Elvis and his beach buddies sing "No More."

Above and right: *In the end, Chad achieved his goal and won the girl, conveyed through the closing musical number "Hawaiian Wedding Song."*

relate something about the characters to the viewers. In this type of musical, characters tend to burst into song at any moment—on the beach, in a car, even on a horse. Elvis disliked this type of musical and was uncomfortable when his character sang in situations where people would not normally sing.

> I GET TIRED OF PLAYING A GUY WHO GETS INTO A FIGHT, THEN STARTS SINGING TO THE GUY HE'S JUST BEAT UP.
>
> —ELVIS PRESLEY, *NEWSWEEK*, AUGUST 11, 1969

Joe Lightcloud (Elvis): *Man, that's what I call one hell of a fight.*
—*Elvis's first use of onscreen profanity, in the comedy* Stay Away, Joe

Because the musical numbers often tell part of the story, it is not unusual for them to include other characters. Most often, Elvis's characters sing to or dance with the leading ladies as a means of winning their love or to symbolize the couple's growing affection. Sometimes the film will feature Elvis singing to a child, a pet, or an elderly woman to help soften the vagabond nature of his characters. In *Blue Hawaii,* Chad gives Maile's grandmother a music box that plays "Can't Help Falling in Love," to which Chad sings along. The scene helps the audience understand that Chad is not the rash, immature young man that his parents believe him to be.

In Kid Galahad, *Elvis plays the role of a boxer.*

Elvis's performing style in *Blue Hawaii* and his later films differs a great deal from that of his 1950s films. Gone are the sensual hip movements, leg swivels, pelvic thrusts, and dramatic hand gestures that drove the ladies wild in *Loving You.* Elvis still moves while he sings, but his style is noticeably toned down. This seemed an appropriate change if Elvis was singing to another character. The notorious performing style of his early career was not suitable for romantic situations or when singing to a child or grandmother. When he wasn't singing to someone else, or when he sang a tune with an upbeat tempo, a bevy of beautiful women often danced in the background. Thus, Elvis no longer needed to move provocatively because a chorus of women did it for him. After all, women dancing in a sexual or provocative way was a more conventional—and therefore more acceptable—sight in mainstream movies.

Singer Patti Page and Elvis were friends; her husband was dance director for the films Elvis made with Hal Wallis at Paramount.

Elvis's toned-down style was less controversial and considered more suited to family entertainment. His musical comedy vehicles were designed to attract a family audience. Elvis, Colonel Tom Parker, Hal Wallis, and Abe Lastfogel wanted to turn Elvis into a mature leading man for the movies. His new singing style and smoother pop-oriented music helped accomplish that. A version of this image had been introduced in *G.I. Blues*, but it was perfected in *Blue Hawaii*, arguably the best of Elvis's musical comedies.

Musical scene from Blue Hawaii

Blue Hawaii was well crafted and shrewdly manufactured to suit Elvis's new image. It was also wildly successful. While it turned Elvis Presley into a highly paid star, it limited the types of roles he could play because it established the formula that his movies followed to the end of his Hollywood career. Much has been written about how Elvis's hopes of becoming a serious actor were foiled by the formula. His potential as an actor was a casualty of his success as a movie star. Because of the significance it holds in Elvis's career, *Blue Hawaii* is both revered and reviled.

MAILE (SOAKING WET): I BOUGHT THIS DRESS TO WELCOME YOU HOME. IT'S THE FIRST TIME I'VE WORN IT.

CHAD (ELVIS): YOU KNOW SOMETHING? ON YOU, WET IS MY FAVORITE COLOR.
—*BLUE HAWAII*

This fanzine refers to Elvis's nickname, the "Million Dollar Actor." In the mid-1960s, he was the highest-paid screen actor.
Right: *Movie publicity photo of Elvis Presley*

Chad the tour guide shows a school group around the island in Blue Hawaii. *Elvis labeled these kinds of movies "Presley travelogues."*

With some notable exceptions, the *Blue Hawaii* formula defines the bulk of his movies, which Elvis disparagingly called "Presley travelogues." Film reviewers and Presley biographers refer to these movies as "vehicles." In Hollywood, a vehicle is a film constructed around a star's image. A star plays a character based on the star's own personality rather than portraying a complex, three-dimensional character. Vehicles showcase a performer's specialty, and in this regard, musical stars tend to benefit more than other actors from appearing in vehicles. Vehicles have showcased many well-respected musical and comedy stars, including Fred Astaire, Ginger Rogers, and Bob Hope. In this context, Hal Wallis's decision to display the talents of Elvis Presley in a series of musical comedies was a logical one.

Elvis enjoyed being behind the camera, too.

Elvis was not the only pop-rock star to appear in a series of lightweight musicals during the 1960s. Everyone from Frankie Avalon to Herman's Hermits bopped through their own musical vehicles, which were marketed to youthful audiences. Some of these teen musicals featured pop-flavored songs that sounded more like some Hollywood executive's idea of what rock music should be, while others included the music of well-known rock 'n' roll bands of the era.

The most famous teen flicks included the series of beach movies produced by American International Pictures starring Frankie Avalon and Annette Funicello. The first, *Beach Party,* was released in 1963 and was so successful it launched four others with the same cast—*Muscle Beach Party, Bikini Beach, Beach Blanket Bingo,* and *How to Stuff a Wild Bikini.* In each film, Funicello played DeeDee, who spent most of the time trying to keep Frankie, played by Avalon, in check. Frankie and Annette's

Beach Party, *starring Frankie Avalon and Annette Funicello, was part of the youth-targeted genre known as teen flicks. Elvis's musical vehicles from the 1960s were also a part of this genre.*

youthful shenanigans were supported by a gang of stock players: dancer Candy Johnson, whose deadly wiggle literally knocked men for a loop; John Ashley, who was often Frankie's rival for DeeDee's affections; and Jody McCrae, a surf bum named Deadhead who had taken one too many spills.

Although their low-budget origins are apparent, the films captured the pleasures of youthful pastimes and the spirit of surfing music, which was so popular during the early 1960s. Several bands known for the "surfin' sound"—Dick Dale and the Del-Tones, the Hondells, the Pyramids, and the Kingsmen—made guest appearances in the beach party movies. In addition, such well-known film actors from past generations as Robert Cummings, Buster Keaton, Dorothy Malone, Mickey Rooney, and Keenan Wynn rounded out the casts, lending this series an aura of legitimacy that was lacking in other teen flicks.

Scene from Paradise, Hawaiian Style

When the beach began to look too familiar, the party moved to the ski slopes. A whole new subgenre was born after producer Gene Corman at American International decided to use a ski resort for the setting of *Ski Party*.

Frankie Avalon courted Deborah Walley this time out, while Dwayne Hickman was paired with Yvonne Craig. Leslie Gore and her pop-flavored songs fit right into the fluffy storyline, but James Brown's highly charged soul numbers burned through the screen when he boogalooed into the scene with his Famous Flames. Still other musicals made use of a college setting in an effort to keep this youth-oriented genre alive, including *Get Yourself a College Girl*, with

Exterior scenes for Paradise, Hawaiian Style *were shot in Hawaii. A Presley picture was often set in an exotic locale or at a vacation resort.*

Annette Funicello and Frankie Avalon in Beach Blanket Bingo

Nancy Sinatra, Mary Ann Mobley, and Chad Everett, and *C'mon Let's Live a Little,* with Bobby Vee and Jackie DeShannon.

Some of the English rock groups that were part of the British Invasion were also packaged into movie vehicles. Peter Noone and Herman's Hermits made a splash with their feature musical, *Hold On,* while the Dave Clark Five made a dismal effort titled *Having a Wild Weekend.* The Beatles' two feature films, *A Hard Day's Night* and *Help!,* belong to this musical genre as well, but the creative direction of Richard Lester lifts them above the exploitative level of the typical teen flick.

The Beatles made two feature films, A Hard Day's Night *and* Help! *Directed by the talented Richard Lester, they represented more creative examples of teen flicks.*

Most of the movies that starred pop-rock singers were meant strictly for teen audiences, but Elvis's musical comedies were family fare. The casts included children as well as older characters who are accepted as wise representatives of past generations. Despite these differences, Elvis's movies fit quite well into the teen musical genre. Many of Elvis's costars, for example, were featured in the beach and ski movies, including Shelley Fabares, Nancy Sinatra, Yvonne Craig, Deborah Walley, Joby Baker, Dwayne Hickman, and Mary Ann Mobley.

Elvis began to fade from the music charts after the Beatles changed the course of rock 'n' roll.

Producers and directors from other teen musicals also worked on Elvis's films. Sam Katzman, the "King of the Quickies," who produced *Get Yourself a College Girl,* had been in the youth exploitation market since he made some of the first rock 'n' roll vehicles during the 1950s. He was responsible for two of Elvis's films, *Kissin' Cousins* and *Harum Scarum.*

Elvis's later musical vehicles were geared to family audiences and often included sentimental scenes with small children, such as actress Vicky Tiu, his costar in It Happened at the World's Fair.

Nancy Sinatra

On his return from the army in 1960, Elvis was scheduled to appear on *The Frank Sinatra-Timex Special,* a television show hosted by Frank Sinatra. Frank sent his daughter Nancy to the airport as Elvis's official greeter. The pair struck up a friendship that lasted for years and provided sparkling chemistry in *Speedway.* Her version of "Your Groovy Self" was included on the soundtrack album, marking the only time another artist sang a solo on a regular RCA Elvis album. In the mid-1960s, Nancy recorded four hit duets with singer-songwriter Lee Hazelwood, who also wrote her best-known hit, "These Boots Are Made for Walking." She earned her third gold record for a duet she sang with her father, "Something Stupid." She also spent a large part of the 1960s cavorting through teen musicals, such as *Get Yourself a College Girl* (1964) and *The Ghost in the Invisible Bikini* (1966). During the mid-1990s, Nancy rode the crest of a nostalgia wave, singing her 1960s hits to a new generation and appearing in *Playboy* magazine.

A young Kurt Russell gives Elvis a kick in the shins in It Happened at the World's Fair.

The settings and plots of Elvis's films paralleled those of other youth-related musicals. When spring break in Fort Lauderdale and other resort areas became a popular subject, as in *Where the Boys Are* and *Palm Springs Weekend,* Elvis starred in his own Fort Lauderdale adventure, *Girl Happy.* When the mod scene in England and Europe was all the rage, Elvis appeared in *Double Trouble,* featuring the swinging discotheques of London and Amsterdam as a backdrop. The considerable number of beach-related films that Elvis made, including *Blue Hawaii, Clambake,* and *Paradise, Hawaiian Style,* was undoubtedly influenced by the popularity of the beach party movies.

Placed within the context of the teen musical, Elvis's movies make perfect sense, even standing out because of their high-quality production values. A critic for *Variety* praised Elvis's movies for this reason in a review of *Easy Come, Easy Go*:

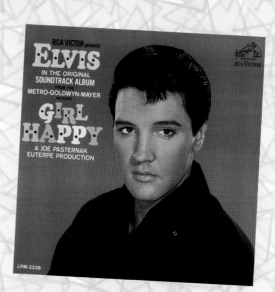

The Girl Happy *soundtrack was a solid collection of pop tunes, except for one song.*

"Anyone who has seen similar films recognizes the superior quality of Presley's films: the story makes sense; the songs are better and are better motivated; cast and direction are stronger; production values are first-rate." The teen musical genre, including Elvis's musical vehicles, is a testament to the popularity of the easy-going, pop-rock music of the mid-1960s and to those teen idols who were part of that scene. Never meant to be serious filmmaking, all of these films are best taken as lighthearted Americana.

Although biographers and film critics continue to condemn Elvis's Hollywood career, his films have always been interesting viewing for fans, who know some of the behind-the-scenes anecdotes and tall tales.

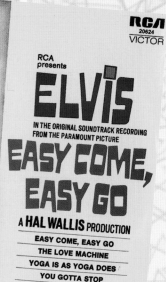

The EP soundtrack of Easy Come, Easy Go *contained all six songs from the movie.*

While in Hollywood, Elvis developed a reputation for dating his costars while a movie was in production. Rumors about Elvis's relationships with actresses were repeated in fan magazines, gossip columns, and the entertainment press. Much of what was said was obviously manufactured for its publicity value, but some of the rumors were undoubtedly true or came close to being true. To his credit, Colonel Parker usually kept information about Elvis's personal life out of the press.

Elvis did not have an exclusive contract with Hal Wallis. He also worked for MGM, United Artists, and Allied Artists. The producers from these other studios followed the musical comedy formula that Wallis had developed, occasionally even improving on it. *Viva Las Vegas,* produced by MGM and released in 1964, features

Football hero Jim Brown and Elvis visited between scenes of Roustabout *in 1964. Jim was filming the Western* Rio Conchos.

Colonel Tom Parker and Priscilla joined Elvis on the set of Stay Away, Joe. *Parker was named technical adviser on 24 of Elvis's films.*

Song List

VIVA LAS VEGAS
THE YELLOW ROSE OF TEXAS
THE LADY LOVES ME
C'MON EVERYBODY
TODAY, TOMORROW AND FOREVER
WHAT'D I SAY
SANTA LUCIA
IF YOU THINK I DON'T LOVE YOU
I NEED SOMEBODY TO LEAN ON
MY RIVAL (ANN-MARGRET)
APPRECIATION (ANN-MARGRET)
THE CLIMB (THE FORTE FOUR)

Elvis as a race-car driver who takes a job as a waiter at the Flamingo Hotel to earn money to enter the Las Vegas Grand Prix. Ann-Margret plays a swimming instructor who is romanced by Elvis's character and by another dashing race-car driver played by Cesare Danova. The movie was shot in and around Las Vegas, using such locations as the Flamingo and Tropicana hotels and the drag strip at Henderson, Nevada.

The inclusion of Ann-Margret made this Presley travelogue a cut above most. Ann-Margret was known at the time as "the female Elvis Presley" for her sensual, rock 'n' roll dancing style. Fans were excited about the potential screen explosion promised by the pairing of Elvis with his female counterpart, and they weren't disappointed. The musical numbers in *Viva Las Vegas* are sparked by an electricity not found in other Elvis movies. The on-screen chemistry between Elvis and Ann-Margret reflected their highly publicized off-screen romance.

Of all his relationships with his costars, Elvis's romance with Ann-Margret was probably the most serious. During the production of *Viva Las Vegas*, Elvis and the redheaded starlet set the publicity mill grinding when they began showing up together at restaurants and clubs around Las Vegas. They shared a mutual love for motorcycles and occasionally rode together, but they were warned to be careful because an accident involving either one of them would have delayed production on the movie.

To avoid injury to either star, mattresses were placed along the paths of the motorcycles during this scene from Viva Las Vegas. Elvis and Ann-Margret loved to ride motorcycles offscreen as well.

Viva Las Vegas *was a major success, thanks to the chemistry between its two high-powered stars, and the publicity surrounding their romance didn't hurt either.*

113

RUSTY (ANN-MARGRET): I'D LIKE YOU TO CHECK MY MOTOR. IT WHISTLES.

LUCKY (ELVIS): I DON'T BLAME IT.

—*VIVA LAS VEGAS*

Other actresses whom Elvis dated during his career in Hollywood included Joan Blackman while working on *Kid Galahad,* Yvonne Craig while shooting *It Happened at the World's Fair,* Deborah Walley during the production of *Spinout,* and Mary Ann Mobley while working on *Girl Happy.*

Some actresses stand out for not dating Elvis during film production. Donna Douglas, costar of *Frankie and Johnny,* was a religious and spiritual person who impressed Elvis because she was so well read. He admired her intellect, and he was inspired by her example to

Ann-Margret, Elvis's love interest in Viva Las Vegas, *was nicknamed "the female Elvis Presley" during the early 1960s because of her sensual, high-spirited dancing style.*

Elvis starred as race-car driver Lucky Jackson in Viva Las Vegas, *released in June 1964.*

Norman Taurog

Norman Taurog directed nine Elvis Presley features, more than any of Elvis's other directors. Elvis always favored Taurog, probably because of his kind nature and lack of ego. After particularly difficult scenes, the fatherly director would pass out candy bars to his cast and crew.

Taurog was known primarily for lightweight vehicles and comedies, a specialty that dated all the way back to 1919 when his directorial career was launched with a series starring silent comedian Larry Semon. The consummate studio director, Taurog directed many major stars in more than 70 films across six decades. He won an Oscar in 1931 for *Skippy,* a vehicle for child star Jackie Cooper, and he was nominated again in 1938 for the classic *Boys Town.* Taurog, who died in 1981, said about Elvis, "I was always proud of his work, even if I wasn't proud of the scripts. I always felt that he never reached his peak."

Actress Shelley Fabares and Elvis, who became good friends, made three movies together.

read more, particularly books on religion and philosophy. Elvis tried desperately to get costar Shelley Fabares to go out with him during the production of *Girl Happy,* but she was heavily involved with record producer Lou Adler and later married him. In lieu of a romantic relationship, Elvis and Fabares became friends. She costarred with him in two other movies, *Spinout* and *Clambake.* Elvis later claimed that she was his favorite costar.

Elvis's musical comedies were relatively inexpensive to produce but always profitable, so Hal Wallis often used them as collateral for financing more prestigious movies. The potential profits from *Roustabout* were enough of a guarantee for investors to back Wallis's production of *Becket,* which later won an Academy Award for best adapted screenplay. After Elvis stopped making movies, he complained bitterly that this practice had made him feel used.

Barbara Stanwyck, Elvis, and Joan Freeman enjoying a carnival ride in Roustabout.

Kissin' Cousins was the first of Elvis's low-budget movies. After he made this movie, the shooting schedules for his musical comedies seemed to get shorter and the budgets seemed to get smaller. Some people say that Colonel Parker thought Elvis's popularity as a movie star was waning, so he began to seek out producers who could lower production costs. He also looked for resorts and hotels that allowed the cast and crew to stay for free. But there's no proof that the Colonel intended to lower the quality of Elvis's movies. The reverse actually may

Elvis was in awe of his famous costar Barbara Stanwyck, and he worked hard to live up to her professional standards.

have been the case, and the decline in production values that went along with lower budgets and shorter schedules may have resulted in a decrease in box-office receipts.

Unfortunately, the music in Elvis's 1960s movies was often not as good as it should have been. Elvis averaged three movies per year between 1960 and 1969, and a soundtrack album was released in conjunction with each movie. After 1964, the Colonel insisted that Elvis record only soundtrack albums. Many of the songs written for Elvis's films were done by hacks who worked for Hill and Range, the publishing house associated with RCA Records. The production values of these albums were erratic. Typically, the songs for a soundtrack album were recorded in two or three all-night sessions. Neither Colonel Parker nor anyone at RCA or Hill and Range was interested in sinking money into securing good material for Elvis when mediocre soundtrack albums were so easy to produce and sold so well. Since the system worked to everyone's advantage, there was no reason to change it. The albums and the movies promoted each other. The release of a soundtrack album reminded fans that a movie would soon be appearing in their neighborhood theater, while the movie served as a glorious advertisement for the soundtrack album.

Elvis's control of the pop, country, and rhythm-and-blues charts faded during the 1960s. After 1960, Elvis didn't have a song on the country charts until 1968, and after 1963, he never again placed a record on the R&B charts. Elvis was able to coast on his reputation until about 1965. That year, he had

Through special effects, Elvis played two characters in Kissin' Cousins—*an Air Force pilot and his country cousin.*

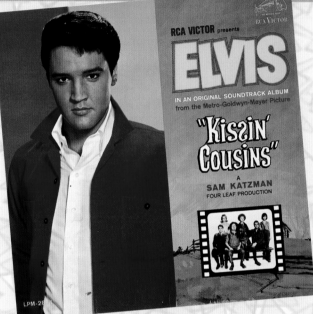

The title song "Kissin' Cousins" reached No. 12 on Billboard's Hot 100 chart.

Opposite page: *The typical Elvis character was a race-car driver, a boat pilot, or an airplane pilot who also happened to sing.*

Change of Habit, *released in 1969, was Elvis's last movie. Ironically, it was a drama and gave him the kind of role he'd been craving. He played a doctor in a ghetto clinic opposite Mary Tyler Moore, who portrayed a nun.*

only one Top-Ten single, "Crying in the Chapel," which he had actually recorded in 1960. His soundtrack albums placed in the Top Ten but just barely. In 1966, only one of Elvis's singles, "Love Letters," made it to the Top 20. By 1967, none of Elvis's singles or albums charted anywhere near the Top 20.

Elvis's music may have declined in quality, originality, and popularity during the 1960s, but the decline was not as rapid as many claim, nor was all the music written for his films mediocre. He recorded some good songs during that decade, even if they were for the soundtracks of his movies. Many of the tunes from *Viva Las Vegas* are comparable to those from his earlier films. Other excellent songs include the title tune from *Follow That Dream*, "Return to Sender" from *Girls! Girls! Girls!*, "Rubberneckin'" from *Change of Habit*, "Wolf Call" from *Girl Happy*, "Can't Help Falling in Love" from *Blue Hawaii*, "Little Egypt" from *Roustabout*, and many more. Although there is little hard-driving rock 'n' roll or rhythm-and-blues in these musical numbers, Elvis's mastery of the pop-rock idiom is smooth and confident.

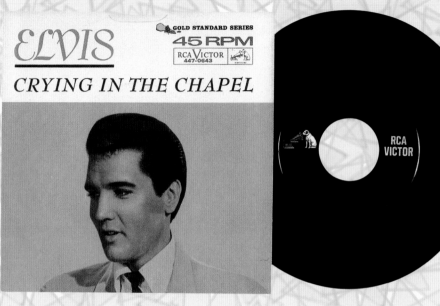

Elvis recorded "Crying in the Chapel" in Nashville in 1960, but it was not released until 1965. The single reached No. 3 on the charts.

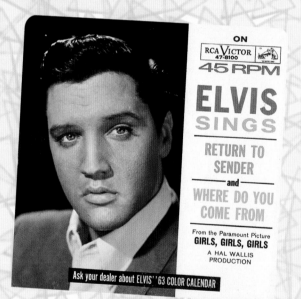

"Return to Sender" hit No. 2 in the U.S.A. and No. 1 in England. Written by Otis Blackwell, the single featured Boots Randolph on saxophone.

What's in a Name?

Hollywood films commonly change their titles during production, but Elvis's musical comedies were notorious for doing this, often at the very last minute. Sometimes the change represented an improvement, as when *Hawaii Beach Boy* was given the much more romantic title *Blue Hawaii*. Usually, however, the final titles were little better than the originals. *Flaming Star* was at various times *Flaming Lance*, *Flaming Heart*, and *Black Star*. *In My Harem* became *Harem Holiday*, which turned into *Harem Scarum* and then finally *Harum Scarum*, with that all-important misspelling so the first word could match the second. The memorable *Kiss My Firm But Pliant Lips* was changed to the forgettable *Live a Little, Love a Little*. *A Girl in Every Port* became *Welcome Aboard*, which became *Gumbo Ya-Ya*, which then became *Girls! Girls! Girls!* Perhaps the worst series of titles belonged to *Spinout* because they were mostly meaningless clichés. Those considered included *Jim Dandy*, *After Midnight*, *Always at Midnight*, *Never Say No*, and *Never Say Yes*. To complicate matters, its British release title was *California Holiday*.

Ursula Andress costarred with Elvis in Fun in Acapulco. *It was the Swiss-born actress's first American movie, although she had been appearing in Italian films since 1954.*

Unfortunately, these well-written songs tend to get lost on soundtracks that feature anywhere from six to fourteen numbers. There is no escaping the fact that Elvis recorded some clunkers during the 1960s. Among the most ridiculous are "(There's) No Room to Rhumba in a Sports Car" from *Fun in Acapulco,* "Fort Lauderdale Chamber of Commerce" from *Girl Happy,* "Queenie Wahini's Papaya" from *Paradise, Hawaiian Style,* "Yoga Is as Yoga Does" from *Easy Come, Easy Go,* "Barefoot Ballad" from *Kissin' Cousins,* "He's Your Uncle, Not Your Dad" from *Speedway,* and "Petunia, the Gardener's Daughter" from *Frankie and Johnny.*

RCA did not market or package Elvis's albums very wisely. His soundtrack albums were a hodgepodge of songs that lacked unity and consistency, and the Colonel and the people at RCA were determined to saturate the market by releasing material at an extremely rapid rate. It was not unusual for RCA to release a Presley soundtrack while an earlier one was still on the charts, even though standard practice was to get as much mileage as possible from a performer's album before releasing the next. Most of Elvis's albums and films secured a profit no matter how hastily they were manufactured. The Colonel continually tied him up with three-film contracts with a number of studios, so even when Elvis decided to stop making movies around 1968, he was contractually obligated to star in several more.

Despite the decrease in box-office revenue for Elvis's films at the end of the 1960s, everyone benefited financially from these vehicles. The budgets of Elvis's films were planned so 50 percent of the total budget was allotted for his salary, and he received a percentage of the profits. Parker received 25 percent of Presley's gross income and whatever he could negotiate as technical adviser, while Abe Lastfogel of William Morris received 10 percent off the top of any film deal.

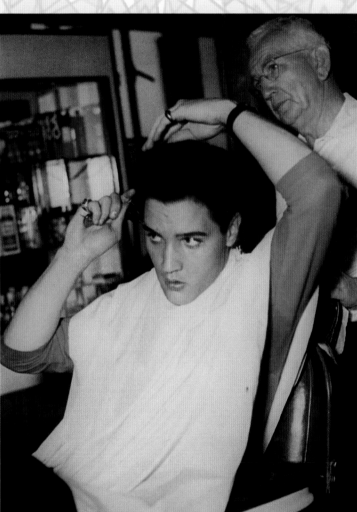

Elvis checked his haircut, a frequent ritual done by the movie studio's barber.

The soundtrack for Fun in Acapulco *remained on Billboard's Top LP chart for 24 weeks.*

Colonel Parker understood the key to the financial success of the films when he told a scriptwriter that there were a quarter of a million die-hard Elvis Presley fans willing to see each movie three times. The fans believed that Elvis's charisma transcended any mediocre material he was given. When the lines formed outside the box offices, the people in those lines came to see Elvis and nothing else.

The many biographers and detractors who search for an explanation as to why Elvis continued to star in the Presley travelogues need look no further than this 1966 fan letter:

"Dear Elvis,
You're [sic] movie played two weeks at Loew's, and I saw it at least twice a day. I can't hardly wait to see it again when it comes to the neighborhood. I have seen it 29 times."

Elvis shows the Girls! Girls! Girls! *script to Scatter, his pet chimp. Elvis became so disillusioned with his later films that he stopped reading scripts.*

What Might Have Been

During the years when Elvis acted in Hollywood, he had several opportunities to star in films that were not "Presley travelogues," but they fell through. Often, the Colonel refused to agree to a film that did not follow the formula or did not showcase Elvis to his best advantage. He turned down the 1956 rock 'n' roll spoof *The Girl Can't Help It*, because the money wasn't good enough and because Elvis had to share the screen with other notable rock 'n' roll acts. Barbra Streisand reportedly asked Elvis to play the male lead in her 1976 remake of the 1954 film *A Star Is Born*. It is said that Elvis was excited about her offer; however, the Colonel was not and turned it down. Kris Kristofferson ended up playing the role. Other roles that Elvis turned down included Hank Williams in *Your Cheatin' Heart* (George Hamilton played Williams) and the singing cowboy in *The Fastest Guitar in the West* (Roy Orbison got the part). Rumors persist that he could have appeared in *Thunder Road*, *The Way to the Gold*, and *The Defiant Ones*, but these tales could have been born of bitterness over Elvis's lost potential as an actor.

Other factors prevented Elvis from appearing in certain films, including the timing of projects and failed deals. Elvis was once set to play a James Bond-like superspy in a comedy adventure called *That Jack Valentine*, but the film was never produced. Other projects that fell through include a proposed musical starring Elvis opposite a classical artist and a comedy teaming Elvis with French legend Brigitte Bardot.

Comeback Hero

Chapter 6

RCA
LSP-4155

VICTOR
STEREO

From
ELVIS
In Memphis

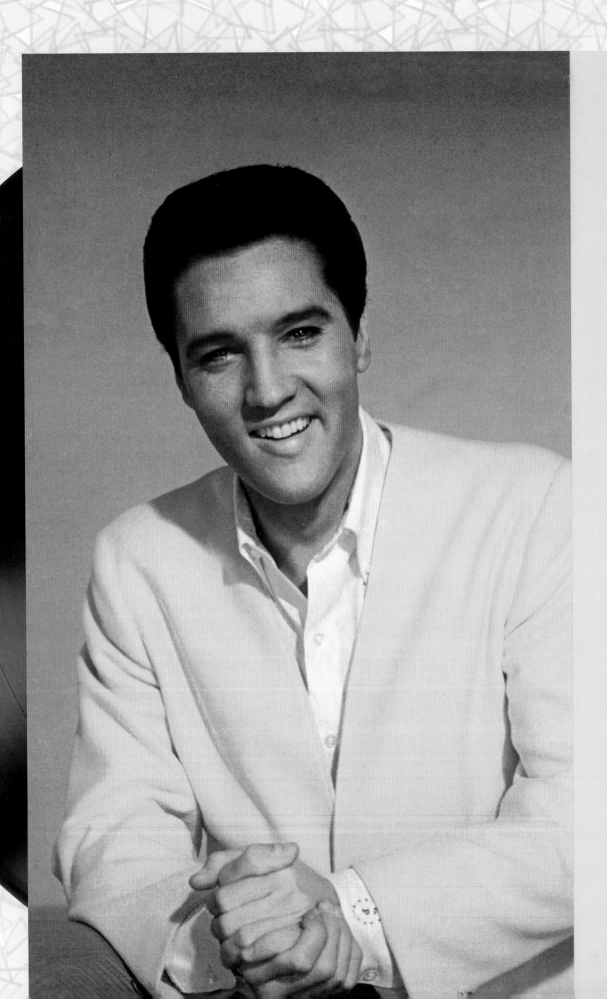

From ELVIS In Memphis

SIDE 1

Wearin' That Loved On Look (BMI 2:41)
Only the Strong Survive (BMI 2:45)
I'll Hold You in My Heart (Till I Can Hold You in My Arms) (BMI 4:31)
Long Black Limousine (BMI 3:41)
It Keeps Right On A-Hurtin' (BMI 2:35)
I'm Movin' On (BMI 2:50)

SIDE 2

Power of My Love (BMI 2:35)
Gentle on My Mind (BMI 3:20)
After Loving You (BMI 3:05)
True Love Travels on a Gravel Road (BMI 2:37)
Any Day Now (ASCAP 2:55)
In the Ghetto (ASCAP 2:44)

FOR YOUR COLLECTION—ELVIS' TV ALBUM

ALSO AVAILABLE ON STEREO 8 CARTRIDGE

THERE IS SOMETHING SPECIAL ABOUT WATCHING A MAN WHO HAS LOST HIMSELF FIND HIS WAY BACK HOME. HE SANG WITH THE KIND OF POWER PEOPLE NO LONGER ASSOCIATE WITH ROCK 'N' ROLL SINGERS. HE MOVED HIS BODY WITH A LACK OF PRETENSION AND EFFORT THAT MUST HAVE MADE JIM MORRISON GREEN WITH ENVY. AND WHILE MOST OF THE SONGS WERE TEN OR TWELVE YEARS OLD, HE PERFORMED THEM AS FRESHLY AS THOUGH THEY WERE WRITTEN YESTERDAY.

—JON LANDAU, ON *ELVIS*—THE '68 COMEBACK SPECIAL

From January 1964 to May 1966, Elvis recorded nothing but movie soundtracks, mostly in Hollywood. Unsatisfied with his life for complex professional and personal reasons, he did not venture into the Nashville studios to cut any album material. When he did finally decide to record new material, he returned to the studio with new musicians and a new producer, Felton Jarvis.

Elvis went to the RCA studios in Nashville in the spring of 1966 to make a gospel album, *How Great Thou Art*. As a child of the South, his sound was steeped in gospel music. Memphis was the center of white gospel music during the 1950s, and as a teenager Elvis had frequently attended all-night gospel sings at Ellis Auditorium. Early in his

Auditorium, Memphis, Tenn.

Postcard of Ellis Auditorium

Felton Jarvis

Chet Atkins served as Elvis's producer in a minimalist way until 1966 when he decided to get away from the night recording sessions that Elvis preferred. Atkins introduced RCA staff producer Felton Jarvis to Elvis when the singer was scheduled to record *How Great Thou Art*, and Jarvis became Elvis's primary producer. Born in Atlanta, Charles Felton Jarvis had been something of an Elvis imitator in his youth, recording "Don't Knock Elvis" in 1959. Jarvis became a producer in 1963 with a Presley soundalike named Marvin Benefield, whom Jarvis renamed Vince Everett after Elvis's character in *Jailhouse Rock*.

Jarvis helped steer Elvis toward better material than the soundtrack albums he had been releasing for the last several years, although his hands were often tied by RCA's strict publishing policies. Jarvis left RCA in 1970 to devote his full attention to Elvis's recordings. After Elvis died, Jarvis produced sessions for Carl Perkins and coproduced the songs sung by Ronnie McDowell for the 1979 biopic *Elvis*. Jarvis died from a stroke in 1981 at the age of 46.

recording career, he developed the lifelong habit of warming up before each session by singing gospel harmonies with the Jordanaires or with his companions.

Elvis loved all gospel music, but he favored the style of four-part harmony sung by male gospel quartets who were associated with the shapenote singing schools of the early 1900s. A quartet usually included first and second tenors, a baritone, and a bass. As a teenager, Elvis's favorite gospel quartets included the Blackwood Brothers, whom he knew personally, and the Statesmen, whose lead singer was the colorful Jake Hess. The Statesmen were known for their emotional, highly stylized delivery, and Hess had a reputation as a flamboyant dresser. So Elvis was delighted when Hess and his latest quartet, the Imperials, joined him in the studio to record "How Great Thou Art," along with a few secular songs that were released later. Also on board were the Jordanaires and a female backup group.

The arrangements for the gospel numbers consisted of Statesmen and Blackwood Brothers material. For most numbers, Elvis sang as the solo artist while one of the quartets backed him up. A high point of the sessions occurred when Elvis and Hess sang a duet on the Statesmen's famous "If the Lord Wasn't Walking by My Side."

Song List

HOW GREAT THOU ART
IN THE GARDEN
SOMEBODY BIGGER THAN YOU AND I
FARTHER ALONG
STAND BY ME
WITHOUT HIM
SO HIGH
WHERE COULD I GO BUT TO
THE LORD
BY AND BY
IF THE LORD WASN'T WALKING
BY MY SIDE
RUN ON
WHERE NO ONE STANDS ALONE
CRYING IN THE CHAPEL

How Great Thou Art *used several Nashville studio musicians, including Ray Stevens (near right) and Charlie McCoy (far right).*

Jake Hess, lead singer of the Statesmen quartet and later the Imperials, sang a duet with Elvis on the gospel album.

How Great Thou Art proved to be a milestone in Elvis's career, winning him the first of his three Grammys, this one in the Best Sacred Performance category. He won Best Inspirational Performance for *He Touched Me* in 1972 and again in that category for the song "How Great Thou Art" from the album *Elvis Recorded Live on Stage in Memphis* in 1974.

Elvis created *How Great Thou Art* during a time of personal and professional struggle. He had been frustrated creatively by the formulaic movies and their conventional soundtrack music. It is most fitting that Elvis should record a gospel album at a time when he was at a creative and spiritual low.

Elvis opened with Elvis striding onstage wearing a sexy leather outfit and singing a scorching rendition of "Trouble."

Grammy Awards

Despite his immeasurable impact on 20th-century popular music, Elvis won only three Grammy Awards during his lifetime. The Grammy is the most prestigious award in the music industry. However, it was particularly coveted during Elvis's lifetime because there were far fewer music awards then. In 1967, Elvis won a Grammy for Best Sacred Performance for the album *How Great Thou Art*. Five years later, he won for Best Inspirational Performance for *He Touched Me*. In 1974, he won Best Inspirational Performance for the song "How Great Thou Art" from the album *Elvis Recorded Live on Stage in Memphis*. Because gospel music played such an important role in Elvis's life, he was especially gratified that he won for his inspirational recordings. In addition to his three awards, Elvis was nominated for Grammys ten times during his career. Also, the cover of *For LP Fans Only* was nominated for Best Album Cover in 1959.

Above and right: Elvis, *aka The '68 Comeback Special, presented four polished musical production numbers.*

Gospel had inspired his interest in music, it had always calmed his nerves before a session or a performance, and as they say in the South, it called him back home.

SINCE I WAS TWO YEARS OLD, ALL I KNEW WAS GOSPEL MUSIC. THAT MUSIC BECAME SUCH A PART OF MY LIFE IT WAS AS NATURAL AS DANCING. A WAY TO ESCAPE FROM THE PROBLEMS. AND MY WAY OF RELEASE.

—ELVIS PRESLEY, REPRINTED IN
ELVIS IN HIS OWN WORDS, 1977

After years of starring in movie vehicles and mainly recording soundtrack material, Elvis had fallen into a rut, devoid of creativity and vitality. The decision to turn Elvis into a big-screen leading man via a series of musical comedies was arguably a good career move in the early 1960s, but by 1968 the movie formula was clearly a dead end. In December of that year, the broadcast of his television special *Elvis* turned his career around by introducing him to hipper recording material and new directions.

Inspired and invigorated by the success of his television special, Elvis walked through the door of tiny American Sound Studios in Memphis in January 1969 to make quality music that would garner him hit records. Elvis had not recorded in his hometown since he left Sun in 1955, but the musical atmosphere at RCA's

In the country-western segment of the TV special, Elvis as the Guitar Man roamed the honky-tonks of the South and found himself in a bar fight.

Chips Moman

Singer Steve Tyrell (left) and Chips Moman

Born in 1936 in LaGrange, Georgia, Chips Moman (near left) made his name as one of the architects of the Memphis Sound, an edgier style of soul music descended from Memphis's blues and rhythm-and-blues. Settling in Memphis in the late 1950s, he helped establish soulful Stax Records in 1958. Six years later, Moman and fellow producer Bob Crewe founded American Sound Studios. Stax and American Sound became the premier champions of the Memphis Sound.

As a songwriter, Moman composed the gritty R&B tune "Dark End of the Street," which was recorded by Percy Sledge, Linda Ronstadt, and Roy Hamilton, and he wrote "Luckenback Texas," made famous by country outlaw Waylon Jennings. As a hands-on producer, Moman became an expert at finding the right material for the right performer. Moman produced a three-year string of hits for such diverse artists as Wilson Pickett, Dusty Springfield, B. J. Thomas, Neil Diamond, and the Box Tops. His work with Elvis in 1969 garnered the singer his first hit singles in years.

During the 1970s, Moman produced in Nashville, but he returned to Memphis in 1985 to open Three Alarm Studios. Partly because of his work with Elvis, Moman gained a reputation for reviving stagnating careers.

Nashville studios had become stale. His friends and associates encouraged him to record at American Sound because Nashville could yield nothing for him at that time.

American Sound Studios, a small studio in a rundown neighborhood, was operated by Chips Moman. With Moman as producer, Elvis worked hard to record his first significant mainstream album in years. In retrospect, *From Elvis in Memphis* may be his most important album because it brought his recording career back from soundtrack purgatory and set a creative standard for the next few years.

The musicians at American Sound Studios (from left): Bobby Wood, Mike Leech, Tommy Cogbill, Gene Chrisman, Elvis, Bobby Emmons, Reggie Young, Ed Kollis, and Dan Penn.

The interior of American Sound Studios.

The material Moman brought to Elvis represented all styles of music. Some songs were from the pens of new country songwriters who had been influenced by the innovative music scene of the 1960s. From Mac Davis came a song with socially conscious lyrics called "In the Ghetto," which was light-years away from the benign movie tunes Elvis had been recording. It became a Top Ten hit for Elvis in the spring of 1969. He also recorded Jerry Butler's rhythm-and-blues hit "Only the Strong Survive."

Elvis recorded 32 songs from a variety of genres, but the 12 cuts on *From Elvis in Memphis* seem weighted toward modern country music. Elvis's intense version of "Long Black Limousine," about a poor country girl who moves to the big city, turned a sentimental country song into a bitter social comment. Other passionately sung country tunes on the album include Eddy Arnold's "I'll Hold You in My Heart (Till I Can Hold You in My Arms)" and "After Loving You." Also among the 32 tracks Moman produced at American Sound Studios were the *(continued on page 132)*

(continued on page 132)

The Elvis TV special team (left to right): Musical producer Bones Howe, producer/director Steve Binder, Elvis Presley, and executive producer Bob Finkel, who won a Peabody Award for his work.

Elvis performed 18 songs on his 1968 special.

129

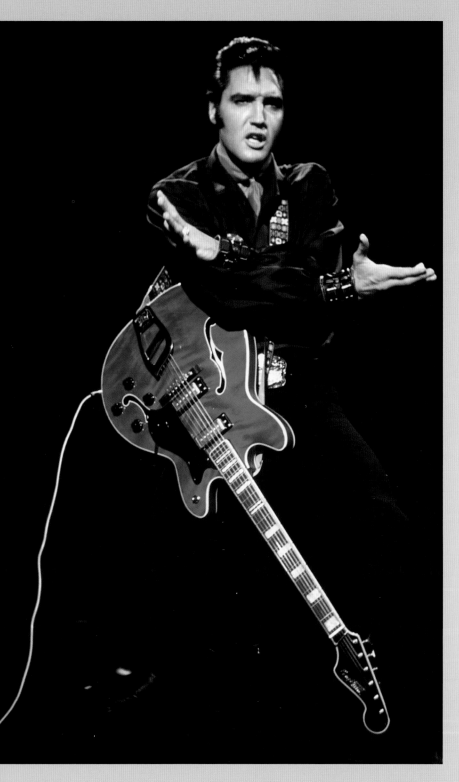

Elvis—The '68 Comeback Special

Elvis delivered knockout performances for the concert segments. It was reported that Elvis could have eaten Mick Jagger for breakfast.

In early 1968, Colonel Tom Parker closed a deal for Elvis to appear in his own television special for NBC. It was taped in late June and aired on December 3. The Colonel's vision of the special had Elvis walking in front of a Christmas tree, singing favorite familiar carols, and then wishing everyone a happy holiday.

However, Steve Binder, the producer of the special, had a different vision. With this program he hoped to capture what he felt was Elvis's genius—the adaptation of rhythm-and-blues to the tastes of mainstream audiences. He wanted to prove that Elvis's original music had been essential to the development of rock 'n' roll and that Elvis was not a relic of the past. Binder had gained a reputation for capturing the high-powered energy of rock music on film with *The T.A.M.I. Show*, a 1964 concert movie featuring a range of acts from the Rolling Stones to James Brown. He had also directed several episodes of NBC's prime-time rock music series *Hullabaloo*. Binder's credentials and conviction helped convince Elvis to defy the Colonel's idea and go along with the young producer's vision.

The Blossoms backed Elvis during the gospel tribute.

For the Elvis *finale, Elvis sang "If I Can Dream." The single became a million-seller and reached No. 12.*

Although he hadn't done a live concert in eight years, Elvis was a powerhouse of talent and charm who held the audience spellbound.

Elvis consists of two concert segments performed before a live audience interspersed with four elaborate musical productions. The concert segments comprise the most famous moments of the show. In these segments, Elvis and four musicians, including his longtime band members Scotty Moore and D. J. Fontana, sat on a small stage surrounded by an audience of mostly female fans. Elvis wore the famous black leather suit designed by Bill Belew, and his hair was fashionably long, yet reminiscent of the past. He performed many of his past hits, including "Hound Dog," "All Shook Up," and "Blue Suede Shoes." However, new arrangements, plus Elvis's lower vocal range, resulted in a slightly different sound. The effect was powerful: An energized, charismatic Elvis thrilled the audience with his first live performance in eight years. In retrospect, these live segments, which were a clever weaving of the old and the new, signify a specific moment in Elvis's career—a turning point. They symbolize the moment when the notorious Elvis returns from the past to reclaim his crown as the King of Rock 'n' Roll.

rock-flavored hits "Suspicious Minds" and "Kentucky Rain," which were not included on *From Elvis in Memphis*. "Suspicious Minds" was included on the follow-up release *From Memphis to Vegas/From Vegas to Memphis*.

The house band at American Sound Studios included musicians who were steeped in all forms of Southern music. Both black and white artists recorded there, and the house band remained generally the same. Many of these musicians, including guitarist Reggie Young (who played Scotty Moore's old guitar on "Suspicious Minds"), bassist Tommy Cogbill, and pianist Bobby Wood, had grown up on Elvis's music. No more fitting group of musicians could have backed Elvis on his return to Memphis.

Released in May 1969, *From Elvis in Memphis* landed on *Billboard*'s Top LPs chart, where it reached No. 13, and the Country LPs chart, where it hit No. 2. The RIAA certified a gold record for the album in January 1970. Most importantly, *From Elvis in Memphis* helped alter Elvis's image as a crooning movie star.

Publicity poster

For the TV special's live segment in the pit, Elvis played with musicians Scotty Moore (right), Charlie Hodge, D. J. Fontana, and Alan Fortas on tambourine.

While performing in Las Vegas, Elvis socialized with a number of fellow entertainers, including Glen Campbell. Campbell had played guitar and sung backup on the soundtrack of Viva Las Vegas.

The year 1969 became a precedent-setting year for Elvis Presley in the way that 1956 and 1960 had been. Just as the events in those years had determined a certain image for Elvis, so did the events of 1969 point Elvis toward a new image and a new sound. His dynamic recordings from the first half of that year helped steer him toward this goal, but his smash engagement in Las Vegas that summer constructed the image that would stay with him for the rest of his career.

After Elvis felt the excitement of singing for a live audience during the performance segment of the comeback TV special, he was excited to return to the concert stage. In early summer of 1969, Elvis was invited to play at the new International Hotel in Las Vegas. The main room of the hotel had not yet been opened, and Elvis was asked to do the honors. When the Colonel decided that Elvis shouldn't risk making his live comeback on an untested stage, the International Hotel booked Barbra Streisand to open the main room in July. It then scheduled Elvis for August and paid him a half million dollars for four weeks. On the marquee was one word: "ELVIS."

International Hotel, Las Vegas, 1969

Elvis had not appeared in a live concert since 1961 when his music had been much simpler. In designing his return to live performing, Elvis chose not to re-create his earlier image or sound. Instead, he planned his act on a broad scale. For his Las Vegas performances, he was joined onstage by pop/gospel quartet the Imperials, female backup singers the Sweet Inspirations, a rock band, and a 35-piece orchestra. The members of his rock band included the well-known Southern blues guitarist James Burton, drummer Ronnie Tutt, bassist Jerry Scheff, keyboard player Larry Muhoberack, and guitarists/vocalists John Wilkinson and Charlie Hodge. (Hodge had been part of the Memphis Mafia ever since he and Elvis had been in the army together.) Part of the reason for such an extensive entourage was doubtless due to

The Sweet Inspirations sang backup vocals for Elvis's concerts.

Elvis went grand scale for his return to live performing. He was backed by not only his rock band but also the Imperials quartet, the Sweet Inspirations, and a 35-piece orchestra.

Priscilla had a ringside table for Elvis's Las Vegas debut.

Although Elvis was anxious about premiering his show in Las Vegas, he seemed confident.

the large 2,000-seat room in which Elvis would perform at the International, but the enormous sound created by Elvis and his musical entourage seemed symbolic of Colonel Parker's favorite billing for his boy—"the World's Greatest Entertainer."

Elvis was terribly nervous about staging his comeback to live performances in Las Vegas, the city where he had bombed when he appeared at the New Frontier Hotel in 1956. The sting of his failure had not diminished with the passing years. Although he did have time for several rehearsals before his engagement at the International, he had no opportunity to iron out any kinks before a live audience, which added to his anxiety. Elvis may have been frightened, but Colonel Parker was in his element as he began promoting Elvis all over Las Vegas. He rented every available billboard and took out full-page ads in the local and trade papers. He filled the lobby of the International with Elvis Presley souvenirs: T-shirts, straw boaters, records, and stuffed animals. The Colonel made sure that Elvis's return to the stage would be the show-business event of the year. Kirk Kerkorian, then owner of the International Hotel, planned to send his own plane to New York to fly in the rock press for opening night.

(continued on page 138)

The Colonel outdid himself promoting Elvis's appearance. He strolled around the hotel's lobby in a topcoat covered with Elvis's name.

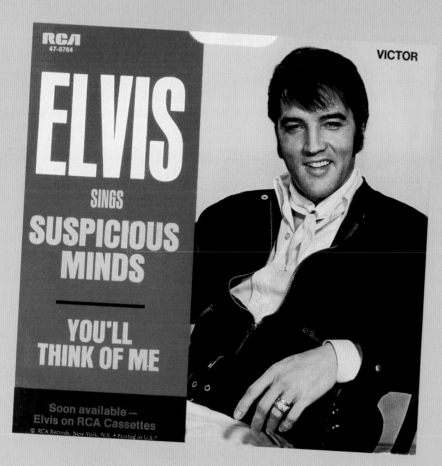

The last No. 1 single Elvis had during his career.

"*Suspicious Minds*"

Elvis's last No. 1 single, "Suspicious Minds," offers an example of the large-scale sound that defined his later style. At four minutes and 22 seconds, it is his longest No. 1 song. In his Las Vegas shows, he stretched it into a powerful, showstopping piece that ran eight minutes. Elvis had introduced the song in Las Vegas on July 31, 1969, when he made his first live performance in eight years at the International Hotel. It was not released as a single until the following September, when it entered *Billboard*'s Hot 100 chart—seven weeks later, it rose to the top.

The song had originally been recorded at American Sound Studios on January 23, 1969, but it was held for release until a later date. "Suspicious Minds" featured backing vocals by Jeannie Green and Ronnie Milsap, a singer-songwriter who later became a prominent country-western star. To help

Elvis onstage at the International Hotel

Above and right: Elvis's Las Vegas show was a resounding success.

Country singer Ronnie Milsap sang backup vocals.

achieve the large-scale sound, Elvis's Las Vegas band was overdubbed on the single at a Vegas recording studio in August. Also, the end of the song was spliced on for a second time. Elvis's producer, Felton Jarvis, supervised this overdubbing and remixing.

After the two recording sessions at American Sound Studios in January and February of 1969, Elvis never recorded there again. Part of the reason was undoubtedly due to a clash over the rights to the songs, including "Suspicious Minds," that producer Chips Moman had suggested for Elvis. RCA and Hill and Range, which oversaw Elvis's own publishing companies, wanted a substantial cut of the songs to which Moman owned the rights. If Moman refused, there was pressure to let those songs slip through the sessions without being recorded. Some quality material was not recorded by Elvis because of the haggling over song rights by Hill and Range. Moman did not want to budge on "Suspicious Minds," and he threatened to cancel the session if Freddie Bienstock of Hill and Range did not back off. Fortunately, Elvis did record "Suspicious Minds," but the tension over song rights took its toll.

The list of celebrities who planned to attend Elvis's opening included Pat Boone, Fats Domino, Wayne Newton, Dick Clark, Ann-Margret, George Hamilton, Angie Dickinson, and Henry Mancini. Elvis personally invited Sam Phillips, the man who had helped him develop his raw talent into a unique musical style.

On July 31, 1969, Elvis performed in front of a sold-out crowd at the International. To the hard-pounding strains of "Baby, I Don't Care," Elvis walked onstage. There was no emcee to introduce him. He grabbed the microphone, struck a familiar pose from the past, and snapped his leg back and forth. The crowd jumped from their chairs and gave him a standing ovation before he sang one note. The audience of 2,000 began to whistle, applaud furiously, and pound on the tables. Some people stood on their chairs. When the ovation began to subside, Elvis launched into "Blue Suede Shoes" with such fury that ten years of his movie music melted away.

Elvis joked with the media.

Elvis looked devastatingly handsome that night. He was dressed in a modified karate suit made especially for him out of black mohair. He was thinner than he had been in his last few films, and his blue-black hair reached down past his collar. Elvis's sideburns were the longest they had been since the 1950s. Never one to take himself too seriously, Elvis joked with the crowd about the old days and the old songs. At one point, he decided to dedicate his next number to the audience and the staff at the International: "This is the only song I could think of that really expresses my feeling toward the audience," he said in all earnestness, before bursting into "Hound Dog." Elvis

Elvis held a press conference to promote his engagement at the International Hotel.

In a back corridor of the hotel, Elvis, with two Memphis Mafia members at his left, approached photographers.

closed his act with "What'd I Say" from *Viva Las Vegas,* and again the sold-out crowd gave him a standing ovation. Elvis came back for an encore and sang "Can't Help Falling in Love," the song with which he closed every show for the rest of his career.

Backstage after the performance, many celebrities and well-wishers, including Cary Grant, were on hand to congratulate Elvis on his triumphant return to live performing. Priscilla Beaulieu Presley, in her account of her life with Elvis, reveals a touching story about Colonel Parker. At this moment of great personal and professional triumph for his one and only client, the Colonel pushed his way backstage. Everyone could see that tears were welling up in his eyes. Where was "his boy" he wanted to know. As Elvis emerged from his dressing room, the two men embraced, too overcome with emotion to say anything. There have been many stories about Colonel Tom Parker over the years, many of them illustrating his greed, his mistakes, or his ruthlessness, yet none reveals the complexity of the relationship between Elvis and the Colonel like this one.

Most members of the rock 'n' roll press, of whom many were teenagers when Elvis began his career, felt ecstatic about his return to the stage and expressed their enthusiasm in glowing reviews. *Rolling Stone* magazine declared Elvis to be "supernatural," while *Variety* proclaimed him a superstar.

Nancy Sinatra and her father, Frank, as well as Fred Astaire, congratulated Elvis on his return to the live stage.

Singer Tom Jones, Priscilla, and Elvis paused for a snapshot. Elvis met Jones in Las Vegas in 1968, and the two became lifelong friends.

The press gave Elvis high praise after his concert.

IT WAS HARD TO BELIEVE HE WAS
34 AND NO LONGER 19 YEARS
OLD . . . .
—*NEWSWEEK, AUGUST 11, 1969*

The next day, the Colonel sat down with the general manager of the International to discuss the enormous success of Elvis's performance. The hotel offered Elvis a five-year contract to play two months a year—February and August—at a salary of $1 million dollars per year. In his typical flamboyant style, the Colonel took out a pen and began scribbling specific terms on the red tablecloth. When he finished, he asked the general manager to sign the cloth to close the deal. The "red tablecloth deal" has become a show business legend, although Parker drew criticism for locking Elvis into a long-term contract that didn't take inflation into account.

Above and left: The International Hotel asked Elvis to open its new main room in the summer of 1969. Elvis declined to open the room but agreed to be the second performer to appear there.

Six months after his first Las Vegas show, Elvis returned to the International for another month of sold-out performances. During this engagement, Elvis wore a jumpsuit on stage. Bill Belew, who had designed the black leather outfit for the comeback TV special, designed a white jumpsuit for this occasion. The costume was slashed down the front to reveal the chest, fitted closely at the waist, and belled out at the legs, which was the fashion of the day. The costume's high collar was inset with semiprecious jewels, and Elvis wore gold and diamond rings on the fingers of both hands. A macramé belt made of gold- and pearl-colored strands accentuated his slender waist.

Elvis struck a pose at one of his performances at the International in August 1969.

Elvis entered the backstage area, greeted by Colonel Parker (far right).

The singer did not identify with the '50s rock revival occurring in '69 and deliberately kept his repertoire new.

Dean Martin attended the opening night of Elvis's second Las Vegas engagement. Elvis sang "Everybody Loves Somebody Sometime" as a tribute to Martin, the pop singer he had always admired. Elvis altered his repertoire for this engagement by emphasizing his current recordings and including some contemporary country and rock ballads. He limited the older material to a few key places during the show, or he covered it in a medley-style arrangement. He was determined not to rest on his laurels so he focused his act on his new material and his new sound, which he had developed with the help of Chips Moman at American Sound Studios.

The success of Elvis's comeback was probably enhanced by the 1950s music revival that began in the late 1960s. Many performers who had helped to develop the rock 'n' roll sound and attitude reaped the benefits of this renewed interest in the roots of rock music. Bill Haley and the Comets, Chuck Berry, and Jerry Lee Lewis were touring once again and attracting large crowds. Elvis not only benefited from the rock-nostalgia craze but also undoubtedly influenced it. Yet, Elvis carefully kept his material new and varied. He didn't identify himself with the rock 'n' roll revival, and his show was never considered to be an oldies act.

Vernon Presley joined his son in Las Vegas for the four-week engagement.

141

Rejuvenated in his professional career, Elvis had also been experiencing a time of personal growth and change in his private life. In 1967, Elvis had married longtime girlfriend Priscilla Beaulieu.

Elvis met Priscilla in 1959 while he was stationed in Germany during his stint in the army. Much has been made of the fact that Priscilla was only 14 when the pair was introduced, but the young girl was mature for her age, and Elvis was mindful of the implications of the situation. Priscilla was photographed by the press at the airport when Elvis left for America, and some of those photos ended up in *LIFE* magazine. Beyond this, there was surprisingly little publicity about their relationship.

Priscilla Beaulieu met Elvis in Germany, just a few months before he was discharged from the army.
Opposite page: *A family portrait of Priscilla, Lisa Marie, and Elvis.*

Priscilla visited Graceland many times over the next couple of years and then Elvis began pressuring her parents to let her stay in Memphis. In 1962, he finally persuaded the Beaulieus to allow her to live with his father and stepmother, Vernon and Dee Presley, and go to school in Memphis. The press would have gone into a feeding frenzy if this information had leaked out, but while Priscilla was finishing high school, her private life remained private. The Colonel was probably responsible for keeping the media at bay because his area of expertise was understanding the press sharks and knowing what and when to feed them. The dozens of stories about Elvis dating his leading ladies in Hollywood—some true, some not— created a smokescreen that protected Priscilla in Memphis.

Immediately following their wedding ceremony, the couple held a reception in a hotel ballroom, mostly for the benefit of the press.

The Presleys released this professional photo to the press after Lisa Marie's birth.

On May 1, 1967, Elvis married Priscilla at the Aladdin Hotel in Las Vegas. The double-ring ceremony took place in the suite of one of the Colonel's associates and lasted merely eight minutes. Only a few of Elvis's friends were allowed to witness the actual event, causing some dissension in the ranks of his buddy-bodyguards. Afterward, a breakfast reception for 100, an event primarily for the press, was held at the Aladdin. Elvis and Priscilla honeymooned in Palm Springs, California, and then divided their time between Graceland and their new home in Beverly Hills. On February 1, 1968, nine months to the day after Elvis and Priscilla were wed, Lisa Marie Presley was born.

Shortly after the marriage, Elvis reported to the set of his next movie, *Speedway*. Although many of the memoirs by Elvis's former friends and bodyguards suggest that Elvis was not comfortable with marriage, actor and costar Bill Bixby recalled that Elvis was content and happy, even ecstatic at times. He had slimmed down and exuded confidence and maturity. The years that encompass Elvis's marriage correspond to his last extended period of creativity.

Above and below: Elvis was a loving father to his baby daughter.

The newlyweds caught a private plane to Palm Springs, where they spent their honeymoon.

ELVIS
Aloha from Hawaii
via SATELLITE

quadradisc
RCA
VPSX-6089
*2 RECORD SET

Vogliamo bene a Elvis

Nous aimons Elvis

Wir lieben Elvis

INCLUDES 8 SONGS
never before recorded by
ELVIS
Recorded Live at the Honolulu International Center,
12:30 AM, Sunday, January 14, 1973
Album Production Supervised by RCA Record Tours

SIDE 1: Introduction:
Also sprach Zarathustra (Theme from 2001: A Space Odyssey)† (1:44)
See See Rider‡ (2:15) • Burning Love‡ (3:20) • Something‡ (3:42) • You Gave Me a Mountain‡ (3:09)
Steamroller Blues‡ (2:42) • Love Me‡ (1:31) • Johnny B. Goode‡ (1:39)
SIDE 2: My Way‡ (2:59) • I'm So Lonesome I Could Cry‡ (2:04)
It's Over* (2:03) • Blue Suede Shoes‡ (1:05) • *SIDE 3: What Now My Love* (3:04)
I Can't Stop Loving You‡ (2:21) • Hound Dog‡ (0:46) • Introductions by Elvis (1:38)
Fever‡ (2:36) • Welcome to My World‡ (1:50) • Suspicious Minds‡ (4:25) • Introductions by Elvis (1:51)
SIDE 4: I'll Remember You‡ (2:27) • *Medley: Long Tall Sally*‡ Whole Lot-ta Shakin' Goin' On‡ (1:42)
American Trilogy* (4:11) • A Big Hunk o' Love‡ (2:01) • Can't Help Falling in Love* (1:42)

*ASCAP ‡BMI †P.D.
Recording Engineers, Dick Baxter and Al Pachucki
Director of Audio, Larry Schnapf
Vocal Accompaniment by The Sweet Inspirations,
J.D. Sumner and The Stamps (courtesy of Heartwarming Records),
and Kathy Westmoreland
Painting of INTELSAT IV satellite based on photo
supplied by Communications Satellite Corporation
Cover Photo—Apollo 15 View of the Earth—
courtesy of NASA (Used by permission)

私達はエルヴィスが好き

Biz Elvis'e seviyoruz

We love Elvis

Queremos a Elvis

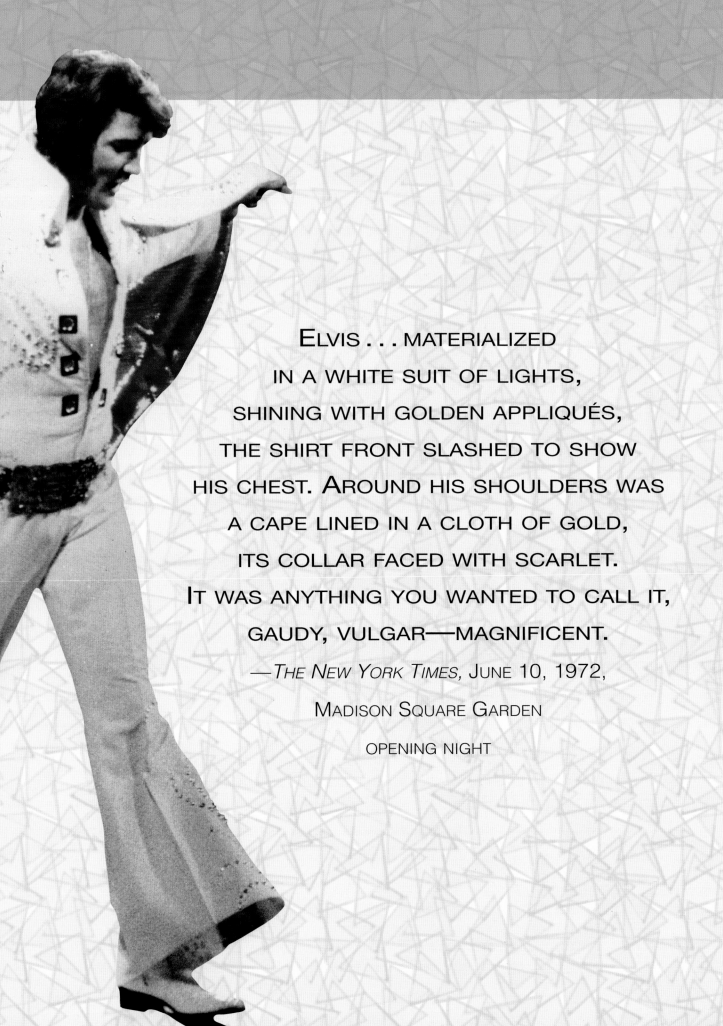

ELVIS . . . MATERIALIZED
IN A WHITE SUIT OF LIGHTS,
SHINING WITH GOLDEN APPLIQUÉS,
THE SHIRT FRONT SLASHED TO SHOW
HIS CHEST. AROUND HIS SHOULDERS WAS
A CAPE LINED IN A CLOTH OF GOLD,
ITS COLLAR FACED WITH SCARLET.
IT WAS ANYTHING YOU WANTED TO CALL IT,
GAUDY, VULGAR—MAGNIFICENT.
—*THE NEW YORK TIMES,* JUNE 10, 1972,

MADISON SQUARE GARDEN

OPENING NIGHT

Following his success in Las Vegas, Elvis took his act on tour. For Elvis's first show on the road, Colonel Parker arranged for him to appear in the Houston Astrodome in conjunction with the Texas Livestock Show. The logic behind choosing such a large arena was simple: Elvis, "the World's Greatest Entertainer," should appear only in magnificent coliseums or showplaces. Besides, Texas had always been good to Elvis. In 1955, East Texas had been the scene of a great surge of Elvis-mania, which helped boost his early career. To return this kindness and perhaps to ensure a sellout, tickets for Elvis's engagement at the Astrodome were greatly reduced in price, with some seats selling for as little as one dollar.

Despite his boost in confidence from the Las Vegas victories, Elvis was overwhelmed by the size of the Astrodome and the thought of having to please 44,500 people. Referring to the Astrodome as an "ocean," he worried about losing some of his energy and dynamism in such a vast arena. Again his fears proved unfounded because the Astrodome sold out each night of his engagement, and the local music critics raved about his personal charisma and his exciting act. For the first time since the 1950s, Elvis was swarmed after his show in a frightening example of mob hysteria. His limousine had been parked by the stage door so he could make a rapid getaway, but the fans were able to reach the car quickly. They surrounded the vehicle; some tried to shove flowers and gifts through the doors and windows while others just wanted to touch their idol.

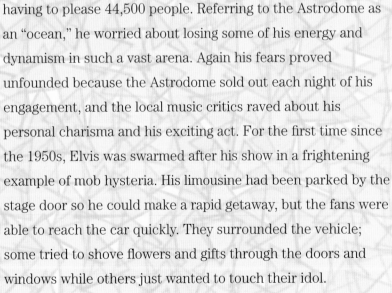

Elvis in concert at the Houston Astrodome

Above and below: *Dressed for the occasion, Elvis held a press conference for his Houston engagement, where he performed twice a day from February 27–March 1, 1970.*

After winning Houston, Elvis continued to tour. He was usually on the road for several weeks out of a month, in addition to playing Las Vegas in February and August. His touring schedule was grueling. By 1971, Elvis was on the road more than most other acts in show business. He would tour for three weeks at a time, taking no days off and doing two shows on Saturday and Sunday. He would rest for a few weeks and then repeat the cycle. Elvis usually played one-night stands, meaning every performance was scheduled for a different arena. Often Elvis and his entourage would arrive in a city and depart again in less than 24 hours. Such a demanding schedule took its toll in terms of Elvis's desire to update or change the material in his act. Eventually, his performances became standardized, even routine. Despite this, Elvis's concerts were almost always sold out.

Above and right: Elvis toured for 21-day periods with no days off, then he rested a few weeks before starting the next tour.

During the final Houston show, Elvis experienced problems with his eyes. Upon returning to Memphis, he checked into Baptist Memorial Hospital where he was diagnosed with glaucoma, a serious eye disease that can eventually result in blindness. Elvis became consumed with an irrational fear that he would be blind by the end of the year. He grew morose, irritable, and reclusive. It took six months for his doctor, his family, and his friends to convince him that his case was treatable. His overreaction to his ailment seemed partly a result of the fatigue and nervousness associated with a demanding schedule.

In September 1972, Elvis told the press in Las Vegas of plans for a worldwide concert tour to be followed by a one-hour TV special featuring the concerts' highlights.

Sweet Inspirations

The female vocal group Sweet Inspirations sang backup for Elvis onstage and in the studio for eight years. Originally with Aretha Franklin, the group recorded several songs on their own in the late 1960s for Atlantic Records. Among these was the soul tune "Sweet Inspiration." The women took their name from the song, which had been written especially for them. After Elvis heard the record, he asked them to join his stage show. The group generally opened each night's performance, sometimes reprising Aretha Franklin's hits.

The Sweet Inspirations joined Rick Nelson's show after Elvis died, then went solo before retiring. Its members were Myrna Smith, Estelle Brown, Sylvia Shenwell, and Cissy Houston (far left), the mother of pop singer Whitney Houston.

The Sweet Inspirations backed Elvis in concert during the 1970s.

Menu from the International Hotel, 1971

Touring and performing in Las Vegas became the basis of Elvis's career during the 1970s. These engagements of 57 or 58 shows generally lasted about one month, a schedule equally as exhausting as being on the road. Plus, the pressure of performing live was as draining as the physical nature of the performances, resulting in sleeplessness, bouts of depression, and exaggerated emotional responses.

Little of this showed in his performances during the early 1970s, and those who saw him on stage marveled at the excitement he generated in his audiences. Indicative of his stage show during this time period is the *Elvis: Aloha from Hawaii* concert, which was not only televised but also recorded and released on an album titled *Aloha from Hawaii via Satellite*. The album hit the top spot on *Billboard*'s album chart, remaining on the charts for 52 weeks. It was Elvis's last album to reach No. 1.

Sign of the times: A macramé belt accented one of Elvis's costumes.

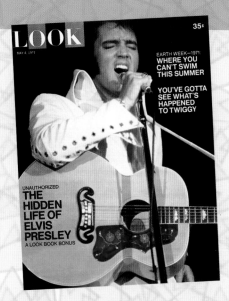

LOOK magazine

Taking advantage of advances in global communications, *Elvis: Aloha from Hawaii* was beamed by the Intelsat IV satellite to countries all over the world on January 14, 1973. Broadcast at 12:30 A.M. Hawaii time, the special was seen in Australia, New Zealand, the Philippine Islands, Japan, and other countries in the Far East. Even parts of Communist China supposedly tuned in. The next day, the show was rebroadcast to 28 European countries. The special consisted of a concert performance by Elvis in front of a live audience at the Honolulu International Center Arena. After the audience left the arena, Elvis was filmed singing five

The '70s Band

A consequence of Elvis's new direction in the 1970s was a change in the core group of musicians who recorded with him, and many of them accompanied him on the road. Chief among these musicians was lead guitarist James Burton, who had worked with Ricky Nelson. An accomplished and respected lead guitar player, Burton later worked with Gram Parsons and Emmylou Harris. Other band members included several Hollywood sessions musicians who had occasionally contributed to Elvis's movie soundtracks: bassist Jerry Scheff, who had worked with the Doors; pianist Larry Muhoberac; and drummer Ronnie Tutt. Elvis's new sound was large-scale, almost operatic. In addition to musicians, he used a male gospel quartet and a female backup group in his recording sessions and on the road. At first the Imperials gospel quartet, with the legendary Jake Hess, backed Elvis vocally, but later J. D. Sumner and the Stamps Quartet took over that role. The Sweet Inspirations fulfilled the duties as female backup voices, and Kathy Westmoreland supplied an additional soprano voice.

On January 14, 1973, Elvis: Aloha from Hawaii *was beamed around the world via the Intelsat IV communications satellite.*

more songs, which were to be included in the U.S. edition of the concert. However, NBC's broadcast of the show on April 4 included only four of the additional songs. The American broadcast of the special was watched by 51 percent of the television viewing audience, more than the number of people who watched the first walk on the moon. When it finished airing around the world, *Elvis: Aloha from Hawaii* was seen in 40 countries by at least 1 billion people.

Happy fans welcomed Elvis at the heliport.

On January 12, Elvis did a full dress rehearsal that was not televised. After seeing a tape of this performance, he decided he needed a haircut. The difference in hairstyles provides a way for the Elvis fan to distinguish between photos of the rehearsal and photos of the special. Both shows were a benefit for the Kuiokalani Lee Cancer Fund and raised about $75,000. Lee was a Hawaiian composer who had died of cancer, and Elvis performed Lee's song "I'll Remember You" in his honor.

Elvis sang a variety of songs throughout the concert special, including his then current hits "Burning Love" and "Suspicious Minds," and past hits "Hound Dog," "Love Me," and "A Big Hunk o' Love." He also sang "My Way," "Steamroller Blues," and other pop and rock tunes, as well as the moving country classic "I'm So Lonesome I Could Cry." During the course of the evening, he doffed his magnificent cape, and later, while singing "An American Trilogy," Elvis tossed his studded belt into the audience.

The 1973 special captures Elvis at one of the best moments in this phase of his career.

For the opening of Aloha from Hawaii, *Elvis's arrival by helicopter at the Hawaiian Village Hotel was filmed.*

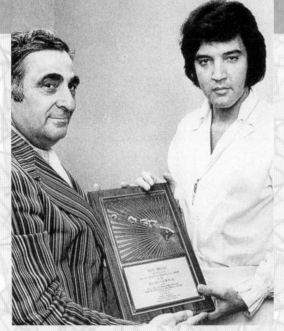

Elvis: Aloha from Hawaii *was a benefit concert for the* Kui Lee Cancer Fund, *based in Hawaii. The organization gave the singer a plaque for his efforts in making the concert a success.*

A LIVE CONCERT TO ME IS EXCITING BECAUSE OF ALL THE ELECTRICITY THAT IS GENERATED IN THE CROWD AND ON STAGE. IT'S MY FAVORITE PART OF THE BUSINESS—LIVE CONCERTS.

—ELVIS PRESLEY, PRESS CONFERENCE PRIOR TO *ELVIS: ALOHA FROM HAWAII* TV SPECIAL

For the finale, Elvis sang his standard closing number, "Can't Help Falling in Love," that built up to the large-scale sound typical of his style of that era. By the time this number began, Elvis had resumed wearing his cape, which typically signaled the end of the show for his band and the audience. Usually, he concluded the number by dropping to one knee in the spotlight, grabbing the ends of his cape in his hands, and

After watching the tape of the dress rehearsal (above), Elvis decided to get a haircut before he did the live broadcast.

Aloha from Hawaii Jumpsuit

The landmark television special *Elvis: Aloha from Hawaii* was telecast live to several countries via satellite. Elvis wanted a costume that signified America, so designer Bill Belew produced a white jumpsuit with an American Eagle patterned in red, gold, and blue gems. The costume's spectacular calf-length cape proved to be too cumbersome during rehearsals, so Elvis ordered a hip-length cape to replace it. A belt decorated with gold American eagles accented the ensemble. During the show, Elvis threw the belt into the audience and later threw the cape into the cheering crowd as he finished the closing song. Elvis ordered a second cape and belt for the jumpsuit and wore the outfit in later performances. By the end of 1974, Elvis stopped wearing capes onstage. Not only were they heavy and uncomfortable, but people in the audience liked to grab the cape edges while he was performing, causing some near accidents.

spreading the garment out behind him—a grandiose gesture befitting the world's greatest entertainer. On this night, he added an extra touch by throwing the gem-laden cape into the crowd, where it was caught by a lucky fan. As the orchestra reprised "See See Rider," Elvis left the stage. As usual, he did not return for an encore. It was simply too hard to top the effect of such sublime imagery.

PRESLEY REMAINS A TRUE AMERICAN ARTIST—ONE OF THE GREATEST IN AMERICAN POPULAR MUSIC, A SINGER OF NATIVE BRILLIANCE AND A PERFORMER OF MAGNETIC DIMENSIONS.

—JIM MILLAR, *ROLLING STONE*

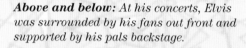

Above and below: *At his concerts, Elvis was surrounded by his fans out front and supported by his pals backstage.*

A typical Presley concert of the 1970s was more like a series of rituals and ceremonies than a performance by a mere entertainer. Elvis made his grand entrance to Richard Strauss's *Also sprach Zarathustra,* popularly known as the "Theme from *2001,*" charging into the spotlight as though propelled by some supernatural force. He incorporated karate kicks and tai chi arabesques into his act as well as other dramatic postures. Elvis also mocked his 1950s sex-symbol image by exaggerating the pelvic thrusts and sexual posturings of his old performing style, while making jokes about the "old days." A peculiar part of his act was wiping the sweat from his brow with his scarf or a towel then throwing it into the audience. This gesture became so popular that dozens of white towels were kept in the wings for Elvis to throw to fans at frequent intervals.

Although Elvis's enormous popularity forced him to live a life secluded from the public, his act onstage gave the illusion of intimacy. His rapport with his audiences was based on treating them as old friends or an extended

Charlie Hodge (right), one of the most loyal of Elvis's buddy-bodyguards, helped out as an equipment technician.

family. Much interaction occurred between Elvis and the audience members, such as the exchange of "gifts." Elvis threw towels and flowers into the audience; fans returned the gesture by throwing underwear, hotel keys, teddy bears, bouquets, and other mementos. In fact, each time Elvis played Las Vegas, the hotel stocked fresh undergarments in the restrooms because women kept tossing their underwear onto the stage while he was performing. Elvis kissed, hugged, and held hands with many of the women in the audience. They lined up just below the stage, like a receiving line for royalty, waiting to be

Elvis established the tradition of tossing scarves and towels to the audience in Las Vegas in 1969 when he returned to performing live concerts.

During his fall 1972 tour, Elvis wore a bright red costume that fans began to call the "Burning Love" jumpsuit.

"Burning Love"

The highlight of Elvis's studio sessions in Hollywood during March 1972 was the recording of "Burning Love." By this point, Elvis and his band were masters of this type of large-scale, fast-rocking number, and his interpretation of the song typifies his 1970s sound.

Dennis Linde composed "Burning Love" especially for Elvis, and the songwriter played guitar on the recording. It was Linde who dubbed in the raucous guitar lick on the bridges of the song. He had occasionally served as a bass guitarist in Elvis's recording band during the 1970s.

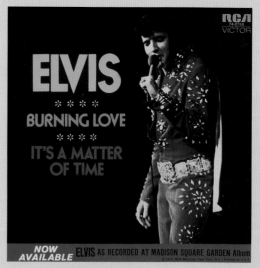

"Burning Love" became a worldwide hit for Elvis in 1972, and it quickly charted on *Billboard*'s Hot 100. Peaking at No. 2, it just missed becoming a No. 1 record. Chuck Berry's "My Ding-a-Ling" prevented "Burning Love" from hitting the top of the charts. The record was certified gold by the RIAA in October 1972 and certified platinum in March 1992.

Unfortunately, Elvis did not follow up on the excitement that the rocking "Burning Love" generated. Instead, his next single release was a ballad, "Separate Ways," backed by "Always on My Mind," which reached only No. 20 on the Hot 100 chart. In addition, RCA buried "Burning Love" and its flip side, "It's a Matter of Time," on an album of old movie tracks creatively titled *Burning Love and Hits from His Movies, Volume 2*. In terms of Elvis's career, this hit song seems to have been lost due to bad marketing decisions.

Ladies always lined up next to the stage, hoping for a touch from the King.

blessed by the King's touch. Audience members expected Elvis to sing specific songs and perform familiar moves, and he always fulfilled their expectations.

This type of interaction can be traced back to Elvis's early career, when audiences became hysterical at his gyrations and performing style. Even then, Elvis exhibited an uncanny instinct for knowing what the fans wanted to see and hear. He teased them with a few hip and leg movements, they responded, and then he cut loose, singling out specific members of the audience to interact with. This phenomenon was reciprocal in nature, forming a strong bond between performer and audience. If Elvis's fans were unusually loyal and demonstrative throughout his career, this interactive aspect of his act—from the beginning of his career to the end—was partially responsible.

Elvis often wore a cape as he took the stage and for the closing numbers.

If there is one symbol that has come to represent this period of Elvis's career, it is the bejeweled jumpsuit. As Elvis launched each new tour or Las Vegas appearance, his jumpsuits became more elaborate. Sometimes accompanied by a waist-length or floor-length cape, these costumes were decorated with real gems, jewels, and semiprecious stones. With the addition of chains and studs, the outfits could weigh as much as 30 pounds. Later costumes were emblazoned with certain symbols that held some significance to Elvis, including eagles, karate emblems, tigers, and sundials.

The Peacock jumpsuit Elvis wore during a 1974 tour proved to be one of his favorites and, at $10,000, the most expensive costume he'd ever had made.

The Bear Claw jumpsuit, also called the Dark Blue Aztec jumpsuit, was designed by Bill Belew for Elvis's June 1975 tour.

Fans refer to these costumes by name, such as the Mexican Sundial, the King of Spades, the Rainbow Swirl, the American Eagle, the Red Flower, the Gypsy, and the Dragon. They can identify specific tours and appearances by the costumes Elvis wore.

Elvis's repertoire of songs varied after the early 1970s, but his style of music and the format of his act did not change. Fans like to find parallels between Elvis's personal life and the songs he chose to sing at certain points in his career. Around 1972, when Elvis and Priscilla were experiencing marital problems, he included "Always on My Mind" and "You Gave Me a

Elvis wore the Tiger jumpsuit only a few times, including an October 1974 concert in Indianapolis.

J. D. Sumner and the Stamps Quartet

When the Imperials quartet left Elvis's stage show, Elvis asked the gospel group J. D. Sumner and the Stamps to sing backup for him in concert and in the studio. John Daniel Sumner had formed the Stamps in the late 1960s after singing for 11 years with the Blackwood Brothers.

J. D. Sumner and the Stamps sang with Elvis from 1972 until the bitter end in 1977. They performed at Elvis's funeral and later recorded two tribute albums, *Elvis's Favorite Gospel Songs* and *Memories of Our Friend Elvis*. Sumner recorded the single "Elvis Has Left the Building." The quartet continued to perform gospel music into the 1990s. Sumner, who had written about 500 songs, was inducted into the Southern Gospel Music Hall of Fame in May 1997 and received a Doctor of Sacred Music degree from Louisiana Baptist University later that year. A bass singer with a deep, clear voice, Sumner was in the *Guinness Book of World Records* for singing the world's lowest note. He and Elvis had known each other since the 1950s, and they shared a devotion to gospel music. In this spirit, it can be said that when J. D. died on November 16, 1998, he joined Elvis once again.

Elvis, pianist Sergio Mendes (center), and singer/songwriter Paul Anka smiled for the press in Las Vegas.

Mountain," two songs about the trials and tribulations of life and love. The following year, Elvis included "My Way" in his act. Paul Anka wrote this powerful song's lyrics, which are about a man reflecting back on his life as death draws near, with Frank Sinatra in mind. Yet, the song became a personal anthem for Elvis, one that seemed to explain his eccentric lifestyle and larger-than-life image. However, a single of this song by Elvis was not released until June 1977.

In 1971, country songwriter Mickey Newbury put together a unique arrangement of three 19th-century songs that he recorded and released as "An American Trilogy." Elvis heard the record and immediately incorporated the medley into his act. This piece has become so associated with Elvis Presley that it is difficult to imagine anyone else performing it with the same showstopping fervor that Elvis put into it. A combination of "Dixie," "The Battle Hymn of the Republic," and the spiritual "All My Trials," the songs reflect Elvis's patriotism, his religious convictions, and his deep affection for his native South.

The International Hotel became the Las Vegas Hilton in 1971 when Barron Hilton bought it. From 1969 to 1976, Elvis performed there on 17 occasions.

Elvis and his band rehearsed several times before opening in Las Vegas.

A Vegas-style comedian always opened Elvis's concerts, even when he was on the road. Rock music aficionados were appalled by the old-fashioned routines and stale jokes of these stand-up comics, particularly because this era saw the rise of a new, more hip generation of comedians with socially relevant material. But, even when he was on the cutting edge of rock 'n' roll in 1956 and 1957, Elvis always toured with an oddball assortment of vaudeville-flavored acts dug up by the Colonel. Therefore, it seems only natural that the Colonel would hire this type of opening act when Elvis returned to live performances in the 1970s. Elvis and the Colonel were accustomed to this kind of show business act, and the humor went over well in Vegas. Sammy Shore opened for Elvis in the early 1970s, and Jackie Kahane did the honors after 1972.

Kahane's responsibilities included announcing, "Ladies and gentlemen, Elvis has left the building," at the end of each performance. Elvis rarely performed an encore, although many times the audience remained behind after the final number, hoping Elvis would respond to the thunderous applause and return for one last song. To avoid any problems with overzealous fans, Elvis always ran backstage immediately after the last song, often while the band was still playing, and dashed into a car waiting at the stage door. Kahane's announcement let the audience know it was truly time to leave.

Despite the predictability of Elvis's live performances during the 1970s, there were still many highlights. On June 9–11, 1972, Elvis played Madison Square Garden in New York City. This was the first time he'd ever performed live in New York. All four shows sold out well in advance. A total of 80,000 people attended, including David Bowie, Bob Dylan, George Harrison, and John Lennon. However, Elvis and his management team feared that the sophisticated New York critics wouldn't like his Las Vegas-style show. On opening night, Elvis was decked out in one of his bejeweled jumpsuits and a gold-lined cape. He wore a gigantic belt emblazoned with "The World Champion Entertainer," in case the critics didn't know who they were dealing with. Throughout the show, particularly while singing his old songs, Elvis maintained an ironic distance from his audience. Sometimes he couldn't resist joking about his former image. At the beginning of "Hound Dog," for example, Elvis dropped dramatically down to one knee, and then said, "Oh, excuse me," and switched to the other knee.

While on tour, Elvis always had a car waiting behind the arena so he could make a quick exit.

At the press conference for Elvis's appearance at Madison Square Garden, reporters teased the flamboyant singer about his costumes. **Left:** *Elvis in the Adonis suit, opening night at Madison Square Garden.*

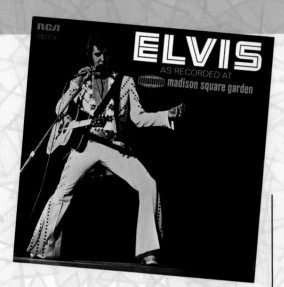

Elvis's performance at the Garden on June 10, 1972, was recorded and made into an album, which achieved gold-record status less than two months after its release.

THE IMAGE IS ONE THING AND THE HUMAN BEING IS ANOTHER . . . IT'S VERY HARD TO LIVE UP TO AN IMAGE.

—ELVIS PRESLEY, PRESS CONFERENCE FOR MADISON SQUARE GARDEN SHOW, JUNE 1972

During the New York engagement, Elvis appeared to be in top physical condition. His voice was strong and clear, and he sang a variety of old and new songs with drama and flair. Most of the New York critics were enthusiastic. RCA recorded all four shows at the Garden for an album titled *Elvis as Recorded at Madison Square Garden*. They mixed the songs, pressed the records, and had the albums in stores in less than two weeks.

MGM produced two film documentaries, *Elvis— That's the Way It Is* and *Elvis on Tour,* that captured Elvis's live performances. *Elvis— That's the Way It Is,* a feature-length movie, is built around Elvis's August 1970 engagement at the International Hotel in Las Vegas. About half of the movie features his performance onstage in the main room. One segment in which Elvis sings "Mystery Train" and "Tiger Man" was filmed at a concert in Phoenix. The rest of the movie documents the excitement Elvis generated as a performer. Elvis is shown in rehearsal for the show, whipping his band into shape and mastering new material for the act. Intercut with the rehearsal footage are shots of the massive promotional buildup in Las Vegas. A film crew was also sent to Luxembourg to record an Elvis Presley convention.

Elvis—That's the Way It Is included the rehearsals for the Vegas show. Elvis directed his band and backup singers to create the musical effect he wanted.

In Denis Sanders's documentary, the camera captured Elvis in rehearsal for his August 1970 Las Vegas engagements.

Elvis—That's the Way It Is was directed by Denis Sanders, who had won an Oscar for Best Documentary for his film *Czechoslovakia 1968*. Expert cinematographer Lucien Ballard caught the excitement of Elvis's performance onstage with eight Panavision cameras. The film was released on November 11, 1970, to good reviews. The *Hollywood Reporter* remarked that Elvis was

161

Elvis—That's the Way It Is

Elvis's 32nd film was not a narrative feature but a documentary showcasing his 1970 summer appearance at the International Hotel in Las Vegas. Elvis began rehearsals July 5 at the MGM studios in Hollywood, where he worked on his material almost until the show opened August 10. The MGM cameras recorded the rehearsals, the opening night, several performances throughout the engagement, and one show at Veterans Memorial Coliseum in Phoenix, Arizona. Performing in a simple white jumpsuit accented with fringe instead of rhinestones and gems, Elvis is captured at the pinnacle of this phase of his career.

Unlike Elvis's musical comedies, *Elvis—That's the Way It Is* offers a realistic portrait of Elvis Presley as a singer and entertainer. During the rehearsal scenes, Elvis freely chats with bystanders, explains the effects he's aiming for with his music, and heckles the camera crew. Later, during the concert sequences, he jokes with the audiences. Between songs, he comments about his appearance on *The Ed Sullivan Show* when the cameras shot him only from the waist up. He mumbles that the incident had occurred a long time ago when he was "a little bitty boy, with little bitty sideburns, and a little bitty shaky leg." A short time later, during his rendition of "Blue Suede Shoes," he replaces the original lyrics in the chorus with "white suede shoes." Elvis emerges from this documentary as a person with a good sense of humor and a star who does not take himself too seriously.

Elvis—That's the Way It Is was directed by documentary filmmaker Denis Sanders and photographed by veteran cinematographer Lucien Ballard. Their skill and expertise are evident in the pacing, which gradually builds in intensity, and in the way they captured Elvis's grace and ease in his milieu.

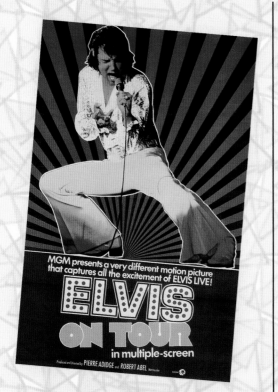

Elvis on Tour, *the second documentary to capture Elvis in performance, focused on his road show.*

probably the only entertainer alive who could draw enough people into a theater to make a documentary profitable at the box office. The film also introduced Elvis as a live performer to an audience who was too young to remember him from the 1950s and knew Elvis only from his movies.

In 1972, MGM released another feature-length documentary about Elvis, which was shot in the spring of that year. *Elvis on Tour* focuses on his road show during a 15-city tour. This film captures the final phase of Elvis's career at its highest point. It was produced by Pierre Adidge and Robert Abel, who had won critical acclaim for their rock documentary *Joe Cocker: Mad Dogs and Englishmen*. Some of the editing was supervised by Martin Scorsese, who also worked on the editing of *Woodstock*. Andrew Solt is credited with doing research on *Elvis on Tour*. He later coproduced the semidocumentary *This Is Elvis* as well as *Imagine,* a film about John Lennon. *Elvis on Tour* won a Golden Globe for the Best Documentary of 1972; it is the only Elvis Presley movie to be honored with an award of any kind.

Slim, healthy, and attractive, Elvis rocked in the Golden Globe-winning Elvis on Tour.

Behind the Scenes

The personal accounts of a couple of his bodyguards relate that Elvis received a death threat during his summer 1970 engagement at the International Hotel. A security guard at the hotel was notified on August 26 that Elvis would be kidnapped some time that night. Feeling protected by extra security, Elvis chose to perform as usual. The next day, Colonel Parker's office received a similar warning over the phone. Again, Elvis appeared that night as usual. On August 28, the wife of Joe Esposito, who was Elvis's foreman, got another threatening phone call at her home in Los Angeles. She was told that Elvis would be shot in the middle of that night's show. With armed bodyguards in the wings, and, according to some, a couple of guns tucked into his costume, Elvis honored that old show business tradition of "the show must go on." Authorities never apprehended the person(s) responsible for the death threats.

Elvis's return to concert performing probably contributed to the disintegration of his marriage to Priscilla. Gone from Graceland much of the time while touring, Elvis saw less of Priscilla and his daughter, Lisa Marie, as his career and lifestyle took a different direction. The horrendous pace of performing in a different city every night made traveling together difficult, and Elvis enforced a "no-wives" rule while on the road, which applied to himself and all members of the Memphis Mafia. Priscilla left Elvis in early 1972, and Elvis sued for divorce the following August. Elvis's lawyer succinctly summed up the problem when he released this statement: "Elvis has been spending six months a year on the road, which put a tremendous strain on the marriage." In October 1973, the couple officially divorced, but it was an amicable split. They held hands during the divorce proceedings and walked out of the courtroom arm in arm.

The years 1969 through 1973 were an incredibly creative time for Elvis. He returned to performing live and developed a new sound and a new image that completely replaced the singing movie-star image that he believed never really matched his talents. Dressed in gold and jewels, this Elvis Presley lived up to the titles "World's Greatest Entertainer" and "The King of Rock 'n' Roll."

Priscilla and Elvis left the courtroom amicably after their divorce was finalized in 1973.

The movie-star image faded away when Elvis re-created himself yet again and became the World's Greatest Entertainer.

In a ruby glass-laden jumpsuit, the performer mesmerized the crowd at one of his Madison Square Garden shows.

Falling Star

Chapter 8

AFL1-2428

ELVIS
MOODY BLUE

ELVIS
MOODY BLUE

SIDE A

1. **UNCHAINED MELODY*** 2:32
Recorded on Tour

2. **IF YOU LOVE ME
(LET ME KNOW)*** 2:57
Recorded on Tour

3. **LITTLE DARLIN'*** 1:52
Recorded on Tour

4. **HE'LL HAVE TO GO**** 4:28
Recorded at Graceland

5. **LET ME BE THERE***** 3:26
Recorded Memphis, Tennessee

SIDE B

1. **WAY DOWN**** 2:37
Recorded at Graceland

2. **PLEDGING MY LOVE**** 2:50
Recorded at Graceland

3. **MOODY BLUE†** 2:49
Strings & Horns arranged by Bergen White
Recorded at Graceland

4. **SHE THINKS I STILL CARE†** 3:49
Strings & Horns arranged by Bergen White
Recorded at Graceland

5. **IT'S EASY FOR YOU**** 3:26
Recorded at Graceland

* J. D. Sumner and The Stamps,
The Sweet Inspirations, Kathy
Westmoreland and Sherrill Nie

** J. D. Sumner and The Stamps,
Kathy Westmoreland, Myrna
Smith and Sherrill Nielsen

*** Voice / J. D. Sumner and The S
The Sweet Inspirations and Kat
Westmoreland

† J. D. Sumner and The Stamps,
Kathy Westmoreland and Myrna
Smith

All selections are BMI except
"Unchained Melody," ASCAP

**EXECUTIVE PRODUCER:
ELVIS PRESLEY**

**ASSOCIATE PRODUCER:
FELTON JARVIS**

RCA

AFL1-2428 STEREO

The trouble is, when a fellow is by himself and starts thinking, the sad things are always stronger in his memory than the happy things.

—Elvis Presley, *Tropic,* April 28, 1968

The nonstop touring and Las Vegas engagements played a part in Elvis Presley's physical and spiritual decline as did his dependency on a variety of prescription drugs. His oppressive performance schedule and his reliance on drugs were connected, at least in Elvis's mind. He claimed he needed drugs to maintain his energy onstage and more drugs to sleep after his performances, but some of the prescription drugs he got his hands on were not designed for those purposes. Some time during the 1970s, Elvis's overuse of drugs evolved into a frightening level of abuse.

In addition, Elvis's record output during the 1970s was extensive, making his recording schedule as grueling as his concert tours. Each year, RCA typically released three to four studio albums, one to two live albums, and various singles.

A misconception exists that Elvis was lazy during the 1970s, that he secluded himself inside Graceland for extensive periods and did very little. Yet, based on his touring and recording schedules, this is clearly untrue. The problem was not inactivity; it was a grinding schedule of repeated routines, the monotony of the road, and a heart heavy from personal disappointments.

Personally downhearted and professionally unchallenged, Elvis grew bored and disaffected. By 1976, no one could get Elvis Presley into the recording studio despite his contractual obligations. Any enthusiasm he had previously mustered for recording was lost by the mid-1970s. Whether it was the end result of a downward spiral or because he thought the drugs had affected the range of his voice is unknown.

Elvis and his entourage, including Dr. Nichopoulos, hurry to board the plane to the singer's next concert venue.

Elvis maintained an arduous schedule of touring and recording.

At a Christmas party at Graceland, the Presley family posed for a group portrait with Mrs. Nichopoulos and Dr. "Nick."

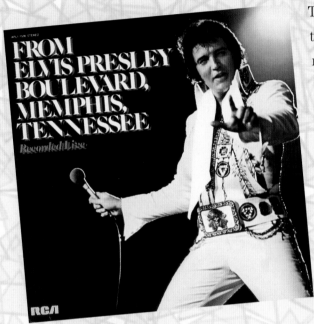

A tired and unwilling Elvis recorded this album at Graceland in 1976.

To appease Elvis by making the recording process easier, RCA sent their recording truck to Graceland in February 1976 so the reluctant singer could work in the convenience of his own home. Technicians set up a makeshift studio in the downstairs back room, known as the Jungle Room because of its decor. They made some technical compromises but, from this session and another session in October 1976, they produced two albums: *From Elvis Presley Boulevard, Memphis, Tennessee* and *Moody Blue*. The October session, resulting in only four completed tracks, was Elvis's last effort at studio recording.

Moody Blue, released in July 1977, consists of leftover tracks recorded at Graceland in 1976, three live songs from concert performances in April 1977, and one previously released cut titled "Let Me Be There." Critics and biographers have overlooked or criticized the album because it is a hodgepodge of tracks representing producer Felton Jarvis's desperate attempts to put together an album on schedule for RCA. While it is not a musical milestone by any standard, *Moody Blue* does tell us something about Elvis Presley and for that reason it deserves consideration and evaluation.

The selection of songs indicates the eclectic nature of Elvis's tastes, while his ability to put them over with a consistency reveals his style. From the country classic "He'll Have to Go" to the pop song "It's Easy for You" by Andrew Lloyd Webber and Tim Rice, Elvis unites disparate sounds and genres of music into a style that is big, dramatic, and unique to him.

Above and right: *Elvis introduced soprano Kathy Westmoreland to the audience. He wore the White Eagle jumpsuit for this 1975–1976 tour.*

If there was one common denominator to his song selection during the last few years of his life, it was his affinity for brooding ballads and other songs of regret and loss. Several songs of this type had been recorded around the time of his separation and divorce from Priscilla, but this preference resurfaced as his personal and professional life continued to deteriorate. If speculation exists as to whether Elvis realized the extent of his decline, the proof of self-awareness lies not in his words or deeds but in the song selections for his final studio albums. "He'll Have to Go," "She Thinks I Still Care," and the title cut "Moody Blue" from this LP are about lost love affairs, bitter endings, and hopeless relationships. These tracks are not great musical innovations, nor did they change the course of music history, but their autobiographical relevance to Elvis's circumstances make their inclusion on this album—released one month before his death—poignant and heartrending.

The King in concert in 1974

Ever patriotic, Elvis had several costumes decorated with the symbolic eagle.

"My Way"

Only Elvis Presley could record a song previously associated with Frank Sinatra and make it his own. Originally a French tune titled "Comme d'Habitude," "My Way" was reworked in 1969 with English lyrics by Paul Anka, with Sinatra in mind. When the Voice recorded it later that year, it sold a million copies and reached No. 27 on the Hot 100 chart.

Elvis sang the song four years later during his 1973 TV special *Elvis: Aloha from Hawaii* and included it in every concert afterward. However, a recording was not produced until June 1977, just two months before Elvis died. The King's version of "My Way" sold a million copies and peaked at No. 22 on the Hot 100, edging out Sinatra's recording by just a few positions. However, the timing of the record's release, so close to Elvis's death, gave the song a biographical meaning, as if it had been a statement of purpose to sum up his life. When Sinatra died in 1998, "My Way" held a similar connotation for him.

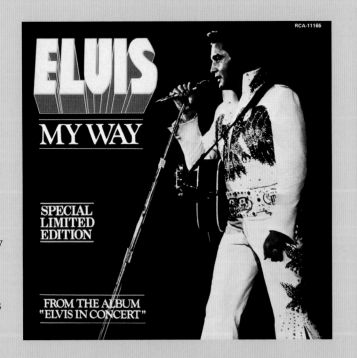

After the 1970 kidnapping and death threats to Elvis, bodyguard Red West was careful not to let strangers near the performer.

Moody Blue reached No. 3 on *Billboard*'s Top LP chart and remained on the charts for 31 weeks. It was certified platinum on September 1, 1977. The original pressing of *Moody Blue* produced 200,000 copies on blue translucent vinyl. Green, red, and gold vinyl were experimented with but quickly discarded for the blue—an obvious choice considering the album's title. After the initial pressing sold out, RCA chose the customary black vinyl for the next run, but later they returned to blue. Fans referred to this album as the "Blue Album," which seemed appropriate not only for its color but also for Elvis's frame of mind.

The reasons, sources, and explanations for Elvis Presley's problems, maladies, and behavior have been discussed, dismissed, interpreted, and exaggerated for decades, often by those who have their own agendas and personal motivations. While separating the reasonable explanations from the angry accusations can be difficult, a common thread among them is Elvis's isolation from the outside world, which resulted in an unconventional lifestyle.

When Elvis began his career, he allowed his fans unprecedented access to himself and his family. Fans tracked him down and visited him in the comfort of his home. As time passed, the fans became too much for him to manage. He was mobbed, pushed down, and sometimes stripped bare by crowds of adoring admirers. Elvis couldn't sightsee, eat in a restaurant, or enjoy himself in public without his fans besieging him. By the time Elvis was discharged from the army, he had begun living as a recluse. He secluded himself at Graceland or his home in California. This isolation, coupled with his boredom when he was between projects, eventually led Elvis to indulge in destructive habits.

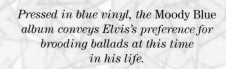

Pressed in blue vinyl, the Moody Blue *album conveys Elvis's preference for brooding ballads at this time in his life.*

Elvis's fame brought him a constant bombardment of adoring fans.

These bad habits accelerated during the 1970s after he returned to performing in concert and a hectic life on the road. His worst problem was obviously his dependence on prescription drugs, which altered his behavior and personality. According to members of the Memphis Mafia, Elvis began using amphetamines and diet pills in the 1960s; the drugs were intended to help Elvis keep his weight down. To counteract the amphetamines, Elvis and his court, who always indulged in whatever Elvis was doing, began to take sleeping pills. By the early 1970s, when he

was touring on a debilitating schedule of one-nighters, Elvis was taking medication for pain and discomfort caused by various afflictions and conditions. These drugs eventually left him in a state of mental limbo. Memphis Mafia members disagree about how many drugs Elvis took, but the fact remains that he took more drugs than his body could cope with.

Elvis's drug problem was the result of prescription drugs, some of which were administered for health problems. He had back pain, digestive troubles, and eye afflictions, including glaucoma. Treatments for these conditions put Elvis in the hospital several times between 1973 and his death four years later. He was also hospitalized for throat ailments, pleurisy, and hypertension. Ironically, Elvis rarely indulged in alcohol and often spoke out against taking illegal drugs.

Above, left, and below: By the mid-1970s, Elvis sometimes looked unfocused onstage, and his performances were peppered with exaggerated mannerisms indicative of drug-influenced behavior.

Elvis had some of his jumpsuits altered to accommodate the extra pounds.

Because of his wealth and position, Elvis's eating habits and choice of foods have been exaggerated and blamed for his weight gain. Some writers reported that the amount of food Elvis consumed was excessive. They told tall tales about Elvis eating so many Spanish omelettes that he created an egg shortage in Tennessee. Elvis did sometimes go on eating binges, usually during his time off between projects. However, the stories about his binges on foods such as bacon, ice cream, and pizza have been repeated so often they infer that Elvis ate this much every day.

Most of Elvis's favorite foods were typical Southern dishes that incorporate a variety of fried meats. Reporters and magazine writers who were not familiar with Southern cooking thought that Elvis's eating habits were peculiar, although many people in the South enjoy the same foods Elvis liked to eat. As early as 1955, when he was 20 and considered an up-and-coming country-western singer, articles about the young singer often mentioned that he liked to down several cheeseburgers at one sitting. In the late 1960s, an article in *Esquire* magazine took a sarcastic but lighthearted tone when describing Elvis's favorite snack of peanut butter and mashed banana sandwiches washed down with plenty of Pepsi. Elvis always had these eating habits, and age and lack of exercise had as much to do with his weight gain as anything else.

Not all of Elvis's excesses were bad for his health. He also liked to collect and wear ostentatious jewelry, which is perhaps an extravagance more befitting the King. During the 1970s, Elvis wore rings on all his fingers, both onstage and off. He also wore heavy medallions, gold-plated belts, and chain-link bracelets. On a gold chain around his neck, Elvis wore a gold Star of David

Elvis liked theatrical jewelry, and he wore big rings and a cross on a gold chain on and off the stage.

The singer enjoyed eating traditional Southern cooking, which eventually increased his waistline.

as well as a crucifix. He also liked to carry walking sticks adorned with tops of silver or gold. Elvis bought expensive jewelry not only for himself but also for the Memphis Mafia, their wives, and his show business friends. He once gave a $30,000 ring to entertainer Sammy Davis, Jr.

Among Elvis's extravagant habits were his buying sprees, particularly of cars, motorcycles, and other vehicles. Elvis had a lifelong love affair with Cadillacs and bought more than 100 during his lifetime, mostly for himself but also for the members of his entourage. If he bought himself a new car, he tended to buy one for the friend or family member who was with him at the time. Later in his life, he was known to buy cars for other customers who were on the car lot at the same time. Sometimes he purchased vehicles to smooth over the ruffled feathers of members of the Memphis Mafia, who tended to feel slighted at the drop of a hat, like kids fighting on a playground.

Elvis Presley also collected guns. He owned thousands of dollars worth of guns, and he lavished gifts of expensive guns on the Memphis Mafia. During the 1970s, he carried a gun much of the time, partly because he had received several death and kidnapping threats. He believed that assassins sought glory or media attention when they attempted to kill a famous person and that he was as likely a target as a president. Elvis carried guns onstage when he performed, during trips in airplanes, and while in his hotel rooms.

Elvis showed off part of his firearms collection.

Elvis had a tendency to bestow expensive gifts on his friends and people he admired. A big fan of Muhammad Ali, he once gave the fighter a robe worth more than $10,000.

Clockwise from above: *Customized for Elvis, the pink 1955 Cadillac Fleetwood has become a symbol of the spirit of rock 'n' roll. When the singer wanted his 1956 Cadillac Eldorado painted purple, he squashed a handful of grapes on the fender to show the color. Stepbrother David Stanley said Elvis's favorite car to drive was a 1975 Dino Ferrari 308 GT4 Coupe that could reach 165 mph.*

Elvis was infatuated with law enforcement most of his life. The entire entourage, including Dr. George Nichopoulos (to Elvis's right), show off their deputy's badges from Shelby County, Tennessee.

Perhaps more than his guns, Elvis was proud of his police badge collection. He was fascinated with law enforcement and collected badges from across the country. The prize of the collection was a federal narcotics badge and a complete set of credentials. He wheedled these out of President Richard Nixon on a spontaneous visit in December 1970. Elvis initiated the meeting by writing a six-page letter to Nixon while on the plane en route to Washington, D.C. The many times that he packed a gun onstage and the many stories about his infatuation with law enforcement reveal a life lived beyond the constraints of the norm.

Elvis Drops in on a President

In December 1970, Elvis made a spontaneous decision to travel to Washington, D.C., to visit Deputy U.S. Narcotics Director John Finlator. Although Elvis said that he was going to Washington to volunteer his help in the antidrug campaign, he was actually hoping to obtain a federal narcotics badge and a complete set of credentials to add to his collection. Finlator turned down Elvis's request for a badge, but this did not stop Elvis. He decided to go over Finlator's head, and with a couple of members of the Memphis Mafia, Elvis called on President Richard Nixon at the White House. The charismatic Presley was able to talk Nixon into giving him an authentic narcotics agent's badge in a matter of minutes. He then asked the President to track down some souvenirs inscribed with the presidential seal for his bodyguards and their wives.

On later trips to Washington, Elvis visited FBI headquarters to offer his assistance in fighting the war on drugs. While it's not surprising that Elvis visited law-enforcement agencies, the fact that he could get in to see the president on a few hours' notice is extraordinary testimony to Elvis's amazing popularity and power. Other entertainers have been honored by invitations to perform at the White House, but the King simply dropped in to get something he wanted.

A life of isolation from the outside world combined with the privileges of stardom eventually led Elvis to self-destruct. He maintained a secluded existence inside the walls of Graceland, where there was no one with enough influence to stop the indulgences of the King. Still, Elvis's dark habits and self-destructive whims are often exaggerated to such a degree that only a fantasy figure could have indulged in proportions of this magnitude. Perhaps normal standards of measurement are simply not adequate when describing the excesses and achievements of Elvis Presley. For all the heartbreaking details that have been revealed since his death, the one part of the legend that remains untarnished is his voice, which rang clear and true from the day he recorded "That's All Right" until June 26, 1977, the day he gave his final performance at Market Square Arena in Indianapolis.

Because of overzealous fans, Elvis felt he had to seclude himself at Graceland, which made for an unusual, isolated existence.

Parker's Folly

Colonel Tom Parker arranged for CBS-TV to tape a concert from Elvis's June 1977 tour for a special titled *Elvis in Concert*. People in the Presley inner circle were amazed at these plans because Elvis was in no shape to appear on national television. Except for an occasional reference to his weight, the media had been more or less indifferent to Elvis Presley in the last two years of his life, but this special threatened to expose his condition on a large scale.

The cameras rolled on the night of June 19, 1977, at the Civic Auditorium in Omaha, Nebraska, but Elvis was in such poor shape that little footage was usable. The crew returned on June 21 to record his performance at Rushmore Civic Center in Rapid City, South Dakota. Elvis died before the special was completed, but CBS chose to air the show on October 3, 1977. His bloated appearance and offbeat manner served to confirm the rumors of drug abuse that had surfaced at the time of his death.

The CBS crew caught a profoundly vulnerable moment in Omaha: After Elvis announced the song "Are You Lonesome Tonight?," he stopped for a few seconds, then added, "and I am, and I was. . . ."

J. D. Sumner and Elvis at Market Square Arena

The Last Concert

On June 26, 1977, Elvis and his entourage flew into Indianapolis, Indiana. It would be his 56th concert performance that year, despite months of head, stomach, and muscle pain, digestive problems, and bouts of vomiting. When the plane landed, Elvis was so fatigued that members of his entourage were concerned about his welfare. He rested at a local hotel before proceeding to Market Square Arena. Backstage before the show, RCA presented Elvis with a special plaque commemorating the two billionth Presley record pressed by RCA. The plaque featured a reproduction of the *Moody Blue* album cover and a brief inscription. That evening, the show went on at 8:30 before a packed crowd of 18,000, and Elvis gave one of his best performances of the year. No one knew it would be his last.

Elvis Presley died at Graceland on August 16, 1977. He was 42 years old. Girlfriend Ginger Alden found him slumped over in the bathroom. Paramedics were called, but they failed to revive Elvis, and he was taken to Baptist Memorial Hospital where further attempts to resuscitate him failed. He was pronounced dead by his physician, Dr. George Nichopoulos, who listed the official cause of death as erratic heartbeat, or cardiac arrhythmia.

Almost immediately, rumors that Elvis was dead began to sift into the Memphis newspaper, radio, and television newsrooms, but reporters took a wait-and-see attitude. They had heard these rumors before. Over the years, many crank calls had come in declaring that Elvis had been killed in a car accident or a plane crash or that he'd been shot by the jealous boyfriend of a woman who was

Physician George Nichopoulos said cardiac arrhythmia was the cause of Elvis's death.

Ginger Alden and her mother waited outside the courtroom where she appeared in 1980 before the Shelby County grand jury, which was investigating Nichopoulos's prescription practices.

hopelessly infatuated with him. Once, someone reported that he had drowned in a submarine. Elvis Presley was a hometown boy and a constant source of news, some of which was manufactured for or by the Memphis press. Newspaper editors and newsroom managers were cautious about sending out their reporters if the rumor that Elvis was dead was just another hoax. But when the staff of the *Memphis Press-Scimitar* learned from a trusted source that Elvis actually was dead, the newsroom became unusually silent. Dan Sears of radio station WMPS in Memphis made the first official announcement, and WHBQ-TV was the first television station to interrupt its programming with the terrible news.

Thousands of mourners wait for the gates of Graceland to open the day of the funeral.

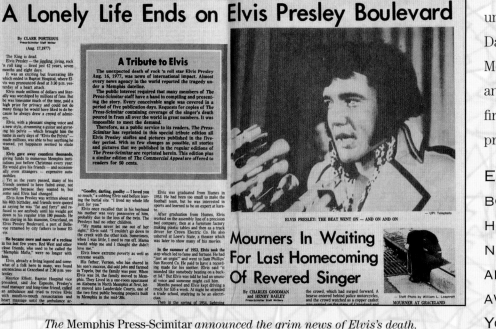

The Memphis Press-Scimitar *announced the grim news of Elvis's death.*

ELVIS WAS A COUNTRY BOY, BUT THE WAY THEY HAD HIM LIVING, THEY NEVER TURNED OFF THE AIR CONDITIONING. TOOK AWAY ALL THE GOOD AIR. YOU GET SICK FROM THAT.

—JAMES BROWN

Singer James Brown, the Godfather of Soul

As the news of Elvis's death spread across the country, radio stations immediately began to play his records. Some stations quickly organized tributes to Elvis while others simply played his music at the request of listeners, many of whom were in a state of shock over his sudden death. Some people called their favorite radio stations just because they wanted

to tell someone their stories about the first time they'd heard Elvis sing or to talk about how much his talent and his music meant to them. In the same way that many people remember exactly where they were when they heard President John F. Kennedy had been killed, most of Elvis's fans remember where they were the day Elvis died. Mick Fleetwood, of rock group Fleetwood Mac, recalls, "The news came over like a ton of bricks. I was driving back from the mountains, and I had the radio on. They were playing an Elvis medley, and I thought, 'Great.' And then they came back with the news."

The manner in which the major television networks handled the news of Elvis's death illustrated his enormous popularity and the tremendous impact he had on America, something few realized until he was gone. Data from the television-ratings service Arbitron revealed that on the day Elvis died, there was a huge increase in the number of televisions tuned to evening news programs. The staffs of television newsrooms considered Elvis's death a late-breaking story. There was not enough time for TV reporters who had been sent to Memphis to file stories for the evening news. Executives had to decide quickly what film footage they could use from their files and where to place the story in relation to the other news of the day.

Above and below: By the day of the funeral, on August 18, 1977, the line of mourners at Graceland extended past the estate and around the block.

Within an hour after the announcement of Elvis's death, mourners began to gather at Graceland. Many stayed until after his funeral.

179

NBC-TV not only rewrote their news lineup to lead off with the story of Elvis's death, but the network also made immediate plans to delay *The Tonight Show* and put together a late-night news documentary. David Brinkley, a national news anchor for NBC at the time, opened his broadcast with three minutes devoted to Elvis's sudden death. ABC-TV also decided to lead with the Presley story. When they learned that NBC would be doing a late-night news special about the significance of Elvis Presley to American music, ABC announced that they would also air a half-hour documentary.

CBS did not follow suit, however. The *CBS Evening News with Walter Cronkite*, featuring the most respected man in broadcasting at that time, had led the news program ratings for more than a decade. CBS executives chose not to open the evening broadcast with the Presley story. Arbitron's records indicate that when millions of viewers realized this they immediately switched the channel to another network. The CBS decision not to lead with Elvis's death gave the *CBS Evening News* its lowest ratings in years. (For the record, Roger Mudd was substituting for Walter Cronkite that evening.) CBS devoted only 70 seconds to its story on Elvis, placing it after a lengthy segment on the Panama Canal. The producer for that evening's news was vehemently opposed to leading off with Elvis's death, in spite of other members of the CBS programming staff suggesting it repeatedly. Interviewed later, the producer agreed that he was out of sync with the national consciousness. Two days later, CBS tried to save face by putting together a documentary on Elvis.

NBC news anchor David Brinkley opened the national news with a three-minute report on Elvis's death. **Left:** *On CBS, reporter Roger Mudd (far left) was substituting for the venerable Walter Cronkite (near left). The program's producer mistakenly chose to disregard the magnitude of the story and buried it after an in-depth report on the Panama Canal.*

THE COMMERCIAL APPEAL

138th Year   No. 229   Memphis, Tenn., Wednesday Morning, August 17, 1977

Death Captures Crown Of Rock And Roll
—Elvis Dies Apparently After Heart Attack

Elvis Went From Rags To Riches
By WILLIAM THOMAS

Hearse Takes Body Of Elvis Presley From Baptist Hospital

'Are You Sure There's No Mistake?'
—The Desired Answer Never Came

By TERRY KEETER and OTIS L. SANFORD

Headlines: August 1977

"Death Captures Crown of Rock And Roll"—*The Commercial Appeal*

"A Lonely Life Ends on Elvis Presley Boulevard" —*Memphis Press-Scimitar*

"The King Is Dead" —*Tupelo Daily Journal*

"All Roads Lead to Memphis" —London *Evening Standard*

"Last Stop on the Mystery Train"—*TIME* magazine

"L'adieu a Elvis" —*France-Soir*

"Elvis Has Left the Building" —*Stereo Review*

IT'S HARD TO IMAGINE ELVIS PRESLEY'S SUCCESS COMING ANYWHERE BUT HERE. HE MOLDED IT OUT OF SO MANY ELEMENTS: COUNTRY AND BLUES AND GOSPEL AND ROCK, A LITTLE MEMPHIS, A LITTLE VEGAS, A LITTLE ARROGANCE, A LITTLE PIETY. . . . HOW COULD WE EVER HAVE FELT ESTRANGED FROM ELVIS? HE WAS A NATIVE SON.

—CHARLES KURALT, CBS NEWS SPECIAL ON ELVIS PRESLEY, AUGUST 18, 1977

Charles Kuralt hosted a CBS news special about Elvis the day after he died.

Even though Elvis never performed in Europe, countries from all over the world sent reporters to Memphis. The press coverage in foreign newspapers and on European television was almost as extensive as the reporting in the United States. Everywhere in the world, people lamented the loss of an irreplaceable entertainer.

Evening Standard CITY PRICES

Mourning fans besiege Presley home
ALL ROADS LEAD TO MEMPHIS

London is marooned after all-night deluge
By Lynda Murdin and Paul Taylor

Newspapers in London and other European cities reported on Elvis Presley's death.

Within one hour after Elvis's death, fans began to gather in front of Graceland. By the next day, when the gates were opened for mourners to view Elvis's body, the crowd was estimated at 20,000. When the gates closed at 6:30 P.M., about 80,000 fans had passed by Elvis's coffin. Many had come from different parts of the country, many from different parts of the world. Eventually, so many mourners arrived that it was impossible for them all to be admitted to Graceland, even with extended calling hours. Law enforcement officials were afraid there might be problems with crowd control, but there were none. However, an unrelated tragic incident occurred: A drunk driver's car careened into three teenagers in the crowd, killing two of them.

A police woman saluted the hearse as it passed through the Music Gates.

As the group of mourners grew around the gates of Graceland, a carnival atmosphere developed; people hawking T-shirts and other souvenirs began to work the crowd. The people who were unable to get into Graceland to pay their last respects to Elvis consoled each other by exchanging anecdotes about their idol. When reporters asked them why they were there, people inevitably gave the same reply: They didn't really know, but they felt they wanted to be where he was this one last time. The hot Memphis weather and the close crush of the crowd caused many people to pass out. A medic was stationed nearby to assist anyone who fainted, but no one left because of the heat.

The white hearse carrying Elvis's casket left Graceland with a police escort.

Elvis's fans sent a tremendous array of flowers, which were set out along the bank in front of the house. Every blossom in Memphis had been sold by the afternoon of August 17, and additional flowers were shipped in from other parts of the country. It was the biggest day in the history of FTD, a floral delivery service. FTD employees claim that more than 2,150 arrangements were delivered. The arrangements were shaped like lightning bolts, guitars, hound dogs, and stars, as well as

As mourners watched, the long motor cortege of all-white automobiles headed toward Forest Hill Cemetery.

Ann-Margret and husband Roger Smith attended Elvis's funeral.

more traditional wreaths and bouquets. Many of the arrangements were sent immediately to Forest Hill Cemetery, the site of the burial. After the funeral, Vernon Presley allowed the fans to take away the flowers as mementos.

Numerous celebrities attended Elvis's funeral, including Caroline Kennedy, country music guitarist Chet Atkins, performers Ann-Margret and George Hamilton, and television evangelist Rex Humbard, who was one of the speakers during the service. Comedian Jackie Kahane, who had opened many of Elvis's concert performances, delivered his eulogy, and a local minister also spoke. Gospel performers sang, including Jake Hess, J. D. Sumner, James Blackwood, and their vocal groups, as well as singer Kathy Westmoreland. The casket was carried to Forest Hill Cemetery in a long motor cortege of all-white automobiles. Later, when someone threatened to steal Elvis's remains, his casket was moved to the Meditation Garden behind Graceland. Gladys's body was also moved to the Meditation Garden in 1977; Vernon Presley died and was buried there in 1979; Minnie Mae Presley, Elvis's grandmother, was laid to rest beside her family in 1980.

The official pallbearers included Joe Esposito, Dr. George Nichopoulos, Billy Smith, Charlie Hodge, and Lamar Fike.

A saddened Sam Phillips paid his last respects to his most famous discovery.

ELVIS WAS A HARD WORKER, DEDICATED, AND GOD
LOVED HIM. LAST TIME I SAW HIM WAS AT
GRACELAND. WE SANG "OLD BLIND BARNABUS"
TOGETHER, A GOSPEL SONG. I LOVE HIM AND HOPE
TO SEE HIM IN HEAVEN. THERE'LL NEVER BE
ANOTHER LIKE THAT SOUL BROTHER.

—JAMES BROWN

In a strange stroke of timing, on August 1, 1977, 15 days before Elvis died, Ballantine Books published the book *Elvis: What Happened?*, put together by Steve Dunleavy. It consisted of interviews with three of Elvis's former bodyguards: Red West, Sonny West, and Dave Hebler. The men were the first to come forward with stories of Elvis's bizarre lifestyle. The book gave accounts of his mood swings, his relationships with women, and his excessive use of prescription drugs. It received almost no publicity until journalist Bob Greene, a columnist for the *Chicago Sun-Times*, interviewed Sonny West. By coincidence, the article happened to run on the day Elvis died. Greene's column provoked a great deal of protest from fans across the country and inspired the wrath of several journalists, including Geraldo Rivera, who blasted Dunleavy on *Good Morning America* for smearing Elvis's name.

(From left) Memphis Mafia members Dave Hebler, Red West, and Sonny West gave accounts of Elvis's private life to author Steve Dunleavy, a former tabloid reporter.

The bodyguards' story was hard to believe for several reasons. Nothing like it had surfaced on a wide scale before because, for the most part, Elvis had been able to keep his eccentric habits and erratic behavior out of the press. Dunleavy also lacked credibility. He had been a reporter for the tabloid newspaper *The National Enquirer*

Elvis was still alive when Dunleavy's tell-all book came out.

when he started working on the book about Elvis, and he was employed by the controversial newspaper the *New York Post* when *Elvis: What Happened?* was published. Dunleavy appeared on the NBC documentary about Elvis that aired the evening he died. The reporter made the mistake of using the term "white trash" in reference to Elvis, and this went over like a lead balloon with the fans. Because Dunleavy wasn't popular with either the public or the press and because Vernon had fired the three bodyguards the previous year, many people believed their outrageous account of Elvis's life amounted to sour grapes over being dismissed. Dunleavy was accused of having manipulated the story to make it as sensational as possible.

Sonny and Red West (above) and Dave Hebler had been fired by Vernon Presley in 1976. Their book was regarded by many as a case of sour grapes.

The autopsy did not reveal any substantive information. The family had requested a private autopsy, and the exact findings were not made public. All reports, notes, and photos related to the autopsy disappeared forever by August 19, and the contents of Elvis's stomach were destroyed before further analysis was done. Any concrete evidence of a drug-related death could only be found in the sealed autopsy report.

Two years later, on September 13, 1979, ABC-TV's news magazine *20/20* aired a report called "The Elvis Cover-Up," and the details surrounding Elvis's death began to take on the character of a mystery novel. This investigative report, produced by Charles Thompson and reported by Geraldo Rivera, marked the first major national media attention devoted to the rumors of a drug-related death. The show attempted to pinpoint the exact cause of Elvis's death and had gone so far as to file a lawsuit on August 10 to obtain a copy of the autopsy report from Dr. Jerry Francisco, the Tennessee medical examiner. When Francisco refused to hand over the report, *20/20* accused him of participating in a cover-up. The medical examiner held a news conference declaring that he

Tennessee medical examiner Jerry Francisco testified before the state medical board hearing for Dr. George Nichopoulos. Francisco never swayed from his opinion that Elvis died from cardiac arrhythmia.

Dr. George Nichopoulos

was not involved in any cover-up. After the *20/20* report, Shelby County officials were pressured to open a criminal investigation of the case, but ultimately they declined to do so. The lawsuit, filed by Thompson and local Memphis reporter James Cole, eventually made it all the way to the Tennessee Supreme Court. In 1982, the court ruled that Francisco was not obligated to release the autopsy results because the postmortem had been requested by the family.

Memphis florists like Frank Gray, Jr., delivered a staggering number of floral pieces for Elvis's funeral. Every flower shop in Memphis was sold out. Floral service FTD reported it delivered more than 2,150 arrangements.

Meanwhile, Elvis's Memphis physician, Dr. George Nichopoulos (Dr. Nick), was brought before the Tennessee Board of Medical Examiners on several charges related to overprescribing drugs to Elvis Presley and other patients. In January 1980, the board suspended his license for three months for indiscriminately prescribing and dispensing controlled substances to ten people, including Elvis and Jerry Lee Lewis. Although the board's conclusions did not challenge Francisco's official ruling about the cause of Elvis's death, the inquiry did reveal stories about the singer's extensive drug use. The exaggerated rumors that had been floating around for more than two years paled in comparison to the damning details that surfaced in Dr. Nick's testimony: Elvis was prescribed over 12,000 pills and vials of potent drugs in the last 20 months of his life; he was hospitalized several times because he was swollen from head to foot from drug misuse; whenever he toured, he carried three suitcases of pills and supplies, which his whole entourage used freely.

Fans expressed their grief at Elvis's crypt. **Left:** *The bodies of both Elvis and Gladys were moved to the Meditation Garden at Graceland in October 1977.*

These stories resurfaced in November 1981 when Nichopoulos was officially charged in a criminal court with 11 felony counts of overprescribing drugs to nine patients, including Elvis and Jerry Lee Lewis. He was acquitted. Five new charges were brought against him in 1992 by the state of Tennessee for overprescribing drugs to Elvis. This time, the State Department of Health was determined to revoke the doctor's medical license permanently.

The President on the King

President Jimmy Carter and First Lady Rosalynn Carter had met Elvis Presley and had seen him in concert on more than one occasion. On August 17, 1977, President Carter presented an official comment on Elvis's death, a comment that was all the more fitting because both men were sons of the South.

"Elvis Presley's death deprives our country of a part of itself. He was unique and irreplaceable. More than 20 years ago, he burst upon the scene with an impact that was unprecedented and will probably never be equaled. His music and his personality, fusing the styles of white country and black rhythm-and-blues, changed the face of American popular culture. His following was immense, and he was a symbol to people the world over of the vitality, rebelliousness, and good humor of his country."

THE KING IS ALWAYS KILLED BY HIS COURTIERS. HE IS OVERFED, OVERINDULGED, OVERDRUNK TO KEEP HIM TIED TO HIS THRONE. MOST PEOPLE IN THE POSITION NEVER WAKE UP.

—JOHN LENNON, ON THE DEATH OF ELVIS PRESLEY

Over the years, the cause of Elvis's death has generally been recognized as polypharmacy, or the interaction of several drugs. This is based on the information revealed by the Nichopoulos trials as well as on statements to that effect by Dr. Eric Muirhead, pathologist at Baptist Memorial, and Dr. Noel Foredo, who was present at the autopsy. Meanwhile, the struggle to have the autopsy results made public continued. In 1991, ABC went to court again to force Francisco to surrender the autopsy report. In May 1993, the Shelby County Commission filed a lawsuit to force the state of Tennessee to reopen an investigation into Elvis's death. As a result, the autopsy notes—but not the report—were given to a forensic pathologist to help settle disputes about the actual cause of death.

Former Beatle John Lennon also met an early death when he was shot in 1980.

Vernon Presley wrote the epitaph inscribed on the bronze plaque that sits atop the grave of his famous son.

The spontaneous outpouring of grief over Elvis's death, the extended coverage by the news media, and the offering of condolences from around the world were reminiscent of the mourning that occurs when a head of state dies. Hundreds of editorials attempted to summarize Elvis's place in our culture. For the first time, the nation as a whole seemed to realize that Elvis had changed the way we look, the way we talk, the music we listen to, and the kind of hero we believe in.

ELVIS WAS THE KING. NO DOUBT ABOUT IT. PEOPLE LIKE MYSELF, MICK JAGGER AND ALL THE OTHERS ONLY FOLLOWED IN HIS FOOTSTEPS.

—ROD STEWART

At the time, many people felt that Elvis's death marked the end of an era, as well as the end of a legendary career, but this has not proved to be true. After Elvis died, the mythology surrounding him continued to grow with each new revelation about his personal life and each new reinterpretation of his contribution to popular culture. Elvis the man died on August 16, 1977, but Elvis the myth continues to flourish. The King is dead—long live the King.

Left and above: During his career, Elvis left an indelible mark on the musical world and on the hearts of his fans.
Below: After Elvis died, many fans with tickets to his concerts kept them as mementos of the legendary singer.

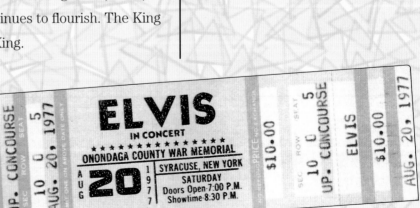

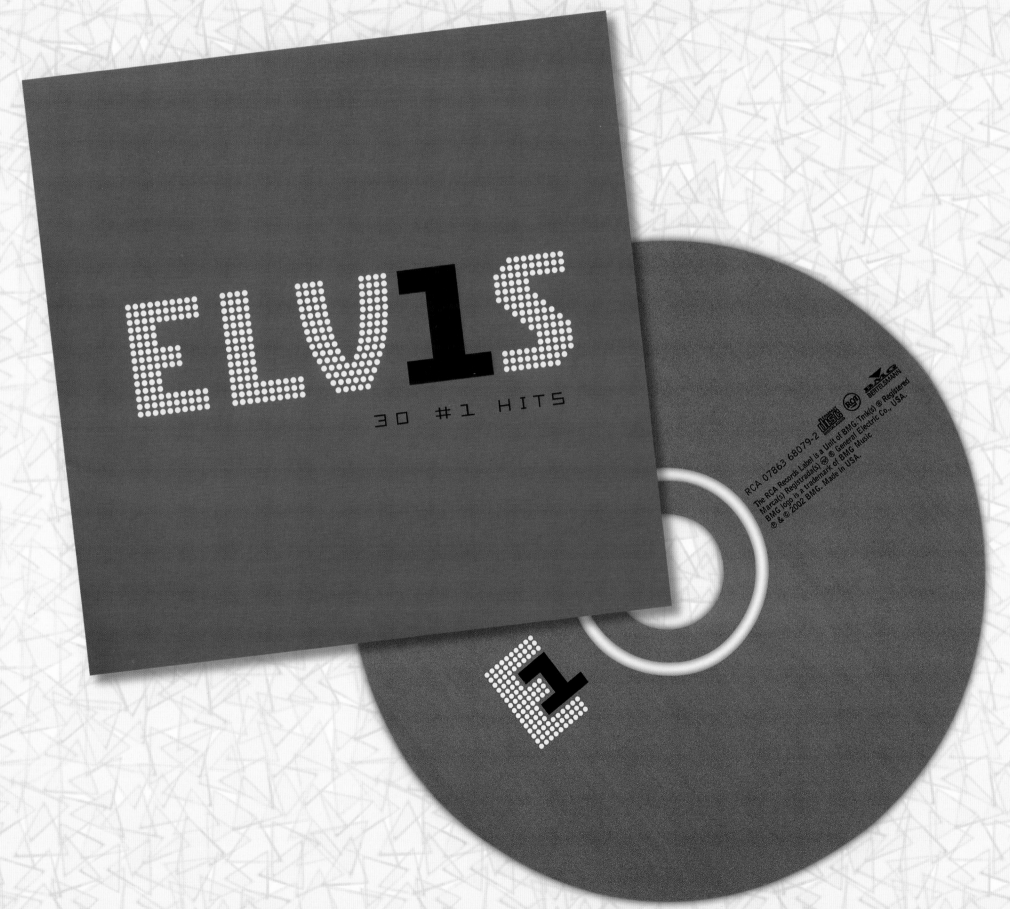

The Legend

Chapter 9

01 heartbreak hotel
02 don't be cruel
03 hound dog
04 love me tender
05 too much
06 all shook up
07 (let me be your) teddy bear
08 jailhouse rock
09 don't
10 hard headed woman
11 one night
12 (now and then there's) a fool such as i
13 a big hunk o' love
14 stuck on you
15 it's now or never
16 are you lonesome tonight?
17 wooden heart
18 surrender
19 (marie's the name) his latest flame
20 can't help falling in love
21 good luck charm
22 she's not you
23 return to sender
24 (you're the) devil in disguise
25 crying in the chapel
26 in the ghetto
27 suspicious minds
28 the wonder of you
29 burning love
30 way down
BONUS TRACK: a little less conversation (JXL Radio Edit Remix)

Mixed and mastered from original master tapes for optimum sound quality.

RCA   BMG
      BERTELSMANN

www.elvisnumberones.com

THERE HAVE BEEN A LOTTA TOUGH GUYS. THERE HAVE BEEN
PRETENDERS. THERE HAVE BEEN CONTENDERS.
BUT THERE IS ONLY ONE KING.

—BRUCE SPRINGSTEEN

$\mathcal{A}$lthough Elvis Presley died in 1977, his name, music, and image have sustained the public's attention. The period after his death has been marked by controversy, acclaim, ridicule, and commercialism: Officials debated the role of drugs in his death, music organizations honored his accomplishments, the media ridiculed the fans, and profiteers made money from it all. From the pits of tabloid headlines to the peaks of awards and honors, Elvis continued to make news. Death was not the end of Elvis Presley's career, it simply marked another phase.

Elvis gave it his all in a recording session for the movie King Creole.

To commemorate Elvis on the 25th anniversary of his death, RCA released a compilation of his No.1 records titled *ELV1S: 30 #1 Hits*. The marketing campaign was designed around the tag line: "Before anyone did anything, Elvis did everything." A clever bit of phrasing, the line succinctly summarized Elvis's contribution to pop culture history while evoking the dynamism of his sound and the danger of his original image.

The world needed to be reminded of this— and it was. *ELV1S: 30 #1 Hits* rocketed to No. 1 when it debuted, selling 500,000 copies in its first week of release. Debuting an album in the top spot on the U.S. charts was an accomplishment Elvis had not managed while he was alive. In addition to America, *ELV1S: 30 #1 Hits* opened at No. 1 in 16 other countries, including Canada, France, the United Kingdom, Argentina, and the United Arab Emirates.

Elvis recording for the first time at RCA.

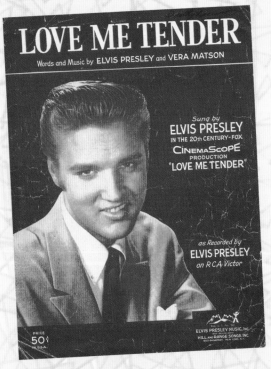

Sheet music of "Love Me Tender"

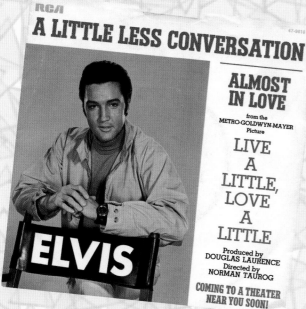

Marketing strategy aside, it was the music that accounted for the CD's success. Arranged in chronological order, the compilation of hits covered Elvis's entire career at RCA—from "Heartbreak Hotel" in 1956 to "Way Down" in 1977. All the songs reached No. 1 on the charts at the time of their original release, either in the United States or the United Kingdom. This fact softens the accusation by rock music historians who claim that Elvis's music went into severe decline during the last few years of his life. His health and career may have suffered, and his sound was no longer rock 'n' roll, but his music was still vital to large portions of the audience.

This could also be said for today's audiences. As a last-minute addition to *ELV1S: 30 #1 Hits,* the producers included a remix of "A Little Less Conversation," a song Elvis originally recorded for the soundtrack of *Live a Little, Love a Little*. Its reworking had been done in early 2002 by Dutch deejay act Junkie XL for a Nike World Cup commercial, but when it was released as a dance-mix single, it became Elvis's first Top Ten single in decades. "A Little Less Conversation" was billed as a bonus track, keeping it separate in concept from the rest of the cuts on the CD.

"A Little Less Conversation" reached No. 69 on the Hot 100 chart in 1968. Remixed in 2002 and released as a dance single, the song soared into the Top Ten.

The BMG/RCA site in Nashville, Tennessee

Elvis in the studio in the 1950s

The team of Ernst Jorgensen and Roger Semon compiled and researched the tracks on *ELV1S: 30 #1 Hits*. Jorgensen and Semon of BMG (which now owns RCA) have researched the Presley song catalog for several years, working hard to restore and repackage his music to its former glory. A group of expert engineers and mixers was hired to optimize the sound in ways that remained true to the original recordings, a difficult assignment considering the condition of the original tapes. Stashed away at RCA's storage facilities in Iron Mountain, Pennsylvania, some of the original tapes had not been played in more than 40 years. Most were deteriorated to some degree, and the first goal was to transfer them onto a digital format for remixing or remastering. Some, including the tape for "Way Down," were in such bad condition they had to be baked in an oven to prevent the oxide from falling off the tape.

The songs from 1956 to 1961 had been recorded on a monaural (mono) system and could not be remixed, only remastered. The ones from 1961 to 1966 had been recorded on a three-track recording system and required an antique three-track machine to help in the remixing process. Only a few of these machines still exist, and the one the remixing team used tended to overheat, further aggravating the process. Later tunes had been recorded on eight tracks, 16 tracks, and even 24 tracks, which were considerably easier to remix. However, the goal was to produce a uniform quality in all the tracks and to ensure that the quality remained whether the CD was played on a home stereo, a computer, or a car stereo. The efforts of these engineers and remixers resulted in a modernization that restores the songs' vitality yet does not detract from Elvis's renditions of the songs.

The Jordanaires, who sang backup vocals for Elvis, premiered on "Hound Dog," recorded at RCA in New York, July 1956.

Elvis recorded "I Want You, I Need You, I Love You" in April 1956 at RCA's Nashville studios. With him on the cut were Bill Black, Chet Atkins, Scotty Moore, D. J. Fontana, pianist Marvin Hughes, and vocalists Ben and Brock Speer and Gordon Stoker.

Signing autographs became almost second nature to the famous singer.

The energy in Elvis's recordings comes in part from the way he worked in the studio. When Elvis entered the studio, he took down the partitions between performer and musician, so he was in the same room as the band. They warmed up by singing a few gospel songs or other tunes, then got down to selecting whatever songs had been brought in by the band, the Memphis Mafia, the Colonel, or anyone who had a suggestion. Elvis sang each take of a song completely through, as if it were a performance before an audience. Each take was enlivened or ruined by interaction between Elvis and the band, a kind of trial-and-error approach that thrived on instinct and spontaneity. Sometimes he moved along with the music in a way that inspired the band to do something a bit different on some takes or hone in on what had worked well in previous takes. All decisions regarding a song were made in the studio during the session, not beforehand. In this way, Elvis was the producer of his work, relying on the immediacy of performance to dictate the recording. He did not generally overdub, nor did he splice together various takes of a song to get a perfect "studio version." The expert remixing and remastering of the songs on *ELV1S: 30 #1 Hits* captures the vitality of Elvis's unique approach to recording, one he never abandoned for easier, more technically driven methods.

Above, right, and below: *For part of the documentary* Elvis—That's the Way It Is, *Elvis was filmed in rehearsal for his August 1970 Las Vegas engagement.*

The astounding success of *ELV1S: 30 #1 Hits* in 2002 steered the spotlight away from the rumors, the mass merchandising, and the antics of the fans in that all-important 25th-anniversary year toward something more significant—his recordings. The story of Elvis's music in the post-death period has not always had such a happy ending.

195

More important than the souvenirs, merchandise, and commemoratives is the music of Elvis Presley, which has been overshadowed by the more peculiar aspects of the phenomenon generated since his death. Before he died in 1977, Elvis sold 250 million records worldwide. Immediately after his death, record stores across the country quickly sold out of Elvis's records. RCA's pressing plants operated 24 hours a day to fill the new orders for Elvis's records that began to pour in. For a while, the record company subcontracted other pressing plants to keep up with the demand. By September, RCA still had not caught up with all the orders. RCA's offices and pressing plants outside the United States were in the same position. Pressing plants operated day and night. One factory in Hamburg, West Germany, only produced Elvis records to meet the demands. By October, sales in the United States were so high that several of Elvis's albums were on the charts again.

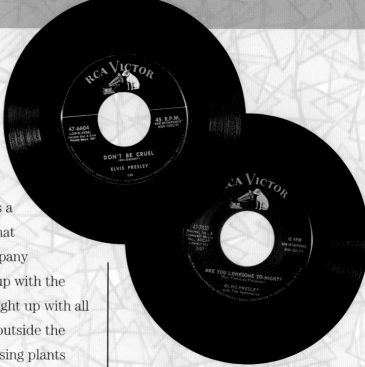

When Elvis died, stores nationwide sold out of his records. RCA ran its pressing plants round the clock and still couldn't keep up with the demand.

RCA continued to release albums of Elvis's music at the rate of two or three per year. As was the case while he was alive, some of the albums were well-received, others were criticized for their inferior quality. The marketing strategy behind the albums varied as much as their quality. Some albums, such as *Guitar Man,* attempted to take advantage of contemporary recording techniques to "improve" Elvis's sound. Other albums, such as *He Walks Beside Me—Favorite Songs of Faith and Inspiration,* contained previously released material repackaged yet again. Still other albums seemed to be the result of RCA searching the vaults for any recording of Elvis's voice. *Elvis—Greatest Hits Vol. 4,* for example, contained previously released cuts in addition to never-before-released "live" material from Las Vegas, Hawaii, and Nashville.

Elvis's continued popularity stems from the loyalty of his fans. Many had followed his career beginning in the 1950s.

Released in 1978, this album was a collection of songs with religious themes. Two cuts were takes that had never been released.

Something for Everybody, *recorded in March 1961, grabbed the No. 1 spot on the Top LPs chart.*

In 1983, a record producer from RCA found master tapes and records stored at Graceland, some of which contained unreleased live performances and offstage conversations with Elvis. Two years later, RCA released much of the musical material on a six-album set that celebrated Elvis's 50th birthday.

RCA has been criticized by purists for tinkering with the recordings of their most famous artist. Over the years the company has released several Elvis Presley albums of older material that was cleaned up for modern audiences. *I Was the One* makes use of modern instruments that were overdubbed to accompany his vocals. Other albums consisted of original mono recordings with "rechanneled stereo." Rock 'n' roll historians claim any attempt to "improve" or "clean up" Elvis's early recordings does not illuminate his contributions to popular music; instead, it distorts them.

A new approach to marketing and releasing Elvis Presley's music began after RCA was sold in 1986 to the German publishing group Bertlesmann Music Group (BMG). BMG formed an international restoration committee two years later to research and restore the Presley catalog of recordings. Representatives from America, England, Germany, Denmark, and Asia comprised the committee, which was ultimately responsible for the high quality of subsequent compilations of Elvis's music.

The BMG committee also researched the actual sales figures for the records and albums that Elvis sold. The Recording Industry Association of America (RIAA) is the official organization to which record companies report sales and request gold and platinum records

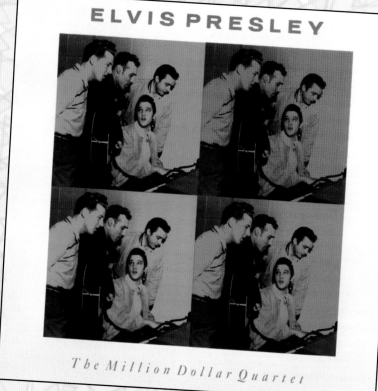

Recorded at the legendary Million Dollar Quartet session in December 1956 at Sun Records, this 17-track album wasn't released until 1990.

The Bertlesmann Music Group (BMG) building is located on Nashville's Music Row.

for their artists. However, the RIAA was not formed until 1958, three years after Elvis had already sold millions of records. Although RCA awarded Elvis various in-house gold records for his pre-1958 hits, they never asked the RIAA for retroactive certification of these records. Also, RCA rarely requested additional certification when Elvis's records went gold or platinum more than once. The BMG committee used Colonel Tom Parker's files to accurately research how many records Elvis sold and which ones deserved gold, platinum, or multiplatinum status. After completing their research, they estimated that Elvis Presley had sold over a billion records worldwide. By August 1992, the committee had updated the status of Elvis's albums and singles. As a result, he was awarded 110 additional gold, platinum, and multiplatinum albums and singles by the RIAA—the largest presentation of gold and platinum records in history.

In the Trophy Room at Graceland, the Hall of Gold displays the magnitude of Elvis's impact as a recording artist.

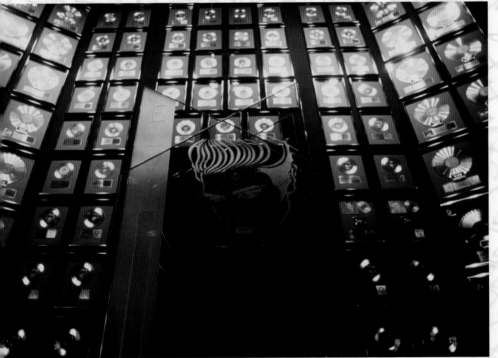

More than 130 of the King's recordings have been certified gold, platinum, or multiplatinum in the U.S.A. alone.

Among the best of the BMG-RCA productions in recent years is the Masters Series, which represents Ernst Jorgensen's and Roger Semon's efforts to not only release Elvis Presley's music commercially but also reframe it historically. Their work has gone a long way toward refocusing attention on his musical triumphs rather than on the personal tragedies of his life or the bizarre aspects of the post-death era.

In 1974 Elvis received a Grammy for Best Inspirational Performance for "How Great Thou Art" on the album Elvis Recorded Live on Stage in Memphis.

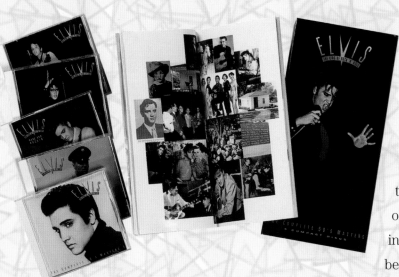

The Complete 50s Masters *(RCA 66050-2) chronicles the most innovative phase of Elvis's career.*

Released between 1992 and 1996, the series consists of *Elvis: The King of Rock 'n' Roll—The Complete 50s Masters, Elvis: From Nashville to Memphis— The Complete 60s Masters I,* and *Elvis: Walk a Mile in My Shoes—The Complete 70s Masters.* Together these three sets of CDs are a faithful audio documentation of Elvis's music from the beginning to the end. The tracks have been digitally remastered from old Sun and RCA recordings, but they maintain the integrity of the originals. Vocal exchanges and banter between Elvis and his musicians capture the camaraderie and the spontaneity of the sessions. An archival and musical achievement, the Masters Series also includes complete session credits and lengthy liner notes by music historians Peter Guralnick and Dave Marsh.

Separately, each set suggests something about Elvis's career that defies a commonly held perception. By following the evolution of Elvis's work from 1954 to 1958, *The Complete 50s Masters* proves that Elvis did not "steal" the sound of black rhythm-and-blues artists and call it his own. Instead, the tracks reveal a blending of influences that coalesced into a commercial sound that inched ever closer toward a mainstream style. *The Complete 60s Masters I* shows that Elvis did not entirely abandon his roots in country, gospel, and

The Essential 60s Masters I *(RCA 66160-2) showcases the mature sounds of a versatile singer.*

rhythm-and-blues after he achieved his pop style— an accusation hurled most often by rock music critics. The smooth, mainstream pop stylings of the movie soundtracks did dominate the period, but his recordings of the blues tunes "Reconsider Baby" and "Such a Night" and his gospel work later in the decade are declarations of his Southern heritage. *The Complete 70s Masters* reveals that Elvis did not grow lazy and rest on his laurels after his comeback to stage performances.

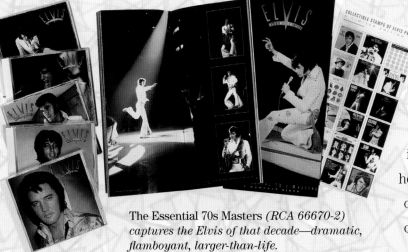

The Essential 70s Masters *(RCA 66670-2) captures the Elvis of that decade—dramatic, flamboyant, larger-than-life.*

A more concise treatment of Elvis's career can be found in *Elvis Presley Platinum: A Life in Music*, which charts the evolution of his style in a four-CD box set. *Platinum* contains 100 tracks, 77 of which were previously unreleased. The unreleased material consists mostly of alternate takes of Presley classics or practice runs of various songs. However, it also includes the newly discovered 1954 demo of Elvis singing "I'll Never Stand in Your Way."

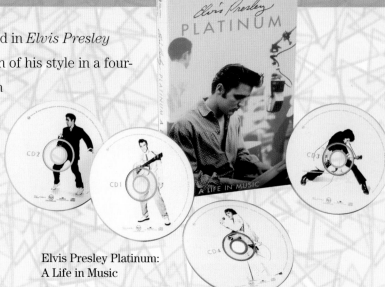

Elvis Presley Platinum:
A Life in Music

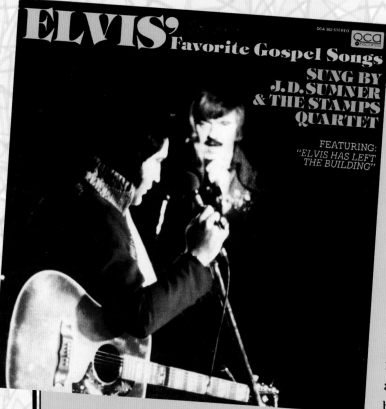

Tributes to the King

No better tribute can be made to a singer than to have other musicians and entertainers perform his or her songs. Singers from all genres and eras of music have recorded Elvis Presley tunes, often for compilation albums produced in tribute to the king. Among the best are *The Last Temptation of Elvis* and *Honeymoon in Vegas*.

The Last Temptation of Elvis, released in 1990, consists of remakes of 26 Elvis songs by performers ranging from rock superstar Bruce Springsteen to progressive country singer Nanci Griffith to the gritty U.K. folk-rock band The Pogues. *Honeymoon in Vegas* is the soundtrack to an offbeat comedy set in gaudy, garish Las Vegas, with its bright lights, noisy casinos, and Elvis impersonators. The soundtrack consists entirely of Elvis songs reworked by prominent pop, rock, and country singers. Willie Nelson performs a unique arrangement of "Blue Hawaii," Billy Joel checks into "Heartbreak Hotel," and Travis Tritt belts out a dynamic "Burning Love."

The high profile of these compilation albums has overshadowed another type of musical tribute to Elvis. Shortly after his death, several performers recorded songs that were *about* Elvis. While well-intended, most of these tunes were poorly written, maudlin affairs. An example is the tritely titled "Elvis Has Left the Building," which can be found on J. D. Sumner and the Stamps' otherwise tasteful tribute, *Elvis's Favorite Gospel Songs*. The best was probably "From Graceland to the Promised Land" by Merle Haggard; the most successful was "The King Is Gone" by Elvis soundalike Ronnie McDowell. Others include "Hound Dog Man's Gone Home" by Lee and Lowe, "Elvis Won't Be Here for Christmas" by Linda Hughes, and "Speaking to Elvis in Heaven" by P. M. Smith (probably a pseudonym).

1969 Hit Enters Grammy Hall of Fame

Thirty years after reaching the top of the charts, Elvis Presley's 1969 song "Suspicious Minds" was honored by an induction into the Grammy Hall of Fame. This made the recording his fourth to be recognized. The Hall of Fame inducted "That's All Right" in 1998, "Heartbreak Hotel" in 1995, and "Hound Dog" in 1988.

Two of Presley's hit songs, "Hound Dog" and "It's Now or Never," rank among the top-selling singles of the 20th century.

The King's music seems destined to reign in the 21st century, too. Recent RCA releases of his legendary recordings include *Sunrise*, a collection of all his Sun Records work, and *Artist of the Century*, a boxed set of CDs. *He Touched Me*, a two-CD compilation of Elvis's gospel recordings, was also released.

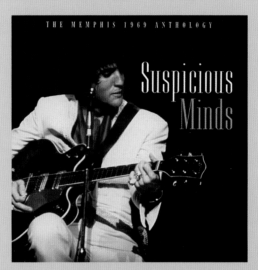

This type of chronological treatment of his music forces listeners to reevaluate the familiar and find a context for the unreleased material. In doing so, a new light is shed on Elvis's music and a full appreciation is gained for the impact of his career. This rings true not only for young audiences, rock 'n' roll listeners, and Presley critics but also for Elvis fans, who remained faithful through the dark years of badly packaged re-releases.

Key to the Elvis phenomenon is the loyalty of his fans. His death left a void that fans have filled with conventions, rituals, fan clubs, and other activities. Their intense devotion results from a complex combination of circumstances, beginning with Elvis's early career on the country-western circuit. Country music followers are among the most loyal of popular music fans. Many people who love country music remain devoted to a particular performer for decades, and they often inspire their children to become fans as well. Many of Elvis's most devoted fans became interested in him when he was regarded as a country singer, and they remained loyal to him after he became a national rock 'n' roll star.

Elvis chats with his fans at the gate of his California house.

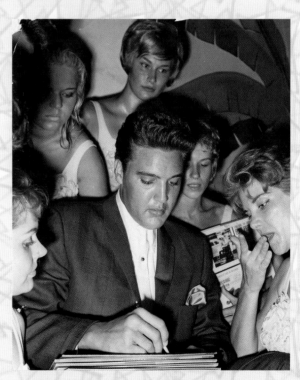

Anxious fans watch as Elvis signs copies of his album Something for Everybody.

Elvis always tried to give his fans what they wanted to see and hear. In the 1950s, his audience came to see his notorious performing style, hoping he would go further at each appearance than he'd ever gone before. Elvis was able to whip his audiences into a frenzy, an experience not understood by those who were not his fans. In the 1960s, his fans paid to see Elvis's musical films. In the 1970s, audiences expected Elvis to perform certain songs, wear his trademark jumpsuits, and strike specific poses—standard parts of his act that he maintained for his fans until he died.

Aloha From Hawaii concert

Opal Remembers

In September 1954, Opal Walker snapped some photographs of a young country singer in the parking lot of the Lamar-Airways Shopping Center in Memphis. To launch the grand opening of the shopping center, the singer and his band performed from a makeshift stage on the back of a flatbed truck. From these humble beginnings, Elvis Presley became the King of Rock 'n' Roll, and Opal became a lifelong fan. Opal's story, in her own words, reveals the charm of an earlier era and also the easy access fans had to Elvis at that time.

Opal recalls: "Elvis had that one record ["That's All Right"] out, and it was a smash locally, and I loved it. I had a girlfriend who was a friend of Dewey Phillips, the first deejay to play him. Dewey doesn't get nearly the credit he deserves for the Elvis phenomenon. Anyway, my girlfriend and I went down and sat in with Dewey while he did his show, and he told us all about Elvis and where he went to church. You can bet we were at First Assembly the next Sunday, and he was there with a friend. After church we flirted with them. He teased me about my long blonde hair.

"This show [at Lamar-Airways Shopping Center] came up and I went alone and took my camera. I rode a streetcar, I believe, and waited for [Elvis] to arrive. They all came in that Chevy, and I asked him to pose and he seemed happy to. There were a lot of people there, but few besides me seemed to know who he was. I had him all to myself. I could have shot a whole roll. But I didn't know then what I know now. He went on stage and started singing and shaking…the girls went wild. Me, too. That was the first time I saw [Elvis] perform, but I didn't miss any opportunities in the future. I saw him around quite a bit after that. I'd go downtown shopping, and he would be shopping. We would talk, and I would get an autograph. I have an autographed photo from '56. He was on the bill with Hank Snow [May 15, 1956, Ellis Auditorium], and I caught him wandering the hall. Later, of course, he got big and I couldn't get to him anymore."

Opal Walker in the mid-1950s

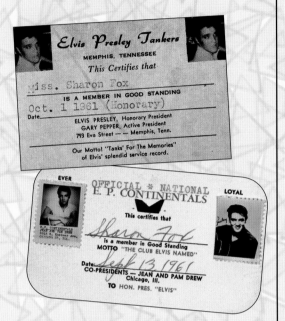

Membership cards from Elvis fan clubs

Elvis, the Colonel, and members of Elvis's family always treated the fans with the utmost consideration from the early days of his success until the very end, when Vernon Presley allowed fans to take flowers from his son's funeral. Elvis believed that his success was dependent on his fans, and he was always grateful for their loyalty and love. When he was young, he allowed them access to his personal life in a way that no other entertainer would dare. Before Elvis moved to Graceland, fans were always hanging around the Presleys' home. At Graceland, fans often gathered at the gate, and Elvis would walk down or ride one of his horses there to sign autographs. Elvis's Uncle Vester was one of the guards at the gate house, and he sometimes stood and talked with fans for hours.

No matter how difficult the fans made Elvis's life by forcing him to live in seclusion, he never complained publicly, and he always had nice things to say to the press about his fans. Colonel Tom Parker

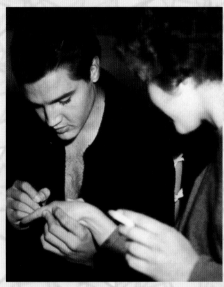

A fan without any paper asked Elvis to sign her hand.

The King's Treasures Fetch $5 Million

The Archives of Graceland, a three-day auction held in Las Vegas in October 1999, brought in $5 million. On the block were 2,000 items that had belonged to Elvis Presley—from a sixth-grade report card to a fleet of automobiles.

Elvis's 1956 Lincoln Continental Mark II commanded the highest bid at a hefty $250,000. The custom-made beaded cape (right) from his 1973 *Elvis: Aloha from Hawaii* concert/TV special sold for $98,000; a longer, calf-length version of the cape, never worn onstage because it was too heavy, sold for $85,000.

People from across the United States and around the world flocked to the MGM Grand Hotel for the chance to outbid each other for the precious memorabilia. The rock legend's first piano, a 1911 Stroud upright made of maple and mahogany that he bought in 1955, went for $90,000. His first contract with RCA Records in 1955 sold for $65,000, and his army fatigues fetched $43,000.

Lisa Marie Presley had recently inherited her father's fortune at the age of 30. While exploring the closets at Graceland, she found a hoard of treasures. Lisa opted to dust off the long-stored belongings and sell them to fund a pet project: Proceeds from the auction were used to build Presley Place, a transitional housing development for the homeless in Memphis.

gave premiums and special offers to Elvis's fan clubs and donated Elvis's personal belongings to be auctioned off for charity. Elvis once presented a car to the president of one of his fan clubs. When he was on tour during the 1950s, Elvis gave as many interviews to the reporters for high-school newspapers and fan-club newsletters as he did to the reporters who worked for big-city papers.

WHBQ-Memphis disc jockey George Klein and Elvis met in high school and became lifelong friends.

Though Elvis accumulated great wealth and success during his lifetime, he never forgot he was a Southern boy from humble beginnings. He chose not to reside permanently in Hollywood but preferred to live in Memphis, where he frequented local businesses and contributed generously to local charities. Elvis never completely lost his Southern accent, and he always preferred down-home cooking and the company of other good ol' boys. Despite his money, position, and power, he never acted as though he was better than his fans. To fans, this meant that Elvis had always been one of them—one of the people. "I guess you could say Elvis was what we'd like to be. He's one of us—and yet he's our ideal," said an anonymous fan, who seems to speak for all fans.

Elvis takes care of autograph business.

Elvis Presley fans have always been intensely devoted, and many have passed on that quality to other generations as a legacy. Elvis's fans are the most genuine testimony to his talent and impact on all of us.

Since his death, the fans' desire to get close to Elvis is gratified through visiting Graceland, where the events of his personal life unfolded. The echoes of Elvis's past linger in the rooms and halls of his private retreat.

The trophies Elvis had been awarded during his career were sorted before going on display at Graceland.

Live Cybercast of Vigil

The year 2000 brought a historical first for Graceland. Elvis admirers could log on and participate in the candlelight vigil held there every August. Fans from around the world watched the cybercast of the ritual on the official Elvis Presley Web site www.elvispresley.com. Nearly a quarter century after Elvis's death, technology enabled those from afar to pay their respects in real time with the 8,000 fans who were assembled at the singer's gravesite.

On the anniversary of Elvis's death, thousands of fans brave the sweltering August heat in Memphis to remember their idol. They organize a week of tributes and memorials that includes visiting Graceland, Sun Records, and other Presley haunts. The week culminates in a candlelight ceremony. On the evening of August 15, fans gather in front of the Music Gate. They sing some of Elvis's songs and swap Elvis stories. At 11:00 P.M., two or more Graceland employees walk down to the gate with a torch that has been lighted from the eternal flame. As the Music Gate swings open, the fans, with their lighted candles, climb silently and reverently up the hill behind the house, where they walk single file past the gravesite. The procession often takes as long as six hours to pass through the Meditation Garden. It is not only a gesture of respect for Elvis and what he represents, but it's also proof that Elvis's fans are as faithful after his death as they were during his lifetime.

I THINK IF ELVIS WERE STILL WITH US THAT . . . HE WOULD REALLY APPRECIATE WHAT HAPPENS EVERY AUGUST SINCE HE HAS PASSED AWAY, THAT THEY [THE FANS] HAVEN'T FORGOTTEN HIM. . . . ELVIS ALWAYS LOVED HIS FANS AND I AM SURE THAT HE WOULD APPRECIATE THE PAIN AND HURT EVERYONE FEELS SINCE HE HAS PASSED AWAY, BUT I BELIEVE HE WOULD RATHER THEY REMEMBER ALL THE GOOD TIMES, THE HAPPY MOMENTS, RATHER THAN TO DWELL UPON THE SAD.

—"ELVIS MEMORIES" AN INTERVIEW WITH GEORGE KLEIN,
BY BOB HEIS, MAY 20, 1981

Each August during the week that marks the anniversary of Elvis's death, fans pay their respects by visiting Graceland and placing flowers on his grave.

The candlelight vigil at Graceland, Elvis Week 1997.

The almost continuous release of biographical information keeps Elvis's name in the news and fuels the phenomenon. Professional writers and scholars have published books about Elvis. Rock-music historian Dave Marsh's eloquent and insightful *Elvis,* published in 1981, concentrated on the singer's contributions to popular music and culture. Peter Guralnick, a noted music historian, wrote two perceptive biographies titled *Last Train to Memphis: The Rise of Elvis Presley* and *Careless Love: The Unmaking of Elvis.*

Members of the Memphis Mafia also published books about Elvis. Jerry Hopkins wrote *Elvis: The Final Years,* and Marty and Patsy Lacker collaborated on *Elvis: Portrait of a Friend.* Both books confirm the stories about Elvis's drug use and destructive lifestyle related in the controversial *Elvis: What Happened?* by Red and Sonny West.

Subsequent biographies by members of Elvis's family acknowledged his bad side but most often balanced these stories with anecdotes about his generosity. The most awaited biography was Priscilla Beaulieu Presley's account of her relationship with Elvis, titled *Elvis and Me.* Published in 1985, the book offers no revelations about his career but does provide some

Priscilla Presley's biography, Elvis and Me, *was published in 1985.*

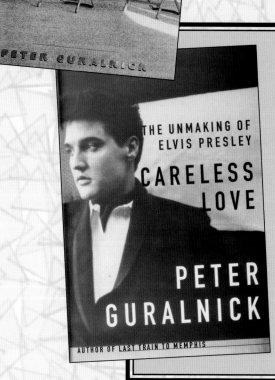

The Definitive Elvis Biography

More books have been written about Elvis Presley than any other entertainer. The Elvis division of the National Popular Culture Association estimates that more than 1,700 books have been written about America's most famous performer. Of these, many have been biographies, including career accounts; personal memoirs by friends, associates, and former members of the Memphis Mafia; and dubious bios by those with personal agendas.

The two-volume biography written by music historian Peter Guralnick in the mid-1990s stands far above the rest. *Last Train to Memphis: The Rise of Elvis Presley* begins at Elvis's birth and concludes with his departure for the army; *Careless Love: The Unmaking of Elvis* picks up the saga in 1958 and follows through to his death. Southern music is Guralnick's specialty, and he has written extensively about country music, blues, and rhythm-and-blues in *Lost Highway, Feel Like Going Home*, and *Searching for Robert Johnson*. His insightful analysis of Elvis's music is one of the strengths of his work. Meticulously researched, this two-volume set is the definitive work on Elvis Presley.

Hollywood Icon

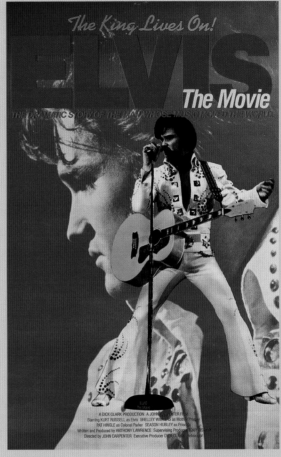

Shortly after Elvis Presley died, Hollywood turned its attention to the singer once again, realizing his enormous popularity had not been diminished by death. In 1979, ABC aired the first of several biofilms on the life of Elvis Presley. Directed by John Carpenter, *Elvis* was a solid attempt to encapsulate the singer's contributions to popular music and to sympathetically portray Elvis the man. Kurt Russell starred as Elvis in a powerful performance that earned him an Emmy nomination.

No other actor had captured Elvis so convincingly until Michael St. Gerard landed the title role in the short-lived television series *Elvis*. It was based on Elvis's real-life experiences but contained a deeper meaning. Some episodes were allegories that alluded to Elvis's impact on popular music, while others commented on the long-lasting effects of poverty on his life. Great care went into the series' production, demonstrated by the beautiful cinematography and poignant writing.

During the 1980s, several movies also made use of the symbolic power of Elvis Presley. *Great Balls of Fire*, the 1989 film biography of Jerry Lee Lewis, used Elvis

Kurt Russell played the King of Rock 'n' Roll in a made-for-TV biofilm.

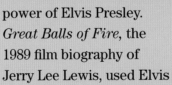

(played by St. Gerard) to represent the zenith of fame and fortune that Lewis was destined never to reach. In 1993, *True Romance* featured a spectral figure of Elvis (played by Val Kilmer) who appears at crucial moments to offer advice to the main character. The ultimate use of Elvis as a symbol occurred in *Mystery Train*, which tells three separate stories of outsiders staying at a run-down Memphis hotel. Elvis never appears in the scenes and none of the stories deals with him directly, but his presence haunts the film via the tacky portraits on the wall and the eerie sound of his version of "Blue Moon" that plays repeatedly in the background.

From the wacky Elvis impersonators that run amuck in the comedy *Honeymoon in Vegas* to the darkly heroic main character in David Lynch's surreal *Wild at Heart*, the complex image of Elvis Presley that has become ingrained in American culture provides filmmakers with a range of interpretations to explore.

Michael St. Gerard starred in the 1990 TV series Elvis.

much-needed insight into his secluded lifestyle during the 1960s. *The Touch of Two Kings* by Elvis's stepbrother Rick Stanley, who is now a minister, recounts Stanley's experiences with his famous relative. *Elvis: We Love You Tender* by Elvis's stepmother Dee Stanley is a compassionate look at his ups and downs during the 1960s and 1970s.

In 1987, to mark the tenth anniversary of Elvis's death, a reappraisal of his musical contributions began to appear in the popular press. After years of negative publicity, the career of Elvis Presley was finally being reevaluated. This appreciation was short-lived, however, because rumors surfaced that Elvis was still alive, undermining any credible assessment of his career.

Initially, the rumors that Elvis Presley had faked his own death served to discredit his standing as an important cultural figure. Fueled by Gail Brewer-Giorgio's self-published book, *The Most Incredible Elvis Presley Story Ever Told,* the "Elvis is alive"

The Presley family monument was created in 1958 when Gladys Presley died.

The Meditation Garden during Elvis Week is a sea of flowers.

Lisa, with her children and musician John Oszajca, leave the Presley Place site.

Grandchildren at Groundbreaking

In June 2000, Lisa Marie Presley, attended by her children Danielle, 11, and Benjamin, 7, dug out the first shovelful of earth at the official groundbreaking for Presley Place in Memphis. Reports said that daughter and son eagerly volunteered to participate in the ceremony. It was a momentous occasion, marking the children's first public appearance in connection to their immortal grandfather.

The Presley Place project is said to be near and dear to Lisa's heart because it represents an intrinsic part of her father's nature—generosity to the people around him and to those in need. She said that he never forgot his humble beginnings and would have been proud of The Elvis Presley Charitable Foundation's (EPCF) efforts to build Presley Place. The transitional housing facility gives qualified homeless families up to one year of rent-free housing. In addition, it provides day care, job counseling, and life skills training to assist them out of the rut of poverty and onto the road of independence.

Presley Place, with 12 apartment units, opened in July 2001. Also funded by EPCF, the Elvis Presley Music Room offers musical instruments and lessons for the resident children and youngsters from other such properties, all managed by the Metropolitan Inter-faith Association.

rumors escalated in 1988 with reported sightings of Elvis in fast-food restaurants in Michigan. Giorgio's book was retitled *Is Elvis Alive?* to take advantage of the media attention surrounding the current surge of interest in Elvis. Included with each book was an audiocassette of Elvis's voice discussing events that occurred after he died. Later an Elvis soundalike came forward, asserting that he had made the recording for a project that never materialized, a claim Giorgio denied.

Ultimately, the authenticity of the tape mattered very little because the rumors and the way they were handled in the press added another dimension to the Elvis Presley phenomenon. The frequency of books, newspaper and tabloid articles, and programs on radio and television indicated that many people—whether or not they believed the rumors—were interested in keeping Elvis Presley "alive." Bumper stickers that sentimentally declared, "Elvis lives in my heart," were replaced with the more emphatic "Elvis Lives." But it was not the historical Elvis Presley who was resurrected—it was Elvis the icon of American popular culture. The "Elvis is alive" stories and the massive amounts of publicity that surrounded their circulation helped refigure the historical Elvis into an American folk hero endowed with as much symbolic significance as Davy Crockett or Wyatt Earp. As an icon, Elvis Presley can evoke any number of ideas, including rebellion, success, excessiveness, and the glory and pitfalls of fame. As a folk hero, he inspires the telling and retelling of anecdotes and stories that are exaggerated and manipulated to illustrate any of these ideas.

In the years since his death, Elvis Presley has been highly honored and sharply criticized. At times a powerful symbol of revolution and at other times a national joke, through it all he has remained the King of Rock 'n' Roll. His crown is intact, only slightly tarnished by criticism, exploitation, and hype. It is a fitting title because it embraces the breadth of an extraordinary career and because it reminds us of the music—his true legacy to American culture.

Just starting out, a young Elvis leaned against a car as he waited to play for the September 1954 opening of Lamar-Airways Shopping Center in Memphis.

Elvis in 1968 at one of the peaks of his musical career.

A statue of Elvis rockin' out stands on Beale Street at Elvis Presley's Memphis Restaurant.

ow does one summarize the impact of Elvis Presley...or measure the magnitude of his career...or convey the significance of this phenomenon? Should it be through anniversaries or commemorative occasions?

It has been 50 years since Elvis stepped into Sun Studios at 706 Union Avenue in Memphis to record for the first time—surely an important anniversary to be remembered by rock 'n' roll fans and an occasion to be marked by the release of another compilation of his music. A half century of fame, whether the artist be alive or dead, is an accomplishment in a celebrity-hungry world where musical stars can burn brightly and then fade away within a matter of months.

Sun Studios today

Should the impact of Elvis be measured in sheer numbers? According to the Elvis Presley estate, Elvis has sold over one billion records worldwide. He has had more than 130 albums and singles certified gold, platinum, or multiplatinum by the Recording Industry Association of America (RIAA). More than 40 Presley songs have made it into the Top Ten on the American charts, with almost 20 reaching No. 1. In September 2002, the CD *ELVIS: 30 #1 Hits* sold over 500,000 copies in the United States during its first week, debuting at No. 1 on the charts. In one month, it was certified multiplatinum.

Thousands of fans gathered at Graceland during Elvis Week 2002.

The month of August had brought the 25th anniversary of Elvis's death, an occasion marked by fans who descended on Memphis to take part in a variety of events designed to celebrate Elvis's life. While the mid-August pilgrimage to Memphis is an annual ritual for thousands of Elvis fans, that year several thousand more people poured into the city to participate in the activities. The grand

Memphis blocks off Beale Street to accommodate the throngs of Elvis admirers that visit every August.

finale for the festivities was *Elvis—The Concert* featuring Elvis. The show drew a sell-out crowd and was attended by the remaining members of the Presley family. Using musical technology of the highest calibre, concert organizers had synched film footage of Elvis with live musicians and backup singers, many of whom were veterans of his concert days. *Elvis—The Concert* had been touring the country for a couple of years, but on this special night the show became a high-profile event because Elvis was playing his hometown once again.

Lisa Marie Presley paid tribute to her father at the Elvis Presley 25th Anniversary Concert on August 16, 2002, in Memphis.

Graceland, Elvis's mansion in Memphis, was opened to the public in 1982 and soon became one of the most visited homes in America. It attracts over 600,000 visitors each year. In mid-August 2002, a record-breaking 35,000 fans made the trek to Graceland to commemorate the 25th anniversary of Elvis's death.

Yet, perhaps awards and honors offer a more telling indication of Elvis Presley's significance to the world. Elvis received 14 Grammy nominations, winning for his gospel albums *How Great Thou Art* and *He Touched Me,* and for the concert recording of the song "How Great Thou Art." In 1986, he was inducted into the Rock 'n' Roll Hall of Fame; in 1987, he was

The Rock 'n' Roll Hall of Fame overlooks Lake Erie in Cleveland, Ohio.

inducted into the Country Music Hall of Fame; and in 2001, he entered the Gospel Hall of Fame. To date, Elvis is the only person who can claim membership in three musical halls of fame.

However, as impressive as the legions of faithful followers and the awards may be, they don't illustrate the man's impact, magnitude, or significance.

The Country Music Hall of Fame in Nashville has a stylized keyboard design.

The key is to return to the music. From the beginning, it was his music that was important. Elvis fused country-western with rhythm-and-blues, along with touches from other musical genres, into a new sound that passed into the mainstream culture as rock 'n' roll. In the early 1950s, country and R&B were indigenous American genres previously unfamiliar to the general public. To combine the two types of music and then to assimilate the result into mainstream culture is the essence of America. It was a musical version of the melting pot. Elvis Presley did not invent rock 'n' roll, other rockers had come before him, but his sound caught the attention of the public on a national scale. Elvis was an innovator in the true sense of the word; he spread the new musical sound quickly, forever changing the course of popular culture.

The original RCA Studios where Elvis recorded in Nashville.

Rock 'n' roll music became synonymous with youthful rebellion, something that Elvis did not intend but still unleashed. Rock 'n' roll gave post-World War II teenagers a culture and an attitude wholly different from their parents, drawing a permanent line in history between their generation and the previous ones. The fact that Elvis the man spent much of his career trying to escape the notoriety of rock 'n' roll is irrelevant. It was Elvis the Pelvis—an icon of rebellion—that American youth needed to free themselves from the constraints of the status quo. Creating controversy and inciting generational conflict began in 1954 with the music of one young man in Memphis, Tennessee—Elvis Presley. Those cultural clashes are now standard for subsequent generations. Each generation, it seems, needs to claim an Elvis Presley to break free from the tastes of their parents.

Elvis's first Sun record that started it all for him in 1954.

The magnitude of Elvis Presley's career is measured through the impact his music had on American culture, granting it a deep-rooted historical significance that no other entertainer can match. The measure of the man is his music.

Vernon Presley placed a rose on his son's grave on the first anniversary of Elvis's death.

A

ABC-TV, 89, 180, 187, 207
Abel, Robert, 163
Acuff, Roy, 16
Adams, Nick, 77
Alden, Ginger, 177
Ali, Muhammad, 174
Allen, Steve, 47
Allied Artists, 112
"All My Trials," 159
"All Shook Up," 37, 41, 130
All the King's Men, 86
"Always on My Mind," 156, 159
American Sound Studios, 127–129, 132, 136, 137, 141
"American Trilogy, An," 152, 159
Andress, Ursula, 119
Anka, Paul, 86, 159, 170
Ann-Margret, 76, 113, 114, 138, 183
"Are You Lonesome Tonight?" 87, 176
Arnold, Eddy, 19, 20, 129
Artist of the Century, 201
Atkins, Chet, 32, 33, 124, 183, 194
Ausborn, Carvel Lee (aka "Mississippi Slim"), 23, 27
Axton, Mae Boren, 33, 34

B

"Baby Let's Play House," 17, 19
Ballard, Lucien, 161, 162
"Battle Hymn of the Republic," 159
Beale Street, 26, 27, 44, 47, 62, 209, 210
Beatles, The, 85, 110
Beck, Jeff, 86
Belew, Bill, 130, 140, 153, 158
Bell, Freddie, and the Bellboys, 39, 40
Benefield, Marvin (aka Vince Everett), 124
Berle, Milton, 44, 45
Berry, Chuck, 82, 141, 156
Bienstock, Freddie, 88, 137
"Big Hunk o' Love, A," 152
Bill Black Combo, 85, 91
Bill Monroe and the Bluegrass Boys, 13
Billboard, 17, 35, 58, 102, 116, 119, 132, 136, 150, 156, 171
Binder, Steve, 129, 130
Bixby, Bill, 144
Black and White Jamboree (aka Saturday Jamboree), 23
Black, Bill, 12, 15–18, 24, 33, 35, 45, 62, 68, 73, 84, 85, 91, 102, 194
Blackman, Joan, 100, 114
Blackwell, Otis, 41
Blackwood Brothers, 26, 75, 125, 158
Blackwood, Cecil, 26
Blackwood, James, 183
Blaine, Hal, 101
Bland, Bobby "Blue," 9
Blossoms, The, 130
Blue Baron Orchestra, 87
"Blue Hawaii," 101, 200
Blue Hawaii (LP), 101, 102
Blue Hawaii (movie), 60, 100–108, 111, 118
"Blue Moon," 207
Blue Moon Boys, 13, 15–18, 20, 86
"Blue Moon of Kentucky," 6, 13, 18
"Blue Suede Shoes" (Carl Perkins), 34, 35
"Blue Suede Shoes" 34, 35, 130, 138, 162
BMG, 193, 197, 198
Boone, Pat, 53, 88, 138
Brewer-Giorgio, Gail, 208, 209
Brinkley, David, 180
Brown, Estelle, 150
Brown, James, 109, 130, 178, 184
Brown, Jim, 112
"Burning Love," 152, 156, 200
Burning Love and Hits from His Movies, Vol. 2, 156

Burton, James, 134, 151
Butler, Jerry, 129

C

Campbell, Glen, 133
"Can't Help Falling in Love," 100, 102, 106, 118, 139, 153
Careless Love: The Unmaking of Elvis, 206
Carpenter, John, 207
Carter, Jimmy, 187
Carter, Rosalynn, 187
Cash, Johnny, 9, 14, 38
"Casual Love Affair," 11
CBS-TV, 48, 49, 176, 180
Change of Habit, 116, 118
Checker, Chubby, 86
Chess Records, 8, 9
Clambake, 104, 111, 115
Clark, Dick, 138
Coasters, The, 60
Cogbill, Tommy, 128, 132
Cohen, Nudie, 42
Cole, James, 186
Cooley, Eddie, 41
Country Music Hall of Fame, 211
Country Song Roundup, 35
Cramer, Floyd, 33, 85, 91
Crewe, Bob, 128
Crosby, John, 46
Crudup, Arthur, 12, 13, 35
"Crying in the Chapel," 116, 118
Cuoghi, Joe, 26, 33
Curtiz, Michael, 73, 76

D

Davis, Mac, 129
Davis, Sammy, Jr., 75, 89, 174
Dean, James, 54, 70, 75, 78
Del Rio, Dolores, 94
"Dixie," 159
Domino, Fats, 138
"Don't Be Cruel," 38, 40–42, 49
Dorsey, Jimmy and Tommy, 19, 43
Double Trouble, 104, 111
Douglas, Donna, 114
"Drums of the Islands," 103
Dunleavy, Steve, 184, 185
Dunne, Philip, 96
Dunnock, Mildred, 67
Durden, Tommy, 34

E

Easy Come, Easy Go, 58, 103, 111, 112, 119
Eden, Barbara, 94
Ed Sullivan Show, The, 48–50, 67, 162
Egan, Richard, 67, 68
Ellis Auditorium, 25, 85, 124, 202
Elvis (book), 206
Elvis (television series), 207
Elvis (The '68 Comeback Special), 126, 127, 129–133
Elvis (movie), 124, 207
Elvis: Aloha from Hawaii (TV Special), 150–153, 170, 202, 203
Elvis: Aloha from Hawaii Via Satellite (LP), 150
Elvis and Jimmy magazine, 78
Elvis and Me, 206
Elvis as Recorded at Madison Square Garden, 161
Elvis' Favorite Gospel Songs, 158
Elvis: From Nashville to Memphis— The Complete 60s Masters I, 199
Elvis—Greatest Hits, Vol. 4, 196
Elvis in Concert, 176
Elvis Is Back!, 84, 86, 87, 101
Elvis on Tour (documentary), 161, 163

Elvis: Portrait of a Friend, 206
Elvis Presley (LP), 35
Elvis Presley Charitable Foundation, The, 208
Elvis Presley Enterprises, 54
Elvis Presley Music, 36, 37
Elvis Presley Platinum: A Life in Music, 200
Elvis Presley 25th Anniversary Concert, 211
Elvis Recorded Live on Stage in Memphis, 126, 198
Elvis's Favorite Gospel Songs, 200
Elvis—That's the Way It Is (documentary), 161, 162, 195
Elvis—The Concert, 211
Elvis: The King of Rock 'n' Roll— The Complete 50s Masters, 199
ELVIS: 30 #1 Hits, 192, 193, 195, 210
Elvis: Walk a Mile in My Shoes— The Complete 70s Masters, 199
Elvis: We Love You Tender, 208
Elvis: What Happened?, 184, 185, 206
Esposito, Joe, 90, 163, 183

F

Fabares, Shelley, 110, 115
"Fever," 41
Fike, Lamar, 90, 91, 183
Finkel, Bob, 129
"Flaming Star," 94, 118
Flaming Star, 94, 96
Fleetwood, Mick, 179
Follow That Dream, 103, 118
Fontana, D. J., 16, 17, 33, 35, 42, 45, 59, 62, 68, 73, 84–86, 91, 102, 130, 132, 194
Foredo, Dr. Noel, 187
Forest Hill Cemetery, 75, 182, 183
For LP Fans Only, 126
Fortas, Alan, 132
Francisco, Dr. Jerry, 185–187
Frankie and Johnny, 114, 119
Frank Sinatra-Timex Special, The (aka Welcome Home Elvis) 89, 90, 111
Freeman, Joan, 115
From Elvis in Memphis, 128, 129, 132
From Elvis Presley Boulevard, Memphis, Tennessee, 169
From Memphis to Vegas/From Vegas to Memphis, 132
Fun in Acapulco, 104, 119

G

Gardner, Hy, 52, 54
"G.I. Blues," 92, 93
G.I. Blues (LP), 92, 93
G.I. Blues (movie), 92, 94, 107
"Girl Happy," 114, 118, 119
Girl Happy, 103, 111, 115
"Girls! Girls! Girls!," 118
Girls! Girls! Girls!, 103, 118, 120
Gladys Music, 36, 37
Gold, Wally, 88
Gooding, Judge Marion W., 51
Good Morning America, 184
Gospel Hall of Fame, 211
Gould, Jack, 46
Graceland, 74, 75, 90, 142, 144, 164, 168, 169, 171, 176–179, 181, 182, 186, 197, 203–205, 210, 211
Graceland Museum, 78
Grammy Hall of Fame, 201
Grand Ole Opry, 18, 27, 28, 91
Great Balls of Fire (movie), 207
Green, Jeannie, 136
Greene, Bob, 184
Guinness Book of Recorded Sound, The, 88

Guinness Book of World Records, The, 158
Gunter, Arthur, 19
Guralnick, Peter, 199, 206

H

Hall of Gold, 198
Haley, Bill, 60, 82, 141
Handman, Lou, 87
Hank Snow Jamboree Attractions, 20, 21
Harris, Emmylou, 151
Harris, Wynonie, 15
Hart, Dolores, 76
Harum Scarum, 104, 110, 118
"Hawaiian Wedding Song," 101, 105
Hawkins, Hoyt, 42
"Heartbreak Hotel," 33–35, 44, 45, 49, 193, 200, 201
Hebler, Dave, 184, 185
Hess, Jake, 26, 125, 151, 183
He Touched Me, 126, 201, 211
He Walks Beside Me, 196
Hill and Range, 36, 37, 41, 88, 116, 137
Hodge, Charlie, 87, 132, 134, 155, 183
Holly, Buddy, 82
Hollywood Walk of Fame, 96
Honeymoon in Vegas, 200, 207
Hopkins, Jerry, 206
Hopper, Hedda, 94
"Hound Dog," 38, 39, 40, 42, 44–47, 49, 58, 59, 88, 130, 138, 152, 160, 194, 201
Houston, Cissy, 150
Hovie Lister and the Statesmen, 26
Howe, Bones, 129
"How Great Thou Art," 125, 126, 198, 211
How Great Thou Art (LP), 124–126, 211
Huffaker, Clair, 94
Humes High School, 15, 24, 25
Huskey, Ferlin, 16
Hy Gardner Calling, 52

I

"I Don't Care if the Sun Don't Shine," 15
"If I Can Dream," 130
"I Forgot to Remember to Forget," 17
"If the Lord Wasn't Walking by My Side," 125
"I Got a Woman," 33
"I'll Never Stand in Your Way," 11, 200
"I'll Remember You," 152
"I'm Left, You're Right, She's Gone," 17, 19
Imperials, 125, 134, 151, 158
"I'm So Lonesome I Could Cry," 152
Ink Spots, 10
"In the Ghetto," 129
Is Elvis Alive?, 208, 209
It Happened at the World's Fair, 104, 110, 111, 114
"It's a Matter of Time," 156
"It's Now or Never," 87, 88, 102, 201
"I Want You, I Need You, I Love You," 47, 194
I Was the One (LP), 197
"I Will Be Home Again," 87

J

Jagger, Dean, 73, 76, 77
"Jailhouse Rock," 58–60, 63
Jailhouse Rock (movie), 60–64, 78, 124
Jailhouse Rock (EP), 59, 60
Jarrett, Hugh, 42
Jarvis, Felton, 124, 137, 169
Jennings, Waylon, 86, 128
John, Elton, 90
Johnson, Nunnally, 94
Jones, Carolyn, 76
Jones, Tom, 139
Jordanaires, The, 33, 38, 40, 42, 49, 72, 73, 85, 91, 102, 125, 194

Jorgensen, Ernst, 193, 198
Junkie XL, 193

K
Kahane, Jackie, 160, 183
Kanter, Hal, 70–72
Keisker, Marion, 9, 10, 11
Ken Darby Trio, 68
Kennedy, Caroline, 183
"Kentucky Rain," 132
Keough, Benjamin, 208
Keough, Danielle, 208
Kerkorian, Kirk, 135
Kid Galahad, 106, 114
Kilmer, Val, 207
King, B. B., 9, 27, 53
King Creole, 60, 66, 73, 76–78, 84, 192
Kissin' Cousins, 110, 115, 116, 119
Klein, George, 204, 205
Kristofferson, Kris, 120
Kuijk, Andreas van, 83
Kuralt, Charles, 181

L
Lacker, Marty, 206
Lacker, Patsy, 206
Lastfogel, Abe, 100, 107, 119
Last Temptation of Elvis, The, 200
Last Train to Memphis: The Rise and Fall of Elvis Presley, 206
Leiber, Jerry, 38, 58–60, 63
Lennon, John, 10, 84, 160, 163, 187
Lewis, Jerry Lee, 9, 14, 38, 41, 66, 82, 83, 91, 141, 186, 207
LIFE magazine, 51, 87, 142
Linde, Dennis, 156
"Little Egypt," 118
"Little Less Conversation, A," 193
Little Richard, 35, 82
Live a Little, Love a Little, 118, 193
Logan, Horace, 17
Long, Shorty, 35, 40
Louisiana Hayride, 16–18, 47, 71, 85, 86
"Love Letters," 118
"Love Me," 58, 152
"Love Me Tender," 49, 66–68, 89, 192
Love Me Tender, 67, 68, 70–72, 78
Loving You, 58, 70–73, 76, 78, 106
Lund, Jana, 71
Lynch, David, 207

M
Marsh, David, 199, 206
Martin, Dean, 28, 36, 66, 75, 141
Matthau, Walter, 73, 76
Matthews, Neal, 42
Mattinson, Bernie, 102
McCoy, Charlie, 92, 125
McDowell, Ronnie, 124, 200
Meditation Garden, 183, 186, 205, 208, 212
Memories of Our Friend Elvis, 158
Memphis Mafia, 90, 134, 138, 164, 172, 174, 175, 184, 195, 206
Memphis Press-Scimitar, 178
Memphis Recording Service, 8–11, 24, 28, 37
Mendes, Sergio, 159
MGM, 64, 112, 161–163
"Milkcow Blues Boogie," 17
Million Dollar Quartet, 38
Million Dollar Quartet, The (LP), 197
Milsap, Ronnie, 136, 137
Milton Berle Show, The, 40, 44–47
Mississippi Slim, 23, 27
Mobley, Mary Ann, 110, 114
Mockridge, Cyril, 94
Modern Records, 8, 59
Moman, Chips, 128, 129, 137, 141

"Moody Blue," 170
Moody Blue (LP), 169, 171, 177
Moore, Bob, 85
Moore, Mary Tyler, 116
Moore, Scotty, 12, 15–18, 33, 35, 45, 62, 68, 73, 84–86, 91, 102, 131, 132, 194
Morgan, Jaye P., 87
Morrow, Vic, 77
Mudd, Roger, 180
Muhoberack, Larry, 134, 151
Muirhead, Dr. Eric, 187
"My Happiness," 9, 24
"Mystery Train," 17, 28, 33, 161
Mystery Train (movie), 207
"My Way," 152, 159, 170

N
National Popular Culture Association, 206
NBC-TV, 47, 130, 152, 180, 185
Neal, Bob, 15, 16, 20, 21, 32
Nelson, Ricky, 42, 75, 150, 151
Newbury, Mickey, 159
Nichopoulos, Dr. George, 168, 175, 177, 183, 185–187
Nixon, Richard, 175

O
Odets, Clifford, 96
"Old Shep," 23, 41
Orbison, Roy, 9, 14
"O Sole Mio," 88, 102

P
Page, Patti, 102, 106
Paget, Debra, 68, 69
Paradise, Hawaiian Style, 91, 103, 109, 111, 119
Paramount Pictures, 66, 70, 73, 76, 106
"Paralyzed," 41
Parker, Junior, 8, 9
Parker, Colonel Tom, 20, 21, 23, 32, 36, 39, 47–49, 51, 53, 54, 64, 73, 82–87, 89, 91, 96, 100, 107, 112, 115, 119, 120, 130, 133, 135, 139, 140–142, 144, 148, 160, 163, 176, 195, 198, 203
Parsons, Gram, 151
Pat Boone Sings…Guess Who?, 88
Perkins, Carl, 9, 14, 34, 35, 38, 86, 124
Phillips, Dewey, 14, 25, 26, 33, 202
Phillips, Sam, 8–16, 19, 28, 32, 34, 37, 38, 84, 138, 183
Pierce, Webb, 18
Poplar Tunes, 26, 33
Presley, Dee, 142
Presley, Gladys, 9, 14, 23, 27, 36, 37, 67, 72, 74, 75, 183, 186, 208
Presley, Lisa Marie, 142, 144, 164, 168, 203, 208, 211
Presley, Minnie Mae, 24, 183
Presley, Priscilla, 26, 112, 134, 139, 142, 144, 159, 164, 168, 169
Presley, Vernon, 14, 23, 24, 27, 36, 37, 72, 74, 75, 141, 142, 183, 185, 187, 203, 212
Presley, Vester, 23, 203
Presley Place, 203, 208

R
Radio Recorders, 100
Rainy, Big Memphis Ma, 27
Randle, Bill, 43, 44
Randolph, Boots, 87, 91, 118
RCA Victor, 32–36, 38, 40–43, 73, 86–88, 111, 116, 119, 124, 127, 137, 156, 161, 168, 169, 171, 177, 192–194, 196–199, 201, 203, 212
"Ready Teddy," 49

"Reconsider Baby," 16, 22, 87, 199
Recording Industry Association of America (RIAA), 42, 102, 132, 156, 197, 198, 210
Red Hot and Blue, 14, 25
"Return to Sender," 41, 118
Rice, Tim, 169
Richards, Keith, 84, 86
Rivera, Geraldo, 184, 185
Robbins, Harold, 73
"Rock-a-Hula Baby," 101
Rock 'n' Roll Hall of Fame, 8, 211
Roustabout, 112, 115, 118
RPM Records, 9
"Rubberneckin'," 118
Russell, Kurt, 111, 207

S
St. Gerard, Michael, 207
Sanders, Denis, 161, 162
Saperstein, Hank, 53, 54
Scheff, Jerry, 134, 151
Schilling, Jerry, 90
Schroeder, Aaron, 88
Scott, Lizabeth, 70
"See See Rider," 155
Semon, Roger, 193, 198
"Separate Ways," 156
"Shake, Rattle, and Roll," 44
Shalimar Music, 41
Shaughnessy, Mickey, 58, 60
Shenwell, Sylvia, 150
"She Thinks I Still Care," 170
Sholes, Steve, 32, 33, 34, 35, 40
Shore, Sammy, 160
Siegel, Don, 94, 96
Sinatra, Frank, 89, 91, 92, 111, 139, 159, 170
Sinatra, Nancy, 89, 110, 111, 139
Smith, Billy, 183
Smith, Myrna, 150
Smith, Roger, 183
"Smokie," 85
Snow, Hank, 20, 21, 25, 27, 42, 202
Something for Everybody (LP), 197, 201
Songfellows, 26
Southern Gospel Music Hall of Fame, 158
Speedway, 111, 119, 144
Speer, Ben, 33, 42, 194
Speer, Brock, 33, 42, 194
Speer Family, 33, 42
Spinout, 114, 115, 118
Stage Show, 19, 43, 44, 64, 65
Stamps Quartet, 151, 158, 200
Stanley, David, 174
Stanley, Dee, 208
Stanley, Rick, 208
Stanwyck, Barbara, 115
Star Is Born, A, 120
Starlight Wranglers, 12, 15, 17, 85
Statesmen Quartet, 125
Stay Away, Joe, 106, 112
Stax Records, 128
Steve Allen Show, The, 38, 47, 48
Stevens, Ray, 125
Stewart, Rod, 188
Stoker, Gordon, 33, 42, 194
Stoller, Mike, 38, 58–60, 63
Stone for Danny Fisher, A, 73, 75
Streisand, Barbra, 120, 133
Strength, Bill, 16
"Stuck on You," 85
"Such a Night," 199
Sullivan, Ed, 47, 48, 49, 50, 90, 91
Sumner, J. D., 151, 158, 177, 183, 200
Sun Records, 8, 9, 11–15, 17, 26, 33–36, 38, 62, 86, 127, 197, 201, 205, 210, 212

"Suspicious Minds," 132, 136, 137, 152, 201
Sweet Inspirations, 134, 150, 151

T
Taurog, Norman, 100, 114
"Teddy Bear," 70
"That's All Right," 12–18, 176, 201, 202
"That's When Your Heartaches Begin," 10, 37
"There's No Tomorrow," 88
This Is Elvis, 163
Thomas, Rufus, 8, 27
Thompson, Charles, 185, 186
Thornton, Willie Mae "Big Mama," 38, 40
Tin Pan Alley, 28, 59, 87
Touch of Two Kings, The, 208
"Treat Me Nice," 58, 59
"Trouble," 126
True Romance (movie), 207
Tubbs, Ernest, and the Texas Troubadors, 27
Turk, Roy, 87
Tutt, Ronnie, 134, 151
"Tutti Frutti," 35
Twentieth Century-Fox, 66, 68
20/20, 185, 186
"Twist, The," 86
Tyler, Judy, 60
Tyrell, Steve, 128

U
United Artists, 112
Universal Studios, 66

V
Vee, Bobby, 86, 110
Viva Las Vegas, 104, 112–114, 118, 133, 139

W
Walker, Opal, 202
Walley, Deborah, 114
Wallis, Hal, 21, 64–66, 68, 70, 71, 73, 75–77, 92, 100, 106–108, 112, 115
Warner Bros., 64, 66
"Way Down," 193, 194
Webb, Robert, 67
Webber, Andrew Lloyd, 169
Weisbart, David, 78
Weld, Tuesday, 96
Wells, Kitty, 16, 42
West, Red, 26, 90, 91, 171, 184, 185, 206
West, Sonny, 26, 90, 184, 185, 206
Westmoreland, Kathy, 151, 169, 183
"What'd I Say," 139
Whitman, Slim, 16, 18
Wilburn Brothers, 16
Wild at Heart, 207
Wild in the Country, 96
Wilkinson, John, 134
Williams, Hank, 18, 27, 120
"Witchcraft," 89
"Wolf Call," 118
Wolf, Howlin', 9
Wood, Anita, 90
Wood, Bobby, 128, 132
Wood, Natalie, 77

Y
Young, Faron, 16, 21
Young, Reggie, 128, 132
"You're a Heartbreaker," 17
"(You're So Square) Baby, I Don't Care," 59, 64, 138